SCOTT FORESMAN • ADDISON WESLEY

Mathematics

Grade 6

Homework Workbook

Editorial Offices: Glenview, Illinois • Parsippany, New Jersey • New York, New York

Sales Offices: Parsippany, New Jersey • Duluth, Georgia • Glenview, Illinois
Coppell, Texas • Ontario, California • Mesa, Arizona

ISBN 0-328-07561-2

Copyright © Pearson Education, Inc.
All Rights Reserved. Printed in the United States of America. This publication, or parts thereof, may be used with appropriate equipment to reproduce copies for classroom use only.

14 15 16 17 V016 14 13 12

Place Value

R 1-1

The 8 in 577,800,000,000,000 is in the hundred-billions place, and its value is 800 billion.

Trillions			Billions			Millions			Thousands			Ones		
hundred trillions	ten trillions	trillions	hundred billions	ten billions	billions	hundred millions	ten millions	millions	hundred thousands	ten thousands	thousands	hundreds	tens	ones
5	7	7,	8	0	0,	0	0	0,	0	0	0,	0	0	0
				9	2,	2	8	2,	0	0	0,	0	0	0

The number 577,800,000,000,000 can be written in different ways.

Standard form: 577,800,000,000,000

Word form: five hundred seventy-seven trillion, eight hundred billion

Short-word form: 577 trillion, 800 billion

Expanded form: 500,000,000,000,000 + 70,000,000,000,000 + 7,000,000,000,000 + 800,000,000,000

1. Write the place and value for the underlined digit.
   7,656,871,228

2. Write 32,600,009,000 in short-word form.

3. Write the number in word form and in standard form.
   9,000,000,000,000 + 8,000,000,000 + 6,000,000 + 5,000 + 1

4. **Writing in Math** What is the value of the 7 in 568,971,433,009? Explain how you know.

Use with Lesson 1-1. 1

Name _____

Place Value

P 1-1

Write the place and value for each underlined digit.

1. 45,287,<u>5</u>21 _____

2. 5,<u>6</u>21,392,835 _____

3. Write 7,208,972,001,010 in short-word form and in expanded form.

_____

_____

_____

_____

_____

4. Write 20 trillion, 310 billion, 670 million, 5 thousand in word form and in standard form.

_____

_____

_____

_____

5. **Number Sense** Write a 6-digit number with a 3 in the hundred thousands place, a 6 in the thousands place, a 0 in the tens place, and a 9 in the ones place.

_____

Test Prep

6. Which shows 76,111 written in expanded form?

   A. 76,000 + 100 + 11
   B. 76,000 + 100 + 10 + 1
   C. 70,000 + 6,000 + 100 + 10 + 1
   D. 70,000 + 6,100 + 10 + 1

7. **Writing in Math** Write 45 million, 67 thousand in three different ways.

_____

_____

_____

Use with Lesson 1-1. **1**

Name _____

Exponents

R 1-2

---

base ⟶ 3^5 ⟵ exponent

The number 3 is the **base**.
It is the factor that is multiplied.

The number 5 is the **exponent**.
It tells how many times the base is used as a factor.

3^5 is read "three to the fifth power."

$3^5 = 3 \times 3 \times 3 \times 3 \times 3$ ⟶ Five factors of 3 are multiplied.

How to write a power as a product and then evaluate:

2^4

The base (2) is used as a factor the number of times as shown by the exponent (4):

$2^4 = 2 \times 2 \times 2 \times 2 = 16$

How to write a product in exponential form:

$5 \times 5 \times 5$

Step 1: Write the base.
5

Step 2: Count the number of times the base is used as a factor. This is the exponent.
5^3

How to use exponents to write a number in expanded form:

$4,512 = (4 \times 1,000) + (5 \times 100) + (1 \times 10) + (2 \times 1)$
$= (4 \times 10^3) + (5 \times 10^2) + (1 \times 10^1) + (2 \times 10^0)$

Write each power as a product and then evaluate.

1. 5^3 _____

2. 2^5 _____

3. 7^3 _____

Write each product in exponential form.

4. $8 \times 8 \times 8$ _____   **5.** $20 \cdot 20 \cdot 20 \cdot 20$ _____

Write the number in expanded form using exponents.

6. $1,324 = (1 \times 10^3) + (3 \times 10^2) + ($ _____ $) + ($ _____ $)$

7. Number Sense Are 2^4 and 4^2 equal? Explain why or why not.

_____

_____

2 Use with Lesson 1-2.

Exponents

Write each power as a product and then evaluate.

1. 3^2

2. 8^3

3. 5^3

4. 10^3

5. 3^5

6. 4 squared

7. **Reasoning** Is 4×2 equal to 4^2? Explain why or why not.

Write each product in exponential form.

8. 35 squared

9. $12 \times 12 \times 12 \times 12$

10. $28 \times 28 \times 28 \times 28 \times 28$

11. 22 cubed

12. Some computer virus programs are based on exponents. A certain program could begin with 4 screens. When it has been cubed, how many screens will be affected?

13. Write $2 \times 2 \times 2 \times 2 \times 2$ in exponential form and as a product in standard form.

Test Prep

14. Which shows 5 squared in exponential form?

    A. 10   **B.** 25   **C.** 5^2 **D.** 5×5

15. **Writing in Math** Zach began with $10 in investments and was able to "triple" his money. Alli also began with $10. She was able to "cube" her money. Who ended up with more money? Explain.

Name _____

Comparing and Ordering Whole Numbers

R 1-3

Here is one way to compare two numbers:

> Which is greater: 452,198 or 452,189?
>
> First, align the numbers. Then, start at the left and compare digits in each place.
>
> 452,1**9**8
> 452,1**8**9
>
> → The numbers in the tens place are different. Since 9 is greater than 8, the top number is larger. So 452,198 > 452,189.

Order 46,525; 44,434; 44,737; and 46,895 from greatest to least.

Order ten thousands.	Order thousands.	Order hundreds.
4 ,	46 ,	46,895
4 ,	46 ,	46,525
4 ,	44 ,	44,737
4 ,	44 ,	44,434

From greatest to least, the numbers are 46,895; 46,525; 44,737; and 44,434.

Use < or > to compare.

1. 445 ◯ 472
2. 354,123 ◯ 345,129
3. 8,367 ◯ 8,381
4. 71,297 ◯ 71,279
5. 5,280 ◯ 5,379
6. 22,420 ◯ 22,421

For 7 and 8, order the numbers from greatest to least.

7. 6,731   67,331   671   6,713

8. 18,910   18,901   18,909   18,919

9. **Number Sense** Which place-value position helps you decide if 312,879 is less than 321,978?

Use with Lesson 1-3.

Name _____

Comparing and Ordering Whole Numbers

P 1-3

Use < or > to compare.

1. 19,878 ◯ 19,898
2. 703,864 ◯ 703,684
3. 856,284 ◯ 856,248
4. 101,010 ◯ 110,101

5. **Number Sense** Write three numbers that are between 456,649 and 456,781.

_____

For 6 and 7, order the numbers from least to greatest.

6. 676   6,760   760   7,060   6,607

_____

7. 87,223   87,232   87,332   87,322   87,233

_____

8. Which whale weighed more, the one found in the Great South Channel or the one found in Massachusetts Bay?

   _____

   _____

Whale	Location	Weight (lb)
A	Florida	112,290
B	Great South Channel	112,336
C	Massachusetts Bay	112,137
D	Cape Cod	112,238

9. Write the weights of the whales in order from greatest to least.

_____

Test Prep

10. Which comparison is correct?

    A. 1,011 > 1,101   B. 1,110 < 1,010   C. 1,001 > 1,111   D. 1,010 > 1,001

11. **Writing in Math** Explain how you would determine if 9,899,989 is greater than or less than 9,898,998.

_____

_____

Name _____

Rounding Whole Numbers

R 1-4

You round numbers when an exact amount is not needed.
Here is how to round numbers.

	Step 1 Find and underline the place you must round to.	**Step 2** Look at the digit to the right of this place.	**Step 3** If this digit is 5 or more, add 1 to the rounding digit. If it is less than 5, leave the rounding digit alone.
Round 3,281 to the nearest hundred.	3,281 ↑ This is the hundreds place.	3,2[8]1 8 is to the right of the hundreds place.	3,281 rounded to the nearest hundred is 3,300. It was "rounded up."
Round 58,241 to the nearest thousand.	58,241 ↑ This is the thousands place.	58,[2]41 2 is to the right of the thousands place.	58,241 rounded to the nearest thousand is 58,000. It was "rounded down."

Round each number to the underlined place.

1. 3,4_5_9

2. 45,_2_48

3. 2_9_2,420

4. 2_2_,654

5. _1_53,744

6. 102,_2_91

7. 9_6_4,499

8. 908,7_4_8

9. _1_,898,234

10. 2,_4_09,158

11. 6,36_5_,054

12. 8,_9_35,102

13. **Number Sense** James has been asked to round 453,215 to the nearest thousand. Which digit and what place will he look at to decide if he should round up or down?

_____

_____

4 Use with Lesson 1-4.

Rounding Whole Numbers

P 1-4

Round each number to the underlined place.

1. 3,8<u>2</u>2

2. 2<u>1</u>,599

3. 962,8<u>9</u>9

4. 6,0<u>0</u>8,012

5. 489,<u>4</u>72,009

6. <u>9</u>25,835,103

7. **Number Sense** Write three numbers that would round to 86,000 if rounded to the nearest thousand.

8. Round the average depth of the Indian Ocean to the nearest thousand.

9. Round the average depth of the Atlantic Ocean to the nearest ten.

Ocean	Average Depth (meters)
Pacific	4,188
Atlantic	3,735
Indian	3,872
Arctic	1,038

10. Round the average depth of the Arctic Ocean to the nearest hundred.

11. Round the average depth of the Pacific Ocean to the nearest thousand.

Test Prep

12. Which shows 869,487 rounded to the nearest ten thousand?

    A. 868,000   B. 869,000   C. 870,000   D. 870,500

13. **Writing in Math** Describe a situation in which it would be better to round to the nearest ten rather than to the nearest hundred or thousand.

Use with Lesson 1-4.

Name _____

Estimating Sums and Differences

R 1-5

Estimate 2,675 − 189.

Determine the greatest place value of the lesser number.	hundreds
Round both numbers to this place.	189 → 200
2,675 → 2,700	
Subtract the rounded numbers.	2,700 − 200 = 2,500

You can also estimate by using front-end estimation with and without adjusting.

Estimate 8,243 + 4,686 + 129.

Front-end Estimation	Front-end Estimation with Adjusting
⑧,243 ④,686 + ①29 ⑫,000 — Add only the first digits that have the same place value to get a rough estimate.	8,②43 4,⑥86 + ①29 ⑫,000 — Add thousands. + ⑨00 — Add hundreds. 12,900 ← Adjusted estimate

Clustering can be used when the numbers are close to each other.

Estimate 252 + 297 + 305 + 327.
↓   ↓   ↓   ↓
300 + 300 + 300 + 300 = 1,200

Estimate each answer. Tell which method you used.

1. 196 + 29 _____

2. 3,769 + 4,109 _____

3. 4,312 − 1,162 _____

4. 369 + 409 + 430 + 378 _____

5. Reasonableness Is 5,500 a reasonable estimate for 5,128 + 921? Why or why not?

_____

_____

_____

Use with Lesson 1-5. **5**

Name _____

Estimating Sums and Differences

P 1-5

Estimate each answer. Tell which method you used.

1. 32,690 − 8,044 _____

2. 8,602 + 7,521 _____

3. 272 + 281 + 264 _____

4. 60,584 − 48,232 _____

5. **Number Sense** Think of two numbers whose sum would be about 3,000.

_____

6. Estimate Mr. Musial's income from January through March.

   _____

7. Estimate Mr. Musial's income from April through June.

   _____

8. Estimate the difference in Mr. Musial's income in March and April.

   _____

Mr. Musial's Income

Month	Income
January	$3,323
February	$3,706
March	$4,542
April	$2,502
May	$3,809
June	$3,238

Test Prep

9. Which shows the estimation of 23,486 + 9,227 + 196 using front-end estimation with adjusting?

   A. 32,000 **B.** 33,000 **C.** 34,000 **D.** 35,000

10. **Writing in Math** Describe a situation in which it would be better to overestimate than underestimate.

_____

_____

_____

Use with Lesson 1-5. **5**

Name _____

Estimating Products and Quotients   R 1-6

Here are two different methods to estimate products and quotients.

Use Rounding Round each factor to its greatest place. Multiply or divide mentally. When both numbers are rounded up, you have an overestimate. When both numbers are rounded down, you have an underestimate.

Estimate 4,698 × 165.

    4,698 →   5,000   Since both numbers were
  × 165 → × 200   rounded up, this is an
                1,000,000   overestimate.

Use Compatible Numbers Think of numbers that are close to the actual ones, but are easier to use. Multiply or divide mentally.

Estimate 718 ÷ 89.

718 ÷ 89   72 and 9 are
 ↓   ↓   compatible
720 ÷ 90 = 8   numbers.

So, 718 ÷ 89 ≈ 8.

Estimate each answer. Tell which method you used.

1. 4 × 19 _____

2. 17 × 59 _____

3. 6,192 × 11 _____

4. 781 ÷ 7 _____

5. 289 ÷ 29 _____

6. 425 ÷ 94 _____

7. 7,248 ÷ 82 _____

8. **Number Sense** Dean estimated 39 × 28 by rounding. He got 1,200 as his estimated product. Is this an overestimate or underestimate? How do you know?

_____

_____

6 Use with Lesson 1-6.

Name _____

Estimating Products and Quotients   P 1-6

Estimate each answer. Tell which method you used.

1. 511 ÷ 12 _____

2. 365 × 466 _____

3. 84,302 ÷ 12,444 _____

4. 28,867 × 303 _____

5. **Number Sense** Give an example of two factors that can be used to give an underestimated product of 2,400.

   _____

6. The distance between Las Vegas, NV, and Los Angeles, CA, is 269 mi. Bob drove between the two cities 6 times. About how many miles did he drive?

   _____

7. The distance between Fargo, ND, and St. Louis, MO, is 870 mi. Seven times the distance from Fargo to St. Louis is about how many miles?

   _____

Test Prep

8. Which is the best estimate for 82,336 ÷ 230?

   A. 200   **B.** 300   **C.** 400   **D.** 500

9. **Writing in Math** You are driving from Portland, Oregon, to Los Angeles, California. The total mileage is 1,892 mi. Your car can travel approximately 325 mi per tank of gas. Use a range to estimate how many tanks of gas you will need for the trip.

   _____
   _____
   _____

6 Use with Lesson 1-6.

PROBLEM-SOLVING SKILL
Read and Understand

R 1-7

Book Donation Mr. Peterson has 10,000 children's books in his personal collection. He wants to donate the books to the 20 elementary schools in Fairmont. If each school is to receive the same number of books, how many books will each school receive?

Read and Understand

Step 1: What do you know?

- Tell the problem in your own words.
  Each elementary school in Fairmont will share the 10,000 books.

- Identify key facts and details.
  There are 10,000 children's books and 20 elementary schools.

Step 2: What are you trying to find?

- Tell what the question is asking.
  You want to know the number of books each elementary school will receive.

- Show the main idea.

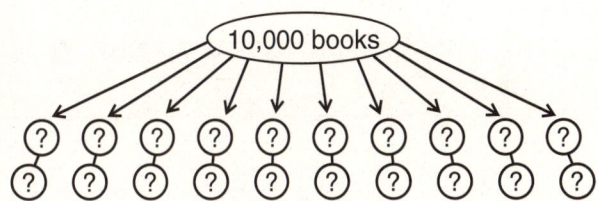

Use division. Each school will receive 10,000 ÷ 20 = 500 books.

Project Sharon's group needs to accumulate 700 points in order to receive an A for their project. The group has earned 532 points so far. The last part of the project is worth 175 points. If they earn all the points for the last part, will they have enough to earn an A on the project?

1. Show the main idea.

2. Solve the problem. Write your answer in a complete sentence.

Use with Lesson 1-7.

Name _____

PROBLEM-SOLVING SKILL P 1-7

Read and Understand

The attendance at a Florida amusement park changes throughout the year. In the winter, the attendance was 917,398. In the spring, it was 940,992. The summer attendance was 1,227,765, while the fall attendance was 824,023. What is the estimated difference between the season with the greatest attendance and the season with the least attendance?

1. Tell what you know about the problem in your own words.

   _____

   _____

2. Identify key facts and details.

   _____

   _____

   _____

   _____

3. Tell what the question is asking.

   _____

   _____

   _____

4. Show the main idea to help solve the problem. Write the answer in a complete sentence.

   _____

   _____

Use with Lesson 1-7.

Name _____

Order of Operations

R 1-8

Order of operations is a set of rules that mathematicians use when computing numbers. Here is how order of operations is used to solve the following problem: 7 + (5 × 4) × 3.

Order of Operations

First, compute all numbers inside parentheses.	7 + (5 × 4) × 3 7 + 20 × 3
Next, simplify exponents. If there are no exponents, go to the next step.	7 + 20 × 3
Then, multiply and divide the numbers from left to right.	7 + 60
Finally, add and subtract the numbers from left to right.	67

How to use parentheses to make a number sentence true:	6 + 2 × 9 = 72
Using order of operations, 6 + 2 × 9 = 24, not 72.	
Place parentheses around 6 + 2 so that this operation is done first:	(6 + 2) × 9 = 72 8 × 9 = 72

Evaluate each expression.

1. 8 + 7 × 5 = _____

2. 18 − 3 × 2 = _____

3. 3 × 7 + 3 × 5 = _____

4. 40 ÷ (2 × 4) = _____

5. 6 × 3 − 6 × 2 = _____

6. 9 + 2^3 = _____

7. 7 + 12 × 3 − 2 = _____

8. 4 × (5 + 5) ÷ 20 + 6 = _____

9. 4^2 − (3 × 5) = _____

10. (3 × 2) + 3^2 = _____

11. Reasoning Which operation should be performed *last* in this problem: 3^2 + 7 × 4? Why?

_____

Use parentheses to make each sentence true.

12. 0 × 6 + 9 = 9 _____

13. 3^2 + 2 × 2 = 13 _____

8 Use with Lesson 1-8.

Name _____

Order of Operations

P 1-8

Evaluate each expression.

1. $3 + 4 \times 7$

2. $88 - 6 \times 6$

3. $8 \times 2 + 7 \times 3$

_____   _____   _____

4. $(5 + 9) + 3 \times 8$

5. $(6 + 3^2) + 5$

6. $9^2 - (7 \times 5) + 3$

_____   _____   _____

7. $48 \div 2 + 6$

8. $26 \div (5 + 8) + 1$

9. $18 + 3 \times (6 \div 2)$

_____   _____   _____

10. **Reasoning** What operation would you perform *last* in this problem: $(2 \times 3) + (7 \times 2)$? _____

Use parentheses to make each number sentence true.

11. $10 + 5 \times 4^2 \div 2^3 = 20$

12. $124 - 6 \times 0 + 15 = 34$

13. $10^2 - 10 + 3 = 93$

14. $7 + 5 \times 3 \div 3 = 12$

15. Mr. Miller's sixth-grade class went on a field trip to hear the symphony perform. Their seats were grouped in the following ways: 2 groups of 3 seats; 3 groups of 4 seats, 4 groups of 2 seats, and 1 seat (for Mr. Miller). Write a number sentence to calculate how many students went on the field trip.

_____

_____

Test Prep

16. Evaluate the expression $(4^2 - 4) + 6 \div 2$.

   A. 4   B. 9   C. 12   D. 15

17. **Writing in Math** Suppose you had to evaluate $9^2 + 5 \times 4$. Tell the order in which you would compute these numbers.

_____

_____

8 Use with Lesson 1-8.

Name _____

Properties of Operations

R 1-9

Commutative Properties You can add or multiply numbers in any order and the sum or product will be the same. **Examples:** 10 + 5 + 3 = 5 + 3 + 10 = 18 7 × 5 = 5 × 7 = 35	**Associative Properties** You can group numbers differently. It will not affect the sum or product. **Examples:** 2 + (7 + 6) = (2 + 7) + 6 = 15 (4 × 5) × 8 = 4 × (5 × 8) = 160
Identity Properties You can add zero to a number or multiply it by 1 and not change the value of the number. **Examples:** 17 + 0 = 17 45 × 1 = 45	**Multiplication Property of Zero** If you multiply a number by zero, the product will always be zero. **Example:** 12 × 0 = 0

Find each missing number. Tell what property or properties are shown.

1. 9 × 5 = 5 × _____

2. _____ × 89 = 89

3. (3 + 4) + 19 = 3 + (_____ + 19)

4. 128 + _____ = 128

5. _____ + 18 = 18 + 12

6. **Reasoning** What is the product of 1 multiplied by zero? Explain how you know.

Use with Lesson 1-9. **9**

Name _____

Properties of Operations

P 1-9

Find each missing number. Tell what property or properties are shown.

1. (32 + _____) + 2 + 7 = 32 + (14 + 2) + 7

   _____

2. 8 + 6 + 12 = _____ + 12 + 6

   _____

3. (8 × _____) × 7 = 8 × (9 × 7)

   _____

4. _____ × 34 × 5 × 6 = 0

   _____

5. 12 × 3 = 3 × _____

   _____

6. 1 × _____ = 288

   _____

7. **Reasoning** Write a number sentence that shows why the associative property does not work with subtraction.

   _____

Test Prep

8. Which property is shown in (23 × 5) × 13 × 7 = 23 × (5 × 13) × 7?

   A. Commutative Property of Multiplication **B.** Identity Property of Multiplication

   C. Associative Property of Multiplication **D.** Associative Property of Addition

9. **Writing in Math** Explain why you do not have to do any computing to solve 15 × 0 × (13 + 7).

   _____

Use with Lesson 1-9. **9**

Name _____

Mental Math: Using the Distributive Property

R 1-10

You can use the Distributive Property to multiply mentally.

Problem A: 6 × (50 + 4)
If you followed the order of operations, you would add the numbers in the parentheses first, then multiply 6 × 54.

Since 6 × 54 is difficult to multiply mentally, use the Distributive Property.

Multiply each number in   6 × (50 + 4)
the parentheses by 6.   (6 × 50) + (6 × 4)
                                      ↓   ↓
Add the products.   300 + 24
                                            324

Problem B: 8(15)   Remember, 8(15) means 8 × 15.
Use the Distributive Property to make it easier to multiply mentally.

                                           8(15)
Break apart 15 into 10 + 5.   8(10 + 5)
Then use the Distributive   (8 × 10) + (8 × 5)
Property to find the products,   80 + 40
and add them together.   120

Find each missing number.

1. 6(5 + 4) = 6(5) + _____(4)   **2.** 2(12 + _____) = 2(12) + 2(7)

3. 9(15) + 9(8) = 9(_____ + 8)   **4.** 8(7 + 3) = 8(7) + _____(3)

5. Number Sense What are two other ways to write 6(24)?

_____

Use the Distributive Property to multiply mentally.

6. 4(21) = _____   **7.** 7(10 + 8) = _____

8. 5(5 + 4) = _____   **9.** (10 + 12)3 = _____

10. 8 × 36 = _____   **11.** 7(89) = _____

10   Use with Lesson 1-10.

Name _____

Mental Math: Using the Distributive Property

P 1-10

Find each missing number.

1. _____(3 + 10) = 9(3) + 9(10)

2. 4(_____ + _____) = 4(7) + 4(9)

3. **Number Sense** Try using the Distributive Property with division to evaluate 12 ÷ (2 + 1). Does it work?

_____

_____

Use the Distributive Property to multiply mentally.

4. 5(3 + 7) = _____
5. 10(5 + 8) = _____
6. 6(15) = _____

7. (3)55 = _____
8. 20(33) = _____
9. (41)8 = _____

10. 11(3 + 7) = _____
11. 6(87) = _____
12. (20 + 3)30 = _____

The chart shows the number of subatomic particles—protons, neutrons, and electrons—in each atom of various elements. Find the total number of subatomic particles in the following elements.

Element	Protons	Neutrons	Electrons
Berylium	4	5	4
Carbon	6	6	6
Nitrogen	7	7	7

13. 2 berylium atoms

14. 3 carbon atoms

15. 5 nitrogen atoms

_____ _____ _____

Test Prep

16. Which is equivalent to 31(3 + 2)?

    A. 150   **B.** 151   **C.** 152   **D.** 155

17. **Writing in Math** Describe how you could use the Distributive Property to multiply mentally: 55(2 + 9).

_____

_____

10 Use with Lesson 1-10.

Name _____

Mental Math Strategies

R 1-11

You can use the properties of operations to compute mentally.
Here are three different strategies you can use.

Strategy A: Break apart the numbers.
Find 47 + 83 using mental math.   47 + 83
Break apart the numbers into   (40 + 7) + (80 + 3)
tens and ones.   (40 + 80) + (7 + 3)
Add the tens. Add the ones.   120 + 10
Add the sums together.   130

Strategy B: Look for multiples of 10 or 100.
Find 20 × 6 × 5 using mental math.
Multiply number pairs   20 × 5 = 100
having a product of 10 or 100.   100 × 6 = 600
Multiply the other number.   So, 20 × 6 × 5 = 600.

Strategy C: Use compensation.
Find 538 − 197 using mental math.
538 − 197
  ↓
  197 + 3   ←   Add 3 to 197.
  ↓
538 − 200 = 338   Since you added 3 to the number
338 + 3 = 341   you subtracted, add 3 to the
                     answer to compensate.

Compute mentally.

1. 43 + 78 = _____   2. 6 × 40 × 5 = _____

3. 2 × 8 × 50 = _____   4. 65 − 22 = _____

5. 94 + 53 = _____   6. 7 + 34 + 16 = _____

7. 125 + 14 + 75 = _____   8. 4 × 9 × 25 = _____

9. 579 − 295 = _____   10. 380 + 20 + 105 = _____

11. 7 × 25 × 4 = _____   12. 801 − 187 = _____

13. **Reasoning** Explain the steps you can use to find 7 × 2 × 50 mentally.

_____

_____

Use with Lesson 1-11.

Name _____

Mental Math Strategies

P 1-11

Compute mentally.

1. 8 × 15 × 50 = _____   2. 634 − 519 = _____

3. 78 + 89 = _____   4. 37 + 66 + 24 = _____

5. 4,922 − 301 = _____   6. 7 × 20 × 4 = _____

7. 34 + 45 + 84 = _____   8. 8 × 8 × 50 = _____

9. **Reasoning** Explain the steps you can use to find 2 × 36 × 50 mentally.

_____

_____

An apartment complex needs to purchase several new appliances. They have made a price list showing the cost of a few of these appliances. Compute mentally.

Appliance	Price
Refrigerator/freezer	$938
Washing machine	$465
Dryer	$386

10. Find the cost of a washing machine and a dryer.

_____

11. How much more does a refrigerator/freezer cost than a dryer? _____

12. Find the total cost for 3 refrigerator/freezers. _____

Test Prep

13. Compute mentally: 450 − 280.

    A. 120   B. 140   C. 170   D. 190

14. **Writing in Math** Explain in your own words why 204 × 6 = (6 × 200) + (6 × 4).

_____

_____

_____

Use with Lesson 1-11. **11**

Name _____

PROBLEM-SOLVING SKILL   R 1-12
Plan and Solve

Twice at Two A clock strikes once at one o'clock, twice at two o'clock, and continues to strike each hour. It does not strike on each half hour. How many total times does the clock strike in 24 hours?

Here are the steps to follow when you plan and solve a problem.

Step 1: Choose a strategy.	Step 2: Stuck? Don't give up. Try these.	Step 3: Answer the question in the problem.
• **Show what you know.** Draw a picture, make an organized list, make a table or chart, or use objects/act it out. • **Look for a pattern.** • **Try, check, and revise.** • **Write an equation.** • **Use logical reasoning.** • **Solve a simpler problem.** • **Work backward.**	• Reread the problem. • Tell the problem in your own words. • Tell what you know. • Identify key facts and details. • Try a different strategy. • Retrace your steps.	What strategy can be used to solve the Twice at Two problem? An organized list can accurately show the information and make the problem easier to solve.

$$1 \text{ o'clock} \ldots\ldots\ldots\ldots\ldots 12 \text{ o'clock}$$
$$\underbrace{1 + 2 + 3 + 4 + 5 + 6 + 7 + 8 + 9 + 10 + 11 + 12 = 78}_{\text{Strikes}}$$
$$78 \times 2 = 156 \qquad (2 \times 12 = 24 \text{ hr})$$

Answer: In 24 hours, the clock strikes 156 times.

Video Games Jane has $80 to buy games. Sports games are $11 each, and adventure games are $13 each. How many different combinations of games can Jane buy without leaving enough money to buy another game? Which combination will allow her to spend the least amount?

1. What strategy might work to solve this problem?

   _____

   _____

2. Give the answer to the problem in a complete sentence.

   _____

   _____

© Pearson Education, Inc. 6

12 Use with Lesson 1-12.

Name _____

PROBLEM-SOLVING SKILL P 1-12
Plan and Solve

Babysitting Margo is saving her babysitting money for a new jacket. The jacket costs $75. If Margo makes $15 each week, how many weeks will it take her to save enough money to buy the jacket?

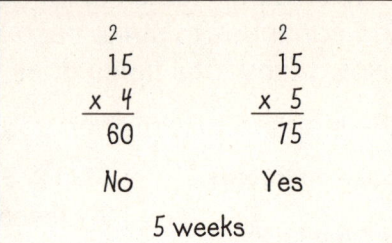

1. What strategy did Tammy use to solve the problem?

   _____

2. Write the answer to the problem in a complete sentence.

   _____

   _____

New CD Joe is making a CD for his collection. The CD holds a total of 70 min of music. Of the songs he wants to put on the CD, 2 are 4 min, 30 sec long; 3 are 5 min, 20 sec long; 4 are 6 min long; and 1 is 3 min long. How many minutes will all the songs take up on the CD?

3. What strategy did you use to solve this problem?

   _____

4. Write the answer to the problem in a complete sentence.

   _____

   _____

Cat's Age Mary adopted a cat from the local animal shelter in 1999. The cat was 3 years old. How old will the cat be in 2012?

5. What strategy did you use to solve the problem?

   _____

6. Write the answer to the problem in a complete sentence.

   _____

   _____

12 Use with Lesson 1-12.

Name _____

Variables and Expressions

R 1-13

Word Phrase	Operation	Algebraic Expression
• six **more than** a number • the **sum of** 5 and a number *t*	Addition	$n + 6$ $5 + t$
• three **less than** a number *n* • the **difference** of 7 and a number *t*	Subtraction	$n - 3$ $7 - t$
• the **product of** 9 and a number *n* • 12 **times** a number *b*	Multiplication	$9 \times n$ or $9n$ or $9 \cdot n$ $b \times 12$
• the **quotient** of a number *g* divided by 3	Division	$g \div 3$ or $\frac{g}{3}$

To evaluate $23n$ for $n = 5$, substitute 5 for *n*, and multiply.

$23 \times 5 = 115$

Write each word phrase as an algebraic expression.

1. 25 more than *p* _____

2. the product of *s* and 7 _____

3. 14 decreased by *e* _____

4. *n* divided by 18 _____

Evaluate each expression for $b = 6$.

5. $b \times 5$ _____

6. $19 + b$ _____

7. $42 \div b$ _____

For 8–11, evaluate each expression for $n = 3, 5,$ and 7.

8. $n - 1$ _____, _____, _____

9. $n + 13$ _____, _____, _____

10. $9n$ _____, _____, _____

11. $\frac{105}{n}$ _____, _____, _____

12. Number Sense Write $11n$ as a word phrase in two different ways.

_____

_____

Use with Lesson 1-13.

Name _____

Variables and Expressions

P 1-13

Write each word phrase as an algebraic expression.

1. twice *n*
2. 3 less than *p*
3. *c* increased by 6

4. *m* times 31
5. 5*d* minus 4
6. 50 divided by *t*

7. **Number Sense** What is a word phrase for 42 + 36 + *n*?

Evaluate each expression for *y* = 2, 6, and 8.

8. *y* + 12 _____, _____, _____
9. $\frac{96}{y}$ _____, _____, _____
10. 5*y* _____, _____, _____
11. $\frac{y}{2}$ _____, _____, _____
12. 11*y* _____, _____, _____
13. 561 − *y* _____, _____, _____

14. A state produces *b* peaches per month. Write an expression for the average number of peaches produced each year.

15. The Oregon Dunes national resource area in Oregon covers 27,212 acres. Another national resource area in New Mexico covers *v* acres. Write an expression that shows the approximate number of acres covered by both areas.

Test Prep

16. Evaluate the expression 10*f* if *f* = 31.

    A. 3.1
    B. 31
    C. 310
    D. 3,100

17. **Writing in Math** Write two different word phrases for 5*h*.

Use with Lesson 1-13.

Name _____

Properties of Equality

R 1-14

To keep both sides of an equation equal, you must do the same thing to both sides.

Balanced Equation	Unbalanced Equation
$1 = 1$ 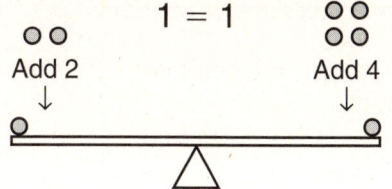 $3 = 3$	$1 = 1$ 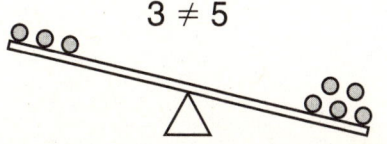 $3 \neq 5$
The equation is balanced because both sides are equal, or have the same amount. We added the same amount to each side of the equation.	The equation is not balanced. 3 does not equal 5. We did not add the same amount to both sides of the equation.

You can use inverse operations to get the variable alone in an equation. Example:

$x + 5 = 21$ The operation is addition, so use its inverse, subtraction.

$x + 5 - 5 = 21 - 5$ Subtract 5 from both sides of the equation to get x alone

$x = 16$ and keep the equation balanced.

Explain how to get the variable alone in each equation.

1. $3p = 27$ _____

2. $10 + h = 54$ _____

3. Reasoning A level pan balance shows $g - 47 = 15$. Explain why you should add to get the variable alone.

_____
_____
_____

Name _____

Properties of Equality

P 1-14

1. You know 16 + 4 = 20. Does 16 + 4 − 4 = 20 − 4? Why or why not?

_____

_____

Explain how to get the variable alone in each equation.

2. $\frac{f}{25} = 3$ _____

3. $54 + t = 132$ _____

4. $m - 8 = 24$ _____

5. $7t = 70$ _____

6. $42 = 6v$ _____

7. $\frac{y}{20} = 70$ _____

8. **Reasoning** Explain why multiplication gets the variable alone in $a \div 32 = 2$.

_____

_____

_____

Test Prep

9. How would you get the variable alone in the following equation: $g \div 9 = 7$?

   A. multiply both sides of the equation by 9

   B. multiply both sides of the equation by 7

   C. divide both sides of the equation by 9

   D. divide both sides of the equation by 7

10. **Writing in Math** To get the variable alone, Ranier added 29 to both sides of $b + 18 = 29$. Was he correct? Explain.

_____

_____

Use with Lesson 1-14.

Name _____

Solving Equations with Whole Numbers

R 1-15

You can use inverse operations and the properties of equality to get the variable alone to solve an equation.

Solve the equation $3d = 51$.

$3d = 51$
$3d \div 3 = 51 \div 3$ To *undo* the multiplication, divide each side of the equation by 3.
$d = 17$

To check your answer, substitute 17 for d in the equation $3d = 51$. If both sides of the equation can be simplified to the same number, the value of the variable is correct.

Check: $3d = 51$
$3(17) = 51$
$51 = 51$

It checks.

Explain how to get the variable alone in each equation.

1. $k + 19 = 34$

2. $37 = f - 24$

_____

_____

3. $17z = 136$

4. $l \div 29 = 10$

_____

_____

Solve each equation and check your answer.

5. $m \times 7 = 21$ _____

6. $15 + n = 35$ _____

7. $8g = 64$ _____

8. $\dfrac{99}{v} = 9$ _____

9. $t - 54 = 1$ _____

10. $44 = p + 13$ _____

11. **Number Sense** How can you check if 24 is the correct value for s in $3s = 78$?

_____

_____

Use with Lesson 1-15.   **15**

Name _____

Solving Equations with Whole Numbers

P 1-15

Explain how to get the variable alone in each equation.

1. $8x = 96$ _____

2. $n - 16 = 2$ _____

3. $\frac{t}{20} = 300$ _____

4. $h + 32 = 81$ _____

5. **Number Sense** What is the solution for $72n = 144$? _____

Solve each equation and check your answer.

6. $k - 52 = 105$

7. $\frac{x}{12} = 5$

8. $m + 18 = 26$

9. $56 = 56s$

10. $g + 43 = 88$

11. $\frac{v}{4} = 15$

12. $7r = 560$

13. $y - 27 = 94$

14. $34h = 0$

15. The Memorial Day Parade featured marching bands from all over the state. There are 5 French horns in each of the bands in the parade and a total of 75 French horns altogether. Solve the equation $5x = 75$ to determine the number of marching bands in the parade.

Test Prep

16. Which shows the solution for $f - 320 = 647$?

   A. 967   B. 337   C. 327   D. 320

17. **Writing in Math** Explain how to get the variable alone in $\frac{m}{16} = 4$.

Use with Lesson 1-15.

Name _____

PROBLEM-SOLVING SKILL
Look Back and Check

R 1-16

Toy Sale Dave and his friends had a toy sale. They charged $6 each for stuffed animals, $5 each for board games, and $4 each for action figures. They sold 15 stuffed animals, 20 board games, and 25 action figures. What was the total amount of money they made?

Kelly's Work

(15 × $6) + (20 × $5) + (25 × $4)
   ↓   ↓   ↓
  $90   + $100   + $100 = $290

Dave and his friends made $290 at the toy sale.

You are not finished with a problem until you look back and check your answer. Here are the steps to follow.

Step 1: Check your answer.

Did Kelly answer the right question?
Yes, she found the total amount of money made at the sale.

Step 2: Check your work.

Kelly could use division and subtraction to check if her answer is correct. $100 ÷ $4 = 25; $100 ÷ $5 = 20; $90 ÷ $6 = 15.
$290 − $100 − $100 − $90 = 0

Equal Amounts Ginger has an equal number of dimes and quarters and no other coins. The total amount of money she has is $2.10. How many of each coin does she have?

Look back and check Tito's work on this problem.

Tito's Work

Dimes	Quarters	Total
1	1	$0.35
2	2	$0.70
3	3	$1.05
4	4	$1.40
5	5	$2.10

Ginger has 5 of each coin.

1. Did Tito answer the right question?

_____

_____

2. Is his work correct?

_____

_____

_____

Name _____

PROBLEM-SOLVING SKILL   P 1-16

Look Back and Check

Party Planning Loren needs to buy supplies for a party. She buys 36 party favors. There are 12 friends coming to the party. How many party favors will each friend get?

Loren's Solution

There are 36 favors and 12 friends.
$12n = 36$
$n = \dfrac{36}{12}$
$n = 2$
Each friend will get 2 favors.

1. Has the right question been answered? Explain.

_____

_____

_____

2. Is her work correct? Explain.

_____

_____

_____

Postage In the United States in 2002, it costs $0.37 to send a letter-sized envelope through the mail. Antonio wants to send invitations to at least 200 people. He has $85 to spend on the postage. Does Antonio have enough money to mail the 200 invitations?

Antonio's Solution

```
    200
 x $0.37
   1400
    600
  $74.00
```

It will cost Antonio $74 to send out all 200 invitations. Since he has $85, he will have $11 left.

3. Has the right question been answered? Explain.

_____

_____

_____

4. Is his work correct? Explain.

_____

_____

_____

Use with Lesson 1-16.

Name _____

PROBLEM-SOLVING APPLICATIONS
In the Driver's Seat

R 1-17

The table below contains the number of automobiles that were imported into the United States from 1998 through 2000 and the nations from which they were imported.

	Japan	Germany	Italy	France	Canada
1998	1,456,081	373,330	2,104	56	1,837,615
1999	1,707,277	461,061	1,697	186	2,170,427
2000	1,839,093	488,323	3,125	134	2,138,811

The table shows that there were 1,697 cars imported from Italy in 1999.

The 6 in 1,**6**97 is in the hundreds place. So, the value of the 6 is 600.

1. How many cars were imported from Japan in 1998? What is the value of the 5 in this number?

2. How many cars were imported from Canada in 1999? What is the value of the 4 in this number?

3. Write the numbers of cars imported in 1998 in order from least to greatest.

4. Round the number of cars imported from Germany in 2000 to the nearest thousand.

5. Estimate the total number of cars that were imported from Italy from 1998 through 2000.

6. **Algebra** Write the word phrase *the product of n and the number of cars imported from France in 2000* as an algebraic expression.

Use with Lesson 1-17. **17**

Name _____

PROBLEM-SOLVING APPLICATIONS
Load That Ship!

P 1-17

Ports are areas where ships are loaded and unloaded with cargo. Most large ports are located in busy cities along large waterways.

Cargo Processed in 1999

Port Name	Cargo (tons)
Houston, TX	158,828,203
New Orleans, LA	87,511,476
South Louisiana, LA	214,196,912
Valdez, AK	53,391,575

1. What is the value of the 4 in the number of tons processed in the South Louisiana port?

   _____

2. Write the number of tons processed in the Valdez port in short-word form.

   _____

3. Round the number of tons processed in the New Orleans port to the nearest thousand.

   _____

4. Round the number of tons processed in the Houston port to the nearest million.

   _____

5. Write the numbers in the table in order from least to greatest.

   _____

6. About how many total tons were processed in both the New Orleans and South Louisiana ports?

   _____

7. **Estimation** Estimate how many more tons were processed in Houston than in Valdez.

   _____

Use with Lesson 1-17. **17**

Name _____

Understanding Decimals

R 2-1

A decimal is a number that uses a decimal point. Each digit in a decimal number has a place and value. You can use a place-value chart to determine a digit's place and value.

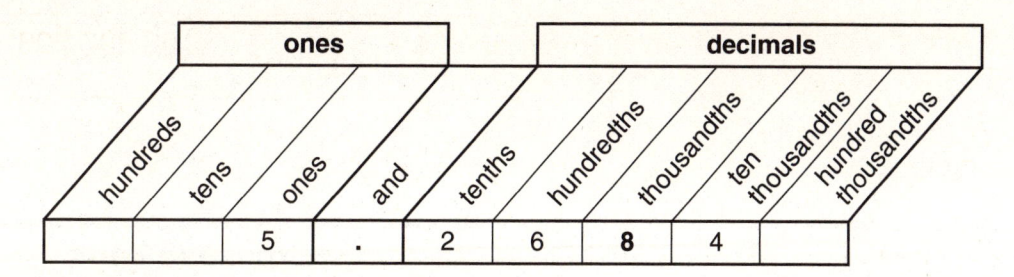

hundreds	tens	ones	and	tenths	hundredths	thousandths	ten thousandths	hundred thousandths
		5	.	2	6	8	4	

(ones | decimals)

The 8 is in the thousandths place. Its value is 8 thousandths, or 0.008.

The standard form of the number is 5.2684. The word form is five and two thousand, six hundred eighty-four ten thousandths.

The expanded form is: _____ + 0.2 + 0.06 + _____ + 0.0004.

Give the place and value of the 9 in each number.

1. 2.195 _____

2. 6.2394 _____

3. 34.32629 _____

Complete the table.

	Standard Form	Short-Word Form	Expanded Form
4.	2.346	2 and 346 thousandths	
5.			1 + 0.6 + 0.0009

6. **Number Sense** Express $\frac{8}{10}$, $\frac{8}{100}$, and $\frac{8}{10,000}$ as decimal numbers.

_____

7. **Writing in Math** Explain how you know that 17 thousandths has more than two places to the right of the decimal point.

_____

_____

18 Use with Lesson 2-1.

Name _____

Understanding Decimals

P 2-1

Give the place and value of the 3 in each number.

1. 56.389 _____

2. 9.6431 _____

3. 0.72536 _____

Complete the table.

	Standard Form	Short-Word Form	Expanded Form
4.		2 and 3 hundredths	
5.			70 + 8 + 0.4 + 0.06

6. **Number Sense** Express $\frac{4}{10}$, $\frac{44}{100}$, and $\frac{444}{1,000}$ as decimal numbers.

_____ _____ _____

Write the total number of points for each event in expanded form.

7. team

_____

8. all-around

_____

Event	Winning Points
Team	154.608
All-around	38.642
Uneven bars	9.862

9. uneven bars

_____

Test Prep

10. Which shows the short-word form for 16.011?

   A. 16 and 11 thousandths   B. 16 and 11 hundredths

   C. 16 and 11 tenths   D. 16 + 0.011

11. **Writing in Math** Explain how to determine the place and value of a number.

_____

18 Use with Lesson 2-1.

Name _____

Comparing and Ordering Decimals   R 2-2

Use a number line

Remember, as you move to the right on a number line, the numbers are greater in value. As you move to the left, the numbers are lesser in value.

Compare 0.332 and 0.323.

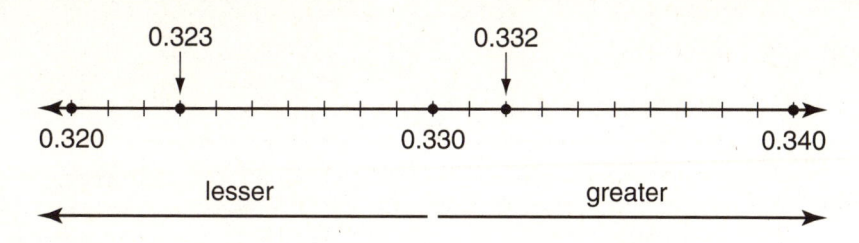

```
          0.323              0.332
    ←——+—+—+—+—+—+—+—+—+—+—+—+—+—+—+—+—+—+—+—+—→
   0.320            0.330              0.340

         ←———— lesser ————|———— greater ————→
```

Since 0.332 is to the right of 0.323, 0.332 > 0.323.

Align the digits

Order 3.27, 4.86, 3.09, and 3.85 from least to greatest.

- Start at the left and compare digits in the same place value.
- Order the digits by place value.

In order from least to greatest, the numbers are:

_____, _____, _____, _____.

Order ones.
3.|27
3.|09
3.|85
4.|86

Order tenths.
3.|0|9
3.|2|7
3.|8|5
4.|8|6

Use >, <, or = to compare each pair of numbers.

1. 3.030 ◯ 3.03

2. 9.3226 ◯ 9.3262

3. 1.39292 ◯ 13.9232

4. 0.135 ◯ 0.0135

Order from least to greatest.

5. 23.4   24.4   24.34   _____

6. 16.03   16.30   16.003   _____

7. 2.5021   2.00251   2.05021   2.00502   _____

8. **Writing in Math** Explain why 37.75 is greater than 37.07.

_____

_____

Use with Lesson 2-2.   **19**

Name _____

Comparing and Ordering Decimals   P 2-2

Use >, <, or = to compare each pair of numbers.

1. 656.07 ◯ 656.23
2. 73.42 ◯ 72.56
3. 0.01 ◯ 0.10
4. 7.999 ◯ 7.998

Order from least to greatest.

5. 639.087, 639.078, 638.088

_____

6. 0.0909, 0.0989, 0.0999

_____

7. 19.235, 19.23, 19.240, 19.2353

_____

8. Order the lung volumes from least to greatest.

   _____

   _____

9. Which animal has a lung volume that is greater than a cow's?

Animal (adult)	Lung Volume (in quarts)
Cat	0.328
Cow	10.565
Mouse	0.001
Whale	105.65

10. Which two animals have the closest lung volume?

Test Prep

11. Which decimal is greater than 3.33 but less than 3.34?

    A. 2.3349   B. 3.305   C. 3.329   D. 3.336

12. **Writing in Math** Explain how to find a number that is between 4.9 and 4.95.

_____

_____

Name _____

Rounding Decimals

R 2-3

Round 0.168 to the nearest hundredth.

Find the rounding place. ⟶ 0.1<u>6</u>8
Look at the digit to the ⟶ 0.16⃞8⃞
right of this place.
If the digit is 5 or greater, add ⟶ 8 > 5
1 to the rounding digit. If the
digit is less than 5, leave the
rounding digit alone.
Drop the digits to the right ⟶ 0.17
of the rounding digit.

So, 0.168 rounded to the nearest
hundredth is 0.17.

Round 0.721 to the nearest hundredth.

The digit _____ is in the hundredths place. The digit to the right is less than 5, so leave the rounding digit alone.

So, 0.721 rounded to the nearest hundredth is _____.

Round to the underlined place.

1. 71.2<u>4</u>7 _____
2. 3.7<u>3</u>1 _____
3. 6.<u>1</u>89 _____

4. 22.6<u>2</u>33 _____
5. 3.0<u>1</u>56 _____
6. 5.10<u>7</u>9 _____

7. 45.451<u>5</u>1 _____
8. 0.00<u>6</u>75 _____
9. 1.<u>5</u>55 _____

10. 4<u>3</u>7.821 _____
11. 10.<u>9</u>711 _____
12. 87.246<u>2</u>7 _____

13. **Number Sense** A number rounds to 5.68. Write one possibility for the number.

_____

14. **Reasoning** Does the number in the tenths place change when you round 3.1678 to the nearest hundredth? Explain your answer.

_____
_____
_____

Rounding Decimals

P 2-3

Round to the underlined place.

1. 0.00<u>4</u>3 _____   2. 8<u>4</u>.638 _____

3. 2.<u>9</u>84 _____   4. 21<u>7</u>.4 _____

5. 0.00<u>1</u>7 _____   6. 2.7<u>0</u>9 _____

7. 371.<u>9</u>02 _____   8. 45.<u>9</u>9 _____

9. **Number Sense** A number rounds to 6.78. List three possibilities for the number.

_____

Departure City	Destination City	Fare
Portland	San Diego	$208.75
San Diego	Denver	$310.45
Denver	Portland	$296.97

Round each of the round-trip fares to the nearest one dollar. Then round to the nearest ten cents.

10. Portland to San Diego _____

11. San Diego to Denver _____

12. Denver to Portland _____

Test Prep

13. Which number can round to 6.766?

   A. 6.7688   B. 6.7669   C. 6.7659   D. 6.7654

14. **Writing in Math** Explain how 1.1, 1.06, and 1.059 can all be rounded forms of 1.0592.

_____

_____

20 Use with Lesson 2-3.

Name _____

Estimating with Decimals

R 2-4

You can use rounding and compatible numbers to estimate with decimals.

Jane bought a shirt for $29.99, a hat for $9.75, and a pair of socks for $5.12. About how much did she spend?

    Round each number to the nearest dollar, then add.

    So, Jane spent about $45.00.

$29.99 ⟶ $30.00
$ 9.75 ⟶ $10.00
+$ 5.12 ⟶ $ 5.00
≈ $45.00

Estimate 78.12 ÷ 3.88.

    Find compatible numbers.

    78.12 is close to 80 and 3.88 is close to 4.
    Four is easy to divide into 80.

80 ÷ 4 = 20

So, 78.12 ÷ 3.88 ≈ 20.

Estimate each answer.

1. 15.03 − 4.89 _____

2. $18.33 + $9.84 _____

3. $11.85 ÷ $4.27 _____

4. $9.66 − $6.12 _____

5. 3.89 × 7.0202 _____

6. 4.03 + 11.0086 _____

7. 23.95 × 9.828 _____

8. 480.456 ÷ 48.003 _____

9. **Writing in Math** Why would it make sense to use compatible numbers to estimate 43.56 ÷ 4.912?

_____

_____

10. **Reasoning** About how much would 11 cans of beans cost? How did you get your answer?

_____

_____

Gene's Groceries	
Can of beans	$0.89
Package of pita bread	$3.75
Package of crescent rolls	$2.99
Large yogurt	$1.81
Salmon fillet	$5.87

11. Wendi needs to buy 5 packages of pita bread and 3 packages of crescent rolls. About how much will she spend?

_____

Use with Lesson 2-4. **21**

Name _____

Estimating with Decimals

P 2-4

Estimate each answer.

1. $36.17 + $42.89 _____
2. 25.9 ÷ 12.8 _____
3. 78.11 × 5.7 _____
4. 132.36 − 48.31 _____
5. $421.90 ÷ $20.10 _____
6. 16.48 × 3.2 _____
7. 94.951 − 67.632 _____
8. $37.55 + $83.69 _____

9. **Number Sense** Is 2 or 4 a better estimate for the quotient 47.8 ÷ 11.6? Explain.

_____

_____

10. Victoria has $10 to spend on her new puppy. Name 3 different items she can buy.

_____

_____

Pet Supplies	
Food dish	$2.69
Water bowl	$2.39
Leash	$5.29
Squeaky toy	$1.32
Rope toy	$2.45
Brush	$4.00

11. Joe has $5 to spend on his dog, Frisky. Can he buy the food dish and a brush? Why or why not?

_____

12. **Mental Math** Estimate the total for all the items.

_____

Test Prep

13. Which is the most reasonable estimate for the total of $22.16 + $57.89 + $46.41?

    A. $110   B. $130   C. $180   D. $250

14. **Writing in Math** You want to buy supplies for a school project. Explain why you would want an estimate to be greater than the exact answer.

_____

_____

Use with Lesson 2-4.

Adding and Subtracting Whole Numbers and Decimals

R 2-5

Find 2.3 + 0.09 + 41.6.

Estimate: 2 + 0 + 42 = 44

Write the numbers, lining up the decimal points. Annex zeros so all numbers have the same number of decimal places.

Add the numbers. Regroup if necessary. Write the decimal point in your answer.

```
   2.30
   0.09
 + 41.60
  43.99
```

Since 43.99 is close to 44, the answer is reasonable.

Find 18.5 − 7.82.

Estimate: 19 − 8 = 11

Write the numbers, lining up the decimal points. Annex zeros so all numbers have the same number of decimal places.

Subtract the numbers. Regroup if necessary. Write the decimal point in your answer.

```
    7 4
  18.5̸0̸
 −  7.82
   10.68
```

Since 10.68 is close to 11, the answer is reasonable.

Find each sum or difference.

1. 45.6 + 26.3

2. 84.84 − 22.7

3. 77 + 3.09

4. 14.25 − 5.17

5. 23.64 − 8.73

6. 29 − 0.45

7. 17.08 + 14.04 + 2.30

8. 5,712.11 + 921.79 + 5.35

9. **Estimation** Estimate the sum of 3.7 and 9.8. _____

10. Find the total distance all three cars have traveled.

Mr. Cortez	Ms. Brown	Gerrie
13052.64	6520.10	920.70

22 Use with Lesson 2-5.

Name _____

Adding and Subtracting Whole Numbers and Decimals

P 2-5

Find each sum or difference.

1. 22 − 0.99 =

2. 9.8347 − 1.26 =

3. 5.011 + 1.23 + 23.7629 =

4. 101.21 − 45.6 =

5. 0.03 + 1.85 =

6. $67.85 + $97.12 =

7. Number Sense Use each of the digits 0, 1, 2, 3, 4, and 5 exactly once to write a decimal subtraction problem. The difference must be the same as one of the decimals in the problem.

8. Find the difference in price between the cost of 1 tube of glue and 1 roll of tape.

9. Find the cost of 2 packs of markers.

Craft Supplies

Poster board	$1.29/sheet
Markers	$4.50/pack
Tape	$1.99/roll
Construction paper	$3.79/pack
Glue	$2.39/tube

10. How much more do 2 packs of markers cost than 4 sheets of poster board?

Test Prep

11. Which is the difference of 8,246.4 − 57.73?

   A. 8,067.03 **B.** 8,144.06 **C.** 8,187.07 **D.** 8,188.67

12. Writing in Math Is 9.008 the correct answer for 9.009 − 0.01? If not, tell why and provide the correct answer.

22 Use with Lesson 2-5.

Multiplying Whole Numbers and Decimals

R 2-6

Find 12.7 × 2.4.

Estimate: 13 × 2 = 26

Multiply as you would with whole numbers.

Count the total number of decimal places in both factors. Start at the right of the product. Move to the left the total number of decimal places in both factors. Sometimes you have to annex zeros to the left of the product to place the decimal point correctly.

```
    1
   1 2
   12.7    ← one decimal place
 × 2.4    ← one decimal place
   508
  1
   2540
   30.48   ← two decimal places
              from the right
```

Place the decimal point in each product.

1. 1.2 × 3.6 = 432

2. 5.5 × 3.77 = 20735

3. 4.4 × 2.333 = 102652

Find each product.

4. 4 × 5.2

5. 2.7 × 2.6

6. 14.8 × 3.7 × 10

7. 4.6 × 0.3 × 100

8. 0.2 × 0.61

9. 17 × 0.087

10. 0.53 × 12.8

11. 8 × 0.06

12. **Number Sense** Two factors are multiplied and their product is 34.44. One factor is a whole number. How many decimal places are in the other factor?

13. **Writing in Math** How many decimal places will be in the product 4.5 × 0.007? Explain.

Use with Lesson 2-6. **23**

Multiplying Whole Numbers and Decimals

P 2-6

Place the decimal point in each product.

1. 3 × 6.892 = 20676 _____

2. 0.3 × 4.57 = 1371 _____

Find each product.

3. 14.3 × 2.1 × 8.9 = _____

4. 0.45 × 0.01 = _____

5. 67.1 × 0.3 × 0.4 = _____

6. 582.1 × 4.2 = _____

7. **Reasoning** Show how to find the product of 16.2 × 4 using addition.

_____

8. Which activity is 6 times faster than the fastest rowing speed?

_____

9. The fastest speed a table tennis ball has been hit is 21.12 times faster than the speed for the fastest swimmer. What is the speed for the table tennis ball?

_____

10. How fast would 1.5 times the fastest rowing speed be?

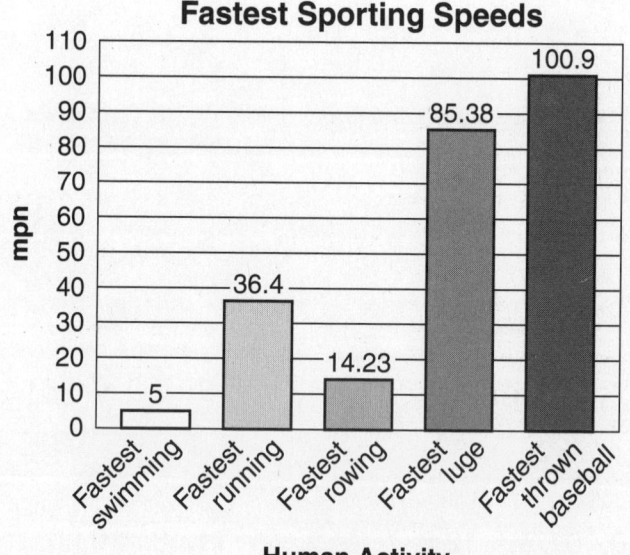

_____

Fastest Sporting Speeds

- Fastest swimming: 5 mph
- Fastest running: 36.4
- Fastest rowing: 14.23
- Fastest luge: 85.38
- Fastest thrown baseball: 100.9

Human Activity

Test Prep

11. Which is the product of 241.82 × 3.8?

   A. 91.8916   B. 918.916   C. 9,189.16   D. 91,891.6

12. **Writing in Math** Explain why multiplying 37.4 × 0.01 gives a product that is less than 37.4.

_____

_____

Use with Lesson 2-6.   23

Name _____

Dividing by a Whole Number

R 2-7

Dividing a decimal by a whole number is similar to dividing whole numbers by whole numbers.

Find 196 ÷ 32.

Estimate: 210 ÷ 30 = 7

Step 1 Divide. Put the decimal point in dividend and quotient.

```
      6.
32)196.
   -192
      4
```

Step 2 Annex a zero. Divide. Subtract then bring down.

```
      6.1
32)196.0
   -192 ↓
       40
      -32
        8
```

Step 3 Repeat until there is no remainder.

```
      6.125
32)196.000
   -192 ↓
       40
      -32↓
        80
       -64↓
        160
       -160
          0
```

Since 6.125 is close to 7, the answer is reasonable.

Find each quotient. Round to nearest hundredth if necessary.

1. 9)20.7

2. 6)31.2

3. 7)22.61

4. 11)93.5

5. 12)4.5

6. 8)401.2

7. Marcus purchased a 12 lb bag of trail mix. He paid $10.80. Find the price per pound.

_____

8. **Writing in Math** Destiny said that 0.6 ÷ 2 = 0.3. Is she correct? Explain why or why not.

_____

24 Use with Lesson 2-7.

Name _____

Dividing by a Whole Number

P 2-7

Find each quotient. Round to the nearest hundredth if necessary.

1. 77 ÷ 4 = _____   2. 3.21 ÷ 6 = _____

3. 14 ÷ 80 = _____   4. $1.13 ÷ 22 = _____

5. 130 ÷ 10,000 = _____   6. 8.6 ÷ 86 = _____

7. 231 ÷ 11 = _____   8. 961.23 ÷ 13 = _____

9. **Number Sense** How can you tell if 54.6 ÷ 3 is greater than or less than 54.6 ÷ 30?

_____

_____

For 10 and 11, write the price per ounce of each type of nut butter to the nearest cent.

10. peanut butter

_____

11. almond butter

_____

Nut Butter	Price per Container
Peanut	12 oz for $1.11
Cashew	11 oz for $3.30
Almond	16 oz for $2.24

12. Which type of nut butter is the most expensive per ounce? _____

Test Prep

13. Find the quotient of 60.82 ÷ 17. Round to the nearest hundredth.

   A. 3.577   B. 3.58   C. 3.59   D. 3.6

14. **Writing in Math** Explain how you determined the price per ounce of a 12 oz jar of peanut butter in Exercise 10.

_____

_____

_____

Name _____

PROBLEM-SOLVING SKILL
Interpreting Remainders

R 2-8

Author Donna is writing a 108-page book. If she plans to write 16 pages per day, how many days will it take her to write the book?

Divide to find the answer.

Estimate: 105 ÷ 15 = 7

Sometimes quotients include a remainder. The remainder represents 12 extra pages that need to be written. Donna will need another day to write the rest of the pages.

Since 6 R12 is close to 7, your answer is reasonable.

```
        6 R12
  16)108
      − 96
        12  ← remainder
```

Donna will need 7 days to write her book.

Sports Cards James collects sports cards. He stores them in plastic carriers. Each carrier holds 9 cards.

1. James has 138 cards. How many carriers will he need to store all his cards? _____

2. What does the remainder or decimal part of your answer represent?

   _____

   _____

3. How many cards are left over? _____

4. How many carriers will be completely filled? _____

Moving Day Mara is moving her CD collection. She has to bring her 235 CDs from her old room to her new room upstairs.

5. Mara can only carry 20 CDs at a time. How many trips will she need to take? _____

6. What does the remainder or decimal part of your answer represent?

   _____

   _____

7. How many CDs will she carry on her last trip? _____

Use with Lesson 2-8. **25**

Name _____

PROBLEM-SOLVING SKILL P 2-8
Interpreting Remainders

Igneous Quarry Company needs to deliver 284 tons of granite to a site that is 1,080 mi away from the company.

1. If each truck can carry a maximum load of 10 tons, how many full trucks will be needed?

   _____

2. How many tons of granite will need to be carried by an extra truck?

   _____

3. If a truck driver drives 600 mi per day, how many days will it take to drive 2,080 mi?

   _____

4. What does the remainder represent?

   _____

5. If the company charged $8,050 for the entire job, how much did it charge per ton for delivery?

   _____

6. What does the remainder represent and how did you adjust your answer to allow for this?

   _____

7. If each truck gets 7 mi to the gallon, how many gallons of gas will be needed for the 1,080 mi? (Round to the nearest hundredth.)

   _____

8. Each truck holds 100 gal of gas. If the drivers start with a full tank of fuel, how many times will they need to refuel?

   _____

Use with Lesson 2-8. **25**

Dividing by a Decimal

R 2-9

Find 4.728 ÷ 0.6.

Estimate: 48 ÷ 6 = 8

Count the number of decimal places in the divisor.

.6)4.728

one decimal place

Step 1 Move the decimal point to make the divisor a whole number.

6.)4.728

decimal point moved to make .6 become 6.

Step 2 Move the decimal point in the dividend the same number of spaces (4.728 × 10 = 47.28). Then write the decimal point in the quotient at the same place.

6.)47.28

moved one decimal place   moved one decimal place

Step 3 Divide the same way you do with whole numbers.

```
       7.88
   6)47.28
     -42 ↓
       5 2
     - 4 8 ↓
         48
       - 48
          0
```

Find each quotient.

1. 0.7)1.75

2. 0.8)3.624

3. 1.1)0.6391

4. 2.2)143

5. 0.09)0.05697

6. 0.15)1.146

7. **Writing in Math** Wendy divided 147 by 0.7. Jan divided 1,470 by 7. Should they both get the same answer? Explain.

Name _____

Dividing by a Decimal

P 2-9

Find each quotient.

1. 8.4 ÷ 0.3 = _____   2. 66.15 ÷ 0.63 = _____

3. 10.5 ÷ 1.5 = _____   4. 86 ÷ 0.4 = _____

5. 72.8 ÷ 1.4 = _____   6. 14.36 ÷ 0.4 = _____

7. 2.87 ÷ 0.01 = _____   8. 78.32 ÷ 0.22 = _____

9. **Reasoning** Why would multiplying both the dividend and the divisor by 10 sometimes make a problem easier to solve?

_____

_____

For each item, find how many times greater the 2002 cost is than the 1960 cost. Round your answer to the nearest hundredth.

Item	1960 Cost	2002 Cost
Movie admission	$0.75	$8.50
Regular popcorn	$0.25	$3.25
Regular drink	$0.35	$2.75

10. movie admission   11. regular popcorn   12. regular drink

_____   _____   _____

13. Which item has increased the greatest amount of times from its original cost? _____

Test Prep

14. Divide. Round to the nearest hundredth. 250.6 ÷ 1.6

    A. 156   B. 156.6   C. 156.61   D. 156.63

15. **Writing in Math** Lynn and Randi got different quotients when they divided 3.60 by 0.12. Whose work is correct? Explain why.

    Lynn: 0.30 / 12)3.60

    Randi: 30.0 / 12)360.

_____

_____

Multiplying and Dividing by Powers of Ten

R 2-10

Multiplying a number by a positive power of ten

Find 3.15×10^3.

Move the decimal point the same number of places to the **right** as the exponent. Annex zeros if you need to.

3.150

So, $3.15 \times 10^3 = 3,150$.

Multiplying a number by a negative power of ten

Find 7.34×10^{-3}. Remember $10^{-3} = 0.001$. So it is the same as 7.34×0.001.

Move the decimal point the same number of places to the **left** as the exponent. Add zeros if you need to.

So, $7.34 \times 10^{-3} = 0.00734$.

Dividing a number by a positive power of ten

Find $42.6 \div 10^3$.

Move the decimal point the same number of places to the **left** as the exponent. Annex zeros if you need to.

042.6

So, $42.6 \div 10^3 = 0.0426$.

Dividing a number by a negative power of ten

Find $24 \div 10^{-4}$. Remember $10^{-4} = 0.0001$. So it is the same as $24 \div 0.0001$.

Move the decimal point the same number of places to the **right** as the exponent. Add zeros if you need to.

So, $24 \div 10^{-4} = 240,000$.

Find each product or quotient.

1. $1,357 \div 10^2 =$

2. $0.00471 \times 10^5 =$

3. $25.346 \times 10^{-3} =$

4. $52.5 \div 10^{-2} =$

5. $139.3 \div 10^6 =$

6. $47.1303 \times 10^{-4} =$

7. **Number Sense** What happens to the dividend when you divide it by a negative exponent?

8. In 2000, the total value of all new cars that Americans bought was $\$274.5 \times 10^9$. Write this number in standard form.

Name _____

Multiplying and Dividing by Powers of Ten

P 2-10

Find each product or quotient.

1. $72.1 \times 10^3 =$ _____
2. $450 \times 10^{-4} =$ _____
3. $3.103 \div 10^3 =$ _____
4. $167.4 \div 10^{-2} =$ _____
5. $0.012 \times 10^{-2} =$ _____
6. $0.012 \div 10^2 =$ _____
7. $0.301 \div 10^{-3} =$ _____
8. $8.235 \times 10^4 =$ _____

9. **Reasoning** Explain in your own words why 10^4 is greater than 10^{-4}.

_____

_____

10. **Number Sense** Write 10, 100, and 1,000 as powers of ten. Do the same for 0.1, 0.01, and 0.001.

_____

11. Write the weight of an ant in standard form.

_____

12. Write the weight of an elephant in standard form.

_____

Weight (in pounds)	
Ant	2×10^{-5}
Hummingbird	2×10^{-2}
Elephant	16×10^3

13. Write the weight of a hummingbird in standard form. _____

Test Prep

14. Which is the quotient of $10.06 \div 10^{-4}$?

   A. 0.001006   B. 0.01006   C. 1,006   D. 100,600

15. **Writing in Math** Explain how you would write one billion as a power of ten.

_____

_____

Use with Lesson 2-10.

Name _____

Scientific Notation

R 2-11

Scientific notation is a way to express very large or very small numbers.

Write 58,300 and 0.00938 in scientific notation.

Number in Standard Form	Step 1	Step 2	Step 3	Number in Scientific Notation
	Move the decimal point to make the number greater than or equal to 1 but less than 10.	Count the number of decimal places you moved the decimal point. Note the direction you moved the decimal point.	Multiply the number by a power of ten. The exponent you use will represent the number of places you moved the decimal point. Move to the left: positive exponent. Move to the right: negative exponent.	
58,300	5.8300	4 places to the left		5.83×10^4
0.00938	0.00983	3 places to the right		9.38×10^{-3}

Give each missing power of ten.

1. $250{,}000 = 2.5 \times$ _____

2. $86{,}900 = 8.69 \times$ _____

3. $0.0054 = 5.4 \times$ _____

4. $0.00000498 = 4.98 \times$ _____

Write each number in scientific notation.

5. 579,000 _____

6. 4,583,000 _____

7. 0.00037 _____

8. 0.097541 _____

9. The energy consumed in South Dakota in 1999: 239,000,000,000,000 btus. _____

10. The diameter of a piece of copper wire: 0.000438 in. _____

11. Writing in Math When expressing a number in scientific notation, how do you know whether to write a positive or a negative exponent?

_____

_____

Use with Lesson 2-11.

Scientific Notation

P 2-11

Give each missing power of ten.

1. $167{,}230{,}000 = 1.6723 \times$ _____

2. $0.000872 = 8.72 \times$ _____

Write each number in scientific notation.

3. 657

4. 978,636,545,232

5. 0.00498

6. 0.000123

7. **Number Sense** Give two examples of situations that might be expressed using scientific notation.

For 8–10, write each number in standard form.

	Pressure (lb per in^2)
Generated by ant jaw	5.12×10^{-3}
Generated by human jaw	8.53×10^{-3}
Sustained by bone	2.40×10^4

8. pressure generated by an ant's jaw

9. pressure generated by a human's jaw

10. pressure sustainable by bone

Test Prep

11. Which is the product of 6.66×10^{-4}?

    A. 0.000666   B. 6.66   C. 6,660   D. 66,600

12. **Writing in Math** Which is greater, 0.003 or 3.2×10^{-3}? Explain why.

28 Use with Lesson 2-11.

Name _____

Solving Equations with Decimals   R 2-12

You solve equations with decimals just as you solve equations with whole numbers. You use inverse, or opposite, operations to solve equations.

Solve $x + 1.3 = 2.64$.   Check: $x + 1.3 = 2.64$

$x + 1.3 - 1.3 = 2.64 - 1.3$ $1.34 + 1.3 = 2.64$

$\qquad x = 1.34$ $2.64 = 2.64$

The inverse of addition is subtraction.

Solve $3.6y = 9.72$.   Check: $3.6y = 9.72$

$\dfrac{3.6y}{3.6} = \dfrac{9.72}{3.6}$ $3.6(2.7) = 9.72$

$\qquad y = 2.7$ $9.72 = 9.72$

The inverse of multiplication is division.

Solve $\dfrac{a}{6} = 3.7$.   Check: $\dfrac{a}{6} = 3.7$

$\dfrac{a}{6}(6) = 3.7(6)$ $\dfrac{22.2}{6} = 3.7$

$\qquad a = 22.2$ $3.7 = 3.7$

The inverse of division is multiplication.

Solve each equation and check your answer.

1. $z + 2.5 = 5.7$ _____   2. $y + 9 = 12.3$ _____

3. $p - 4.2 = 8.2$ _____   4. $s - 7.3 = 4.5$ _____

5. $2k = 14.6$ _____   6. $\dfrac{m}{1.6} = 6$ _____

7. $6.9 = 2.3x$ _____   8. $\dfrac{n}{3.7} = 5$ _____

9. **Reasonableness** Is 3.5 a reasonable answer to $3y = 24.6$? Explain.

_____

_____

10. Mya and Eric work in a bakery. Mya has 3 times as much flour as Eric. Mya has 15.81 lb of flour. Use the equation $3f = 15.81$ to find how much flour Eric has.

_____

Use with Lesson 2-12.   **29**

Solving Equations with Decimals

P 2-12

Solve each equation.

1. $a + 0.6 = 3$

2. $s - 17.2 = 36.7$

3. $x + 0.031 = 0.348$

4. $9.76 = t - 1.66$

5. $1.8x = 54.198$

6. $y \div 0.91 = 32$

7. $d - 160.9 = 426.84$

8. $p \div 5 = 6.46$

9. **Number Sense** What inverse operation would you use to solve $m + 15.6 = 0.204$?

In 2002, the cost to mail a single letter through the U.S. Postal Service was $0.37 for the first ounce plus $0.23 for each additional ounce. To find the weight of a letter, subtract $0.37 from the cost and then use the equation $0.23w$ = (new cost). Remember to add the first ounce to your answer.

10. How many ounces did a letter weigh if it cost $2.21 to mail?

11. Janice spent $4.05 mailing her letter. How much did it weigh?

Test Prep

12. Solve $x \div 16.9 = 57.58$.

    A. 973.102   B. 40.68   C. 3.41   D. 0.29

13. **Writing in Math** Explain how you would check $x = 0.81$ for the equation $x + 43.6 = 44.41$.

Name _____

PROBLEM-SOLVING STRATEGY
Write an Equation

R 2-13

Vacation Spending Margot budgeted $110.50 to spend on her 7-day vacation. After spending 4 days on her vacation, she has spent $58.89. How much money will Margot have left for the remaining 3 days?

Read and Understand

What do you know? Margot has $110.50 to spend on her 7-day vacation. She has already spent $58.89 during 4 days of the vacation.

What are you trying to find? The amount of money Margot has left to spend for the remaining 3 days

Plan and Solve

What strategy will you use? **Strategy:** Write an equation.

Show the main idea:

$110.50	
m	$58.89

Let m = the amount Margot has left to spend.
$m + \$58.89 = \$110.50$ ⟵ Use addition.
$m + \$58.89 - \$58.89 = \$110.50 - \$58.89$
$m = \$51.61$
Margot has $51.61 left to spend.

Look Back and Check

Is your work correct? Yes, $58.89 + $51.61 = $110.50

Write an equation to solve each problem. Give the answer in a complete sentence. Check to see that your answer is reasonable.

1. There is 4.5 times the seating capacity of the balcony on the main floor of a concert hall. If the main floor can seat 1,053 people, how many people can be seated in the balcony?

   _____

   _____

2. Gina's book has 349 fewer pages than Terri's. If Gina's book has 597 pages, how many pages does Terri's book have?

   _____

30 Use with Lesson 2-13.

Name _____

PROBLEM-SOLVING STRATEGY   P 2-13

Write an Equation

Write an equation to solve each problem. Give the answer in a complete sentence. Check to see that your answer is reasonable.

Recycling Prices

Item	Price per Pound (rounded to the nearest cent)
Aluminum cans	$0.31
Glass	$0.25
Newspaper	$0.15
Plastic	$0.12

1. Maria received $5.58 for aluminum cans that she brought to the recycling center. How many pounds of cans did she recycle?

_____

2. Andy wants to make $51. How many pounds of plastic would he have to recycle to make this amount?

_____

3. Antonio recycled a total of 527 lb of newspaper. He made 2 trips to the center. If he recycled 133 lb on the first trip, how many pounds did he recycle on the second trip?

_____

4. Pedro brought 87 lb of recyclables to the recycling center. He brought 54 lb of glass, and the rest was plastic. How many pounds of plastic did Pedro recycle?

_____

5. If there are 31 cans in 1 lb, how many cans are in 40.5 lb?

_____

PROBLEM-SOLVING APPLICATIONS

Book It!

R 2-14

Bookstore Naomi and Wendell work at a bookstore. A new shipment of 38 boxes of books came in today. Wendell can carry 3 boxes at a time to the storage room. How many trips will Wendell have to make to move all 38 boxes?

You can divide to solve this problem.
You know that Wendell can carry
3 boxes during one trip and that
he needs to move 38 boxes.

```
    12 R2
3)38
   -30
     8
   - 6
     2
```

So, Wendell will have to make 13 trips to carry all the boxes: 12 trips with 3 boxes and 1 trip with 2 boxes.

1. Suppose another shipment of books came in with 27 boxes in the order. Naomi can carry 2 boxes at a time. How many trips will Naomi have to make to move all 27 boxes?

2. How many boxes will Naomi carry on her last trip?

Write an equation to solve each problem. Give the answer in a complete sentence. Check to see that your answer is reasonable.

Bookshelves Juanita works at the public library. The librarian asked her to help take inventory of the books in the different sections.

3. The first bookshelf in the literature section can hold 2,492 books. The bookshelf has 7 shelves. Each shelf can hold the same number of books. How many books can each shelf hold?

4. The music section has 729 books. The librarian asked Juanita to donate some of the books to the local community center. Now there are only 643 books in the music section. How many books did Juanita donate to the community center?

Use with Lesson 2-14.

PROBLEM-SOLVING APPLICATIONS
Masses of Planets

P 2-14

Masses of Planets Relative to Earth

Earth	1.00
Jupiter	317.8
Mars	0.107
Mercury	0.0553
Neptune	17.15
Pluto	0.0021
Saturn	95.16
Uranus	14.54
Venus	0.815

1. Write the relative mass of Mercury in short-word form.

   _____

2. Round the relative mass of Venus to the nearest hundredth.

   _____

3. What is the difference between the relative mass of Mercury and the relative mass of Pluto?

   _____

4. What would the relative mass of a planet be if it had a relative mass that was 0.2 times that of Jupiter?

   _____

5. Round the relative masses of Venus and Mercury to the nearest tenths place. Then divide the relative mass of Venus by the relative mass of Mercury.

   _____

   _____

6. Which planet's relative mass does the product of 21×10^{-4} represent? _____

7. **Writing in Math** Explain how you would write the relative mass of Mercury in scientific notation.

   _____

   _____

   _____

Use with Lesson 2-14. **31**

Name _____

Factors, Multiples, and Divisibility

R 3-1

You can use these divisibility rules to determine if a number is divisible by another number.

A whole number is divisible by	Examples
2 if the ones digit is 0, 2, 4, 6, or 8.	2, 8, 24, 96, 300
3 if the sum of the digits of the number is divisible by 3.	144 1 + 4 + 4 = 9 9 ÷ 3 = 3
4 if the last two digits of the number are divisible by 4.	124 Last two digits are 24. 24 ÷ 6 = 4
5 if the ones digit is 0 or 5.	205; 300; 1,005; 270
6 if the number is divisible by both 2 and 3.	522 Divisible by 2 because ones digit is 2 Divisible by 3 because 5 + 2 + 2 = 9 9 ÷ 3 = 3
9 if the sum of the digits of the number is divisible by 9.	3,123 3 + 1 + 2 + 3 = 9 9 ÷ 9 = 1
10 if the ones digit is 0.	20; 40; 150; 2,570

Tell whether each number is divisible by 2, 3, 4, 5, 6, 9, or 10.

1. 25 _____ **2.** 32 _____ **3.** 124 _____

Tell whether the first number is a multiple of the second.

4. 45; 2 _____ **5.** 155; 5 _____

6. 240; 6 _____ **7.** 320; 10 _____

8. Number Sense Name 3 factors of 40. _____

There are 100 members in the U.S. Senate. There are 435 members in the U.S. House of Representatives.

9. Is the total number of U.S. senators divisible by 2, 3, 4, 5, 6, 9, or 10?

_____

10. Could the members of the U.S. House of Representatives be evenly divided into committees with 3 members on each? 5 members on each? 8 members on each?

_____

Use with Lesson 3-1.

Name _____

Factors, Multiples, and Divisibility

P 3-1

Tell whether each number is divisible by 2, 3, 4, 5, 6, 9, or 10.

1. 27 _____
2. 86 _____
3. 348 _____
4. 954 _____

Tell whether the first number is a multiple of the second.

5. 78; 2 _____
6. 535; 3 _____

7. **Number Sense** Name 3 numbers that are factors of both 15 and 30. _____

The sixth graders at Washington Middle School researched the history of their city. The students then gave a presentation to the other students at the school.

8. If there were 64 sixth graders, list all of the ways they could have been divided equally into groups of 10 or fewer students.

_____

_____

9. Only 60 sixth graders were present. Of the 60, 14 were needed to run the light and sound equipment during the presentation. How could the remaining students be divided into equal groups of 6 or fewer students to read the presentation?

_____

10. The 60 students were transported in vans to the high school to share their presentation. If the vans carry a maximum of 7 students each, what was the minimum number of vans required to carry the students to the high school? _____

Test Prep

11. Which of the following numbers is divisible by both 9 and 4?

    A. 24,815   B. 18,324   C. 9,140   D. 9,126

12. **Writing in Math** If a number is divisible by both 2 and 6, is it always divisible by 12? Use examples in your answer.

_____

_____

Use with Lesson 3-1.

Prime and Composite Numbers

R 3-2

A prime number has exactly two factors: 1 and itself.

    Example: 17 is prime. Its factors are 1 and 17.

Composite numbers have more than two factors.

    Example: 10 is composite. Its factors are 1, 2, 5, and 10.

You can make a factor tree to find the prime factorization of a number.

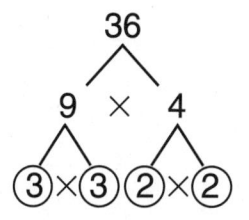

```
        36
       /  \
      9  ×  4
     /\    /\
    3×3  2×2
```

1. Begin with any two factors of the number.
2. Continue to write factors until all the factors are prime.
3. Circle the prime factors.

$36 = 2 \times 2 \times 3 \times 3$

4. Write the prime factors from least to greatest.

$36 = 2^2 \times 3^2$

5. Write the factors in exponential form.

Tell whether each number is prime or composite.

1. 45 _____   2. 57 _____

3. 36 _____   4. 97 _____

5. 29 _____   6. 39 _____

Write the prime factorization of each number.

7. 18 _____   8. 42 _____

9. 50 _____   10. 66 _____

11. 36 _____   12. 30 _____

13. **Number Sense** How can you tell that 642 is divisible by 3?

_____

_____

Use with Lesson 3-2. **33**

Name _____

Prime and Composite Numbers

P 3-2

Tell whether each number is prime or composite.

1. 65 _____   2. 97 _____

3. 53 _____   4. 116 _____

Write the prime factorization of each number.

5. 80 _____   6. 22 _____

7. 84 _____   8. 124 _____

9. **Number Sense** Is the sum of two prime numbers always a prime number? Use an example in your answer.

_____
_____
_____

Maria and Josh created a code using prime numbers as substitutes for letters.

10. If Maria and Josh used consecutive prime numbers to substitute for the letters of the alphabet, what number should they use for the letter *I*?

_____

Prime Number Code				
A	B	C	D	E
2	3	5	7	11
F	G	H		
13	17	19		

11. Using this system, what number should Maria and Josh use to substitute for the letter *K*? _____

Test Prep

12. Which of the following correctly shows the prime factorization of 324?

    A. $2^4 \times 3^2$ **B.** $2^2 \times 9^2$ **C.** $2^2 \times 3^3$ **D.** $2^2 \times 3^4$

13. **Writing in Math** Are more prime numbers even or odd? Explain your answer.

_____
_____
_____

Name _____

Greatest Common Factor

R 3-3

Here are two different ways to find the greatest common factor (GCF) of 12 and 40.

List the Factors

Step 1: List the factors of each number.
12: 1, 2, 3, 4, 6, 12
40: 1, 2, 4, 5, 8, 10, 20, 40

Step 2: Circle the factors that the numbers have in common.
12: 1, ②, 3, ④, 6, 12
40: 1, ②, ④, 5, 8, 10, 20, 40

Step 3: Select the greatest factor the numbers have in common. The numbers have 2 and 4 in common, but 4 is greater.
The GCF is 4.

Use Prime Factorization

Step 1: List the prime factors of each number.
12: 2 × 2 × 3
40: 2 × 2 × 2 × 5

Step 2: Circle the factors that the numbers have in common.
12: ②×②× 3
40: ②×②× 2 × 5

Step 3: Multiply the common prime factors.
2 × 2 = 4
The GCF is 4.

Find the GCF for each set of numbers.

1. 10, 70 _____
2. 4, 20 _____
3. 18, 24 _____

4. 18, 90 _____
5. 36, 42 _____
6. 14, 28 _____

7. **Number Sense** Name two numbers that have a greatest common factor of 12.

_____

8. Name two numbers that have a greatest common factor of 9.

_____

9. Name two numbers that have a greatest common factor of 5.

_____

10. The swim team has 45 members and the diving team has 27 members. If the coaches wished to divide the teams into groups and have all of the groups from both teams be the same size, what is the greatest number of team members who could be in a group?

_____

Name _____

Greatest Common Factor

P 3-3

Find the GCF for each set of numbers.

1. 12, 48 _____   2. 20, 24 _____   3. 21, 84 _____

4. 24, 100 _____   5. 18, 130 _____   6. 200, 205 _____

7. **Number Sense** Name three pairs of numbers that have 5 as their greatest common factor. Use each number only once in your answer.

_____

8. The bake-sale committee divided each type of item evenly onto plates, so that every plate contained only one type of item and every plate had exactly the same number of items with no leftovers. What is the maximum number of items that could have been placed on each plate?

Bake Sale Donations	
Muffins	96
Bread sticks	48
Rolls	84

_____

9. Using this system, how many plates of rolls could the bake-sale committee make? _____

10. Using this system, how many plates of muffins could the bake-sale committee make? _____

Test Prep

11. Which of the following pairs of numbers is correctly listed with its greatest common factor?

    A. 20, 24; GCF: 4   B. 50, 100; GCF: 25

    C. 4, 6; GCF: 24   D. 15, 20; GCF: 10

12. **Writing in Math** Explain one method of finding the greatest common factor of 48 and 84.

_____

_____

_____

_____

34 Use with Lesson 3-3.

Name _____

Least Common Multiple

R 3-4

There are different ways to find the least common multiple (LCM) of two numbers. Here are two ways of finding the LCM of 4 and 5:

List Multiples

Step 1: List multiples of each number.
4: 4, 8, 12, 16, 20, 24, 28, 32, 36, 40, 44, 48…
5: 5, 10, 15, 20, 25, 30, 35, 40, 45, 50…

Step 2: Check the multiples the numbers have in common.
4: 4, 8, 12, 16,⓴ 24, 28, 32, 36,㊵ 44, 48…
5: 5, 10, 15,⓴ 25, 30, 35,㊵ 45, 50…

Step 3: Determine which of the common multiples is the least.

20 and 40 are both common multiples, but 20 is the least.

The LCM of 4 and 5 is 20.

Use Prime Factors

Step 1: List the prime factors of each number.
4: 2 × 2
5: 5

Step 2: Circle the greatest number of times each different factor appears.
4: (2 × 2)
5: (5)

Step 3: Find the product of the factors you circled.
2 × 2 × 5 = 20
The LCM of 4 and 5 is 20.

Find the LCM of each set of numbers.

1. 6, 7 _____
2. 4, 5 _____
3. 10, 15 _____

4. 2, 5, 10 _____
5. 6, 21 _____
6. 8, 10 _____

7. 12, 20 _____
8. 5, 10, 25 _____
9. 7, 8 _____

10. **Number Sense** If you know the LCM of 4 and 5, how could you find the LCM of 40 and 50?

_____
_____

11. Peter says the least common multiple of 4, 6, and 12 is 24. Do you agree or disagree? Explain.

_____
_____
_____

Name _____

Least Common Multiple

P 3-4

Find the LCM of each set of numbers.

1. 15, 20 _____
2. 4, 50 _____
3. 8, 12 _____

4. 14, 42 _____
5. 21, 30 _____
6. 3, 7, 10 _____

7. 6, 7, 8 _____
8. 16, 20 _____
9. 12, 16 _____

10. At what times of the day between 10:00 A.M. and 5:00 P.M. do the chemistry presentation and the recycling presentation start at the same time?

_____

_____

Science Museum
— Show Schedule —
Chemistry — Every 30 minutes
Electricity — Every 20 minutes
Recycling — Every 40 minutes
Fossils — Every 45 minutes
The first showing for all shows is at 10:00 A.M.

11. The museum does shows in schools every Monday and shows in public libraries every fifth day (on both weekdays and weekends). If the museum did both a school show and a library show on Monday, how many days will it be until it does both shows on the same day again?

_____

Test Prep

12. Which of the following pairs of numbers is correctly listed with its LCM?

    A. 5, 15; LCM: 30
    B. 20, 30; LCM: 60
    C. 24, 36; LCM: 12
    D. 7, 9; LCM: 21

13. **Writing in Math** What method would you use to find the LCM of a group of four numbers? Explain and give an example.

_____

_____

_____

_____

Use with Lesson 3-4.

Name _____

PROBLEM-SOLVING STRATEGY:
Make a Table

R 3-5

Some problems can be solved by making and using a table.

Dan can cut 2 lawns per day in the summer. How many lawns can he cut if he works 12 days?

Here is how to make and use a table for this problem:

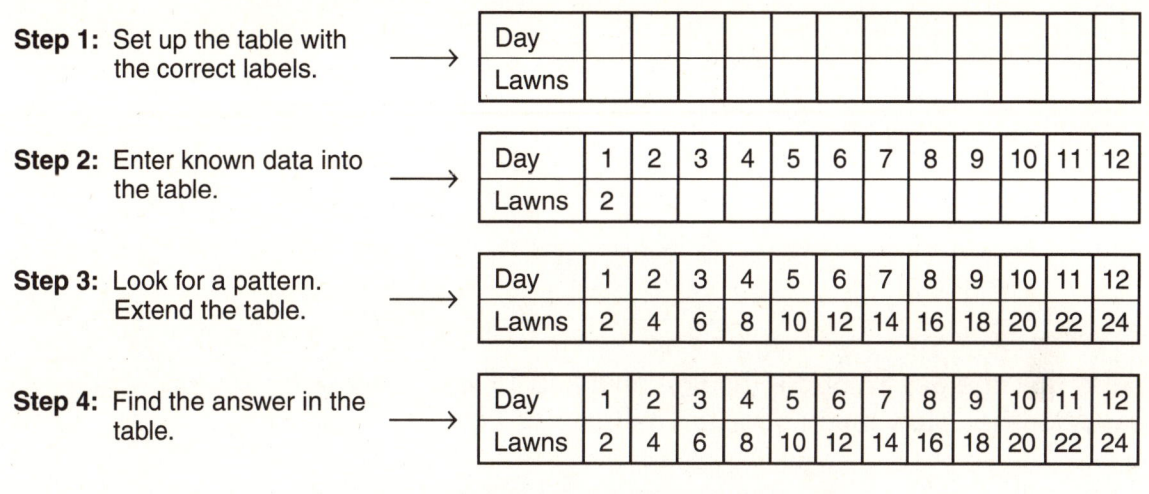

Step 1: Set up the table with the correct labels. →

Day												
Lawns												

Step 2: Enter known data into the table. →

Day	1	2	3	4	5	6	7	8	9	10	11	12
Lawns	2											

Step 3: Look for a pattern. Extend the table. →

Day	1	2	3	4	5	6	7	8	9	10	11	12
Lawns	2	4	6	8	10	12	14	16	18	20	22	24

Step 4: Find the answer in the table. →

Day	1	2	3	4	5	6	7	8	9	10	11	12
Lawns	2	4	6	8	10	12	14	16	18	20	22	24

Dan can cut 24 lawns in 12 days.

Make a table to solve the problem. Write the answer in a complete sentence.

1. Marie studied seeds in science class. She noticed that 25 seeds sprouted at 55°F. She also noticed that for every degree warmer she kept the seeds, 6 more sprouted than at the previous temperature. How many seeds sprouted at 60°F?

2. Lee did chores for his neighbor each week. For the first chore he received $2.00. For each additional chore he earned $0.75. If he did 6 chores one week, how much money did he earn?

36 Use with Lesson 3-5.

Name _____

PROBLEM-SOLVING STRATEGY P 3-5
Make a Table

Make a table to solve each problem. Write each answer in a complete sentence.

1. The recycling club started a program to recycle waste from the cafeteria. The first week 50 lb of waste were collected. Each week after, 15 lb more were collected than the previous week. How much recycling was collected on the fourth week?

   _____

   _____

2. Metro taxi charges $4.00 for the first mile and $1.25 for every mile after that. How much does a 7 mi taxi ride cost?

   _____

   _____

3. The music club sells T-shirts to raise money. The club purchases the T-shirts for $7.50 each and sells them for $10.00 each. How many T-shirts does the music club need to sell to make a profit of $10.00?

   _____

   _____

Use with Lesson 3-5.

Understanding Fractions

R 3-6

Fractions are used to show parts of a whole, or parts of a set. They can also indicate division.

Situation	Fraction	Division Expression
(rectangle split in 3, 2 shaded)	$\frac{2}{3}$	2 ÷ 3
(paperclip on ruler, 3/4 inch)	$\frac{3}{4}$	3 ÷ 4
(circle split in 8, 5 shaded)	$\frac{5}{8}$	5 ÷ 8

Write a fraction for the shaded portion of each picture.

1. (rectangle with 5 parts, 3 shaded) _____

2. (7 circles, 2 shaded) _____

3. (ruler showing shaded portion) _____

4. (grid with 10 squares, 3 shaded) _____

Draw a picture to show each fraction.

5. $\frac{3}{8}$ as a part of a set

6. $\frac{5}{10}$ as a part of a whole

7. **Number Sense** If you show $\frac{1}{3}$ as a part of a set by shading, what portion of the set is not shaded? _____

Use with Lesson 3-6. **37**

Name _____

Understanding Fractions

P 3-6

Write a fraction for the shaded portion of each picture.

1.

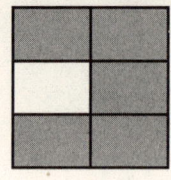

2.

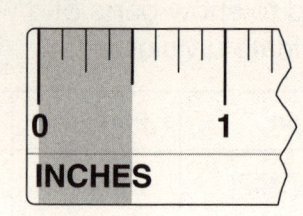

_____   _____

Draw a picture to show each fraction.

3. $\frac{5}{9}$ as part of a set

4. $\frac{4}{15}$ as a part of a whole

5. Write a division expression for $\frac{7}{8}$.   _____

6. Write $5 \div 20$ as a fraction.   _____

7. **Number Sense** A regulation football field is 120 yd long, including the two end zones. Each end zone is 10 yd long. What fraction of the football field is made up of the two end zones?   _____

Test Prep

8. Which pair of fractions correctly describes the points on the number line?

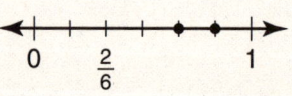

   A. $\frac{4}{6}, \frac{5}{6}$ B. $\frac{3}{6}, \frac{5}{6}$ C. $\frac{4}{5}, \frac{5}{5}$ D. $\frac{3}{5}, \frac{4}{5}$

9. **Writing in Math** Two families each used $\frac{1}{2}$ of a garden plot. A third family moved to the neighborhood and wished to share the garden equally with the first two families. To share the garden equally, should each of the first two families give $\frac{1}{2}$ of their garden space to the new neighbor? Why or why not?

_____

_____

Use with Lesson 3-6. **37**

Name _____

Equivalent Fractions

R 3-7

Two fractions that are equivalent will always be the same when expressed in simplest form.

How to Write Equivalent Fractions

One Way: Use multiplication.

Multiply both the numerator and the denominator by the same nonzero number.

Example:

$\frac{16}{20} = \frac{16 \times 2}{20 \times 2} = \frac{32}{40}$ $\frac{16}{20} = \frac{32}{40}$ They are equivalent.

Another Way: Use division.

Divide both the numerator and the denominator by the same nonzero number. Choose a common factor to divide by.

$\frac{16}{20} = \frac{16 \div 4}{20 \div 4} = \frac{4}{5}$ $\frac{16}{20} = \frac{4}{5}$ They are equivalent.

4 is a common factor, so divide 16 and 20 by 4.

How to Write Fractions in Simplest Form

One Way: Use divisibility rules.

Divide the numerator and the denominator by a common factor. Repeat until 1 is the only common factor.

$\frac{16}{20} \div \frac{2}{2} = \frac{8}{10} \div \frac{2}{2} = \frac{4}{5}$

Another Way: Divide by the GCF.

Divide the numerator and the denominator by the greatest common factor (GCF).

$\frac{16}{20} = \frac{16 \div 4}{20 \div 4} = \frac{4}{5}$

The GCF of 16 and 20 is 4.

Find two fractions equivalent to each fraction.

1. $\frac{5}{7}$ _____   2. $\frac{3}{5}$ _____   3. $\frac{25}{35}$ _____

Rewrite each pair of fractions with a common denominator.

4. $\frac{1}{5}, \frac{1}{10}$ _____   5. $\frac{2}{3}, \frac{4}{5}$ _____   6. $\frac{2}{3}, \frac{1}{6}$ _____

Write each fraction in simplest form.

7. $\frac{2}{10}$ _____   8. $\frac{12}{16}$ _____   9. $\frac{18}{26}$ _____

10. **Number Sense** If two fractions have the same denominator, how can you determine if they are equivalent?

_____

_____

_____

38 Use with Lesson 3-7.

Equivalent Fractions

P 3-7

Find two fractions equivalent to each fraction.

1. $\frac{5}{6}$ _____ 2. $\frac{15}{30}$ _____ 3. $\frac{45}{60}$ _____

Rewrite each pair of fractions with a common denominator.

4. $\frac{5}{8}, \frac{3}{4}$ _____ 5. $\frac{2}{5}, \frac{1}{2}$ _____ 6. $\frac{9}{9}, \frac{5}{7}$ _____

Write each fraction in simplest form.

7. $\frac{9}{54}$ _____ 8. $\frac{20}{40}$ _____ 9. $\frac{100}{110}$ _____

10. **Number Sense** Are the fractions $\frac{5}{1}, \frac{5}{5}$, and $\frac{1}{5}$ equivalent?

_____

11. The United States currently has 50 states. What fraction of the states had become a part of the United States by 1795? Write your answer in simplest form.

    _____

12. In what year was the total number of states in the United States $\frac{3}{5}$ the number it was in 1960?

    _____

Number of States in the United States

Year	Number of States
1795	15
1848	30
1900	45
1915	48
1960	50

13. The United States currently has 50 states. What fraction of the states had become a part of the United States by 1915? Write your answer in simplest form.   _____

Test Prep

14. Which of the following pairs of fractions are equivalent?

    A. $\frac{1}{10}, \frac{3}{33}$ B. $\frac{9}{5}, \frac{5}{9}$ C. $\frac{5}{45}, \frac{1}{9}$ D. $\frac{6}{8}, \frac{34}{48}$

15. **Writing in Math** In what situation can you use only multiplication to find equivalent fractions to a given fraction? Give an example.

_____

_____

Name _____

Improper Fractions and Mixed Numbers

R 3-8

A mixed number combines a whole number with a fraction. It is greater than one.

An improper fraction has a numerator that is larger than its denominator.

How to Write an Improper Fraction as a Mixed Number

Write $\frac{12}{5}$ as a mixed number.

Divide the numerator by the denominator.

The quotient is the whole number in the mixed number.

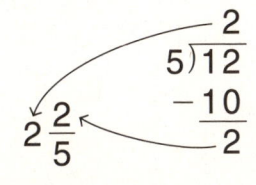

$2\frac{2}{5}$ $5\overline{)12}$
           $\underline{-10}$
              2

The remainder is the numerator. The denominator stays the same.

$\frac{12}{5} = 2\frac{2}{5}$

How to Write a Mixed Number as an Improper Fraction

Multiply the denominator by the whole number. $3\frac{2}{5}$

$5 \times 3 = 15$

Then add the numerator. $15 + 2 = 17$

Write this number for the numerator. ⟶ $\frac{17}{5}$
Use the original denominator.

$3\frac{2}{5} = \frac{17}{5}$

---

1. Draw a picture to show $4\frac{2}{3}$.

Write each improper fraction as a whole number or mixed number in simplest form.

2. $\frac{60}{40}$ _____   **3.** $\frac{33}{10}$ _____   **4.** $\frac{12}{7}$ _____

Write each mixed number as an improper fraction.

5. $4\frac{1}{3}$ _____   **6.** $1\frac{20}{50}$ _____   **7.** $8\frac{7}{8}$ _____

8. Reasoning Write 6 as an improper fraction with a denominator of 10. _____

Use with Lesson 3-8. **39**

Name _____

Improper Fractions and Mixed Numbers

P 3-8

1. Draw a picture to show $\frac{9}{7}$.

2. Draw a picture to show $3\frac{4}{5}$.

Write each improper fraction as a whole number or mixed number in simplest form.

3. $\frac{25}{5}$ _____

4. $\frac{47}{9}$ _____

5. $\frac{52}{7}$ _____

Write each mixed number as an improper fraction.

6. $4\frac{4}{5}$ _____

7. $13\frac{3}{4}$ _____

8. $9\frac{5}{8}$ _____

9. **Reasoning** Write 8 as an improper fraction with a denominator of 4. _____

Which letter on the number line corresponds to each number?

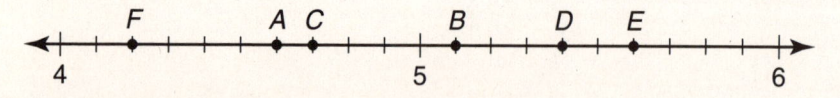

10. $5\frac{2}{5}$ _____

11. $4\frac{7}{10}$ _____

12. $\frac{23}{5}$ _____

Test Prep

13. Which number does the picture show?

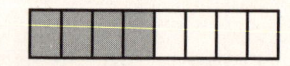

   A. $\frac{12}{8}$
   B. $2\frac{1}{8}$
   C. $2\frac{1}{4}$
   D. $\frac{20}{8}$

14. **Writing in Math** Can you express $\frac{9}{9}$ as a mixed number? Why or why not?

_____

_____

Use with Lesson 3-8. **39**

Estimating Fractional Amounts

R 3-9

You can use benchmark, or common, fractions to estimate fractional amounts. Some benchmark fractions are $\frac{1}{4}$, $\frac{1}{3}$, $\frac{1}{2}$, $\frac{2}{3}$, and $\frac{3}{4}$.

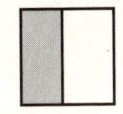

About $\frac{1}{2}$ of the square is shaded.

You can also use rounding to estimate fractional amounts.

97 out of 386 workers surveyed said they prefer to drive to work. About what fraction prefer to drive?

$\frac{97}{386}$ 97 is close to 100.
       386 is close to 400.

$\frac{97}{386}$ is close to $\frac{100}{400}$, and

$\frac{100}{400} = \frac{1}{4}$, so $\frac{97}{386}$ is about $\frac{1}{4}$.

$\frac{1}{4}$ of the workers prefer to drive.

Estimate the shaded part of each.

1. _____

2. _____

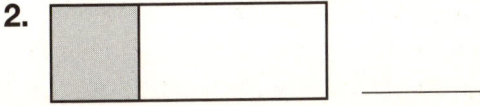

3. Which benchmark fraction is close to $\frac{297}{400}$? _____

4. Which benchmark fraction is close to $\frac{31}{97}$? _____

5. Which benchmark fraction is close to $\frac{39}{64}$? _____

6. Which benchmark fraction is close to $\frac{89}{190}$? _____

7. **Reasoning** The state of Rhode Island has an area of 1,545 sq mi. It has 500 sq mi of land that is covered by water. About what fraction of the state's land is covered by water? _____

Use with Lesson 3-9.

Name _____

Estimating Fractional Amounts

P 3-9

Estimate the shaded part of each.

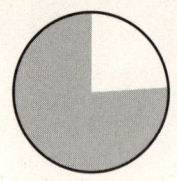

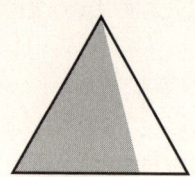

1. _____   2. _____   3. _____

4. Which benchmark fraction is close to $\frac{94}{156}$? _____

5. **Reasoning** A deli sold 81 sandwiches one day. If 59 of the sandwiches had veggies, about what fraction of the sandwiches sold did not have veggies? _____

6. About what fraction of students said that fossils were their favorite part of the museum?

_____

— Museum Trip — Favorite Exhibits	
Fossils	22 students
Insects	32 students
Rain Forests	46 students

7. About what fraction of students said that insects were their favorite part of the museum?

_____

Test Prep

8. About what fraction of students participated in the drama workshop?

    A. $\frac{3}{4}$ B. $\frac{2}{3}$
    C. $\frac{1}{2}$ D. $\frac{1}{4}$

Student Workshops	
Cooking	13 students
Drama	52 students
Basketball	75 students
Camping	61 students

9. **Writing in Math** What benchmark fraction could represent the combined number of students who participated in the cooking and camping workshops? Explain.

_____

_____

_____

Connecting Fractions and Decimals

R 3-10

A fraction and a decimal can both be used to represent the same value.

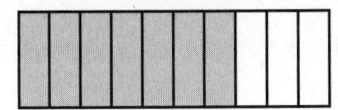

7 of the 10ths are shaded.

$\frac{7}{10} = 0.7$

fraction   decimal

How to Convert Decimals to Fractions

Write 0.35 as a fraction.

$0.35 = 35$ hundredths $= \frac{35}{100}$

Write $\frac{35}{100}$ in simplest form. $\frac{35}{100} = \frac{7}{20}$

So $0.35 = \frac{7}{20}$.

Write 3.50 as a mixed number.

$3.50 = 3 + 0.50$

$0.50 = 50$ hundredths $= \frac{50}{100}$

$\frac{50}{100} = \frac{1}{2}$ $3 + \frac{1}{2} = 3\frac{1}{2}$

So $3.50 = 3\frac{1}{2}$.

How to Convert Fractions to Decimals

Write $\frac{5}{9}$ as a decimal.

Divide the numerator by the denominator. Apply zeros if necessary.

```
  0.555
9)5.000
 -4 5
   50
  -45
   50
  -45
    5
```

The decimal 0.555 is a repeating decimal. Place a bar over the repeating digit.

So $\frac{5}{9} = 0.\overline{5}$.

Write a decimal and a fraction in simplest form for each shaded portion.

1. _____

2. _____

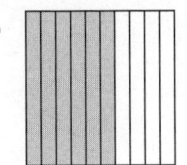

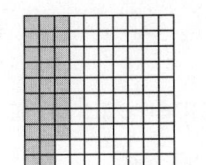

Write each decimal as a fraction or a mixed number in simplest form.

3. 0.45 _____   **4.** 2.18 _____   **5.** 3.25 _____

Write each fraction or mixed number as a decimal.

6. $\frac{20}{100}$ _____   **7.** $\frac{1}{10}$ _____   **8.** $3\frac{1}{5}$ _____

Use with Lesson 3-10.   41

Name _____

Connecting Fractions and Decimals   P 3-10

Write a decimal and a fraction in simplest form for each shaded portion.

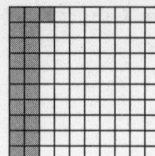

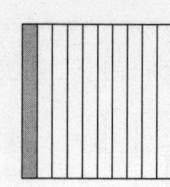

1.

_____

2.

_____

Write each decimal as a fraction or a mixed number in simplest form.

3. 0.15 _____   4. 2.67 _____   5. 5.705 _____

Write each fraction or mixed number as a decimal.

6. $\frac{56}{60}$ _____   7. $2\frac{7}{8}$ _____   8. $\frac{90}{200}$ _____

9. **Number Sense** How could you show $\frac{46}{200}$ using only one hundredths grid? What decimal does the model show?

_____

_____

10. A gram is a metric measurement of weight equal to 0.04 oz. What is this decimal expressed as a fraction? _____

11. One inch equals 2.54 cm. Express the number of centimeters in an inch as a mixed number. _____

Test Prep

12. What is a mixed number equivalent to 3.750?

    A. $3\frac{76}{100}$ B. $3\frac{6}{8}$ C. $3\frac{2}{3}$ D. $3\frac{1}{4}$

13. **Writing in Math** Name one situation in which you would use fractions to express a number less than one. What is one situation in which decimals seem to work better?

_____

_____

Use with Lesson 3-10.   **41**

Comparing and Ordering Fractions and Decimals

R 3-11

How to Compare Fractions

Compare $\frac{1}{4}$ and $\frac{3}{5}$.

Write the fractions with a common denominator.

$\frac{1}{4} = \frac{1 \times 5}{4 \times 5} = \frac{5}{20}$

$\frac{3}{5} = \frac{3 \times 4}{5 \times 4} = \frac{12}{20}$

(The LCD is 20.)

Compare the numerators.

$\frac{12}{20} > \frac{5}{20}$, so $\frac{3}{5} > \frac{1}{4}$.

How to Order Fractions

Order $\frac{1}{8}$, $\frac{2}{5}$, and $\frac{3}{4}$ from greatest to least.

Write the fractions with a common denominator.

$\frac{1}{8} = \frac{1 \times 5}{8 \times 5} = \frac{5}{40}$

$\frac{2}{5} = \frac{2 \times 8}{5 \times 8} = \frac{16}{40}$

$\frac{3}{4} = \frac{3 \times 10}{4 \times 10} = \frac{30}{40}$

Compare the numerators.

$\frac{30}{40} > \frac{16}{40} > \frac{5}{40}$, so the order from greatest to least is $\frac{3}{4}, \frac{2}{5}, \frac{1}{8}$.

How to Compare or Order Fractions and Decimals

Order $\frac{1}{4}$, $\frac{4}{5}$, and 0.35 from greatest to least.

First write the fractions as decimals.

$\frac{1}{4}$ $\frac{4}{5}$ 0.35

↓   ↓   ↓

0.25 0.80 0.35

Then compare the decimals.
0.8 > 0.35 > 0.25, so the order from greatest to least is $\frac{4}{5}$, 0.35, $\frac{1}{4}$.

Use <, >, or = to compare.

1. $\frac{5}{10}$ ◯ $\frac{4}{5}$
2. $\frac{4}{8}$ ◯ $\frac{1}{10}$
3. $\frac{14}{5}$ ◯ $\frac{22}{10}$
4. $\frac{14}{21}$ ◯ $\frac{30}{90}$
5. 0.7 ◯ $\frac{2}{8}$
6. 1.3 ◯ $1\frac{2}{5}$

Order from least to greatest.

7. 0.7, $\frac{25}{30}$, $\frac{6}{10}$ _____

8. 2.6, 2.07, $2\frac{70}{100}$ _____

9. **Writing in Math** Describe how you would use a number line to compare two fractions with different denominators.

_____

_____

_____

Comparing and Ordering Fractions and Decimals

P 3-11

1. Use a number line to compare 0.7 and $\frac{7}{8}$.

Use <, >, or = to compare.

2. $\frac{3}{9}$ ◯ $\frac{3}{12}$
3. $\frac{10}{100}$ ◯ 0.01
4. 13.6 ◯ $13\frac{3}{5}$
5. $\frac{6}{16}$ ◯ 0.40
6. 4.1 ◯ $4\frac{1}{12}$
7. $\frac{35}{105}$ ◯ 0.2

Order from least to greatest.

8. 1.3, $\frac{27}{24}$, $1\frac{2}{5}$ _____

9. 0.4, 0.6, $\frac{5}{10}$ _____

10. **Number Sense** Compare the decimals 0.6 and 0.600. Is one greater than the other?

_____

11. The basketball hoop used by the youngest students at Middleport School was set at 6.45 ft. The gym teacher suggested that the hoop be set no higher than $6\frac{2}{3}$ ft high. Does the basketball hoop need to be moved to meet the gym teacher's suggestion? Explain.

_____

Test Prep

12. Which is the decimal equivalent to $\frac{450}{500}$?

    A. 0.45   B. 0.450   C. 0.9   D. 1.0

13. **Writing in Math** Explain one method for comparing a decimal with a fraction.

_____

_____

Name _____

PROBLEM-SOLVING SKILL:
Multiple-Step Problems

R 3-12

Word problems often contain hidden questions. Sometimes you cannot answer the problem until you have answered these hidden questions.

James and Raul have both designed and printed T-shirts for school spirit week. If James had 50 T-shirts printed and Raul had 3 times that number printed, would there be enough T-shirts for 300 students to each buy one?

   Hidden question: How many T-shirts are available?

      James has 50 T-shirts.

      Raul has $3 \times 50 = 150$ T-shirts.

      Total: 200 T-shirts

Now you can answer the question in the problem. There are not enough T-shirts for all 300 students.

Write and answer the hidden question or questions in each problem and then solve the problem.

1. During a week-long dry spell the water level in a pond decreased by 4 in. per day, except for two days when it decreased by half that amount. How much did the water level decrease in the pond in one week?

   _____

   _____

   _____

2. The school store offers a discount for purchases made during lunchtime. If the usual price of pencils is $0.25, and the discount price during lunchtime is $0.15 per pencil, how much can you save by buying 5 pencils during lunchtime?

   _____

   _____

3. **Writing in Math** Explain one way you can organize the information in a problem with hidden questions.

   _____

   _____

Name _____

PROBLEM-SOLVING SKILL

P 3-12

Multiple-Step Problems

Write and answer the hidden questions in each problem and then solve the problem.

1. NASA's space shuttle takes $8\frac{1}{2}$ min to reach orbit. It takes 90 min for the space shuttle to orbit Earth. How long after launching would the space shuttle have orbited Earth three times?

    _____

    _____

    _____

2. At a school concert the orchestra plays 8 songs that are 4 min long and 1 song that is twice as long as each of the others. Is the concert longer or shorter than one hour?

    _____

    _____

    _____

    _____

    _____

    _____

3. A shoe store sold 52 pairs of shoes on Monday and 35 pairs on Tuesday. On Wednesday the store sold as many pairs as Monday and Tuesday together. How many pairs of shoes did the shoe store sell from Monday through Wednesday?

    _____

    _____

    _____

Use with Lesson 3-12.

Name _____

PROBLEM-SOLVING APPLICATIONS R 3-13

Prime Time

It is estimated that for every 24 hr in a day the average TV station broadcasts for about 16 hr. For what fraction of each day does the average TV station broadcast?

Remember, fractions show the parts of a whole.

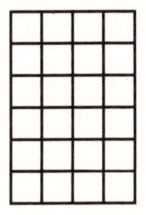

24 hours 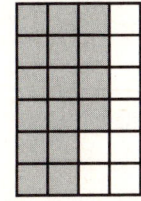   16 of 24 hours

$\frac{16}{24}$ part whole

Reduce to simplest form:

$\frac{16 \div 8}{24 \div 8} = \frac{2}{3}$

So, the stations broadcast for $\frac{2}{3}$ of every day.

It is estimated that there are about 48 million hours of "original" or new programs on TV each year in the world.

1. Is 48 divisible by 16? _____

2. Is 9 a factor of 48? _____

3. **Writing in Math** Find all the factors of 48. Explain how you found your answer.

   _____

   _____

It is a rule in America that for every 60 min of children's TV programs there can be a maximum of only 12 min of commercials.

4. Write a fraction for the maximum number of minutes allowed for commercials for every 60 min of children's TV-program broadcasts. Then write an equivalent fraction that uses a different denominator.

   _____

   _____

44 Use with Lesson 3-13.

Name _____

PROBLEM-SOLVING APPLICATIONS P 3-13

Extreme Weather

1. Find the greatest common factor of 120 and 100. _____

2. Find the least common multiple of 100 and 2. _____

The National Weather Service monitors the daily changes in weather throughout the United States. As of the year 2000, the state of Alaska had the coldest recorded temperature, −80°F. The coldest recorded temperature in Hawaii is 12°F.

3. Of the 50 states, 23 have record low temperatures between 2°F and −39°F. Write a fraction for these states that uses 50 in the denominator. _____

4. About $\frac{1}{5}$ of the states have record high temperatures between 100°F and 109°F. Write $\frac{1}{5}$ as a decimal. _____

5. **Writing in Math** Which value is greater, $\frac{1}{5}$ or 0.25? Explain.

_____

_____

6. A report on the precipitation in the 48 continental states gave the following information for June 2002: 11 of the 48 states had "above normal" precipitation; 15 of the 48 states had "below normal" precipitation; 4 of the 48 states had "much below normal" precipitation; and 18 of the 48 states had "normal" precipitation. Complete the precipitation table for the month of June 2002 for the 48 continental states.

Precipitation in the 48 Continental U.S. States—June 2002

Amount of Precipitation	Number of States	Fraction for the Number of States
Above normal	11	
Normal		$\frac{18}{48}$
Below normal	15	
Much below normal		

44 Use with Lesson 3-13.

Name _____

Adding and Subtracting Fractions with Like Denominators

R 4-1

How to find sums or differences of fractions with like denominators:

Find $\frac{2}{14} + \frac{6}{14}$.	The fractions have like denominators, so you can just add the numerators.
$\frac{2}{14} + \frac{6}{14} = \frac{8}{14}$	Write the sum over the common denominator.
$\frac{8}{14} = \frac{4}{7}$	Simplify if possible.

Find $\frac{5}{7} - \frac{2}{7}$.	The denominators are the same, so you can subtract the numerators.
$\frac{5}{7} - \frac{2}{7} = \frac{3}{7}$	$\frac{3}{7}$ cannot be simplified, so
	$\frac{5}{7} - \frac{2}{7} = \frac{3}{7}$

Find each sum or difference. Simplify your answer.

1. $\frac{1}{6} + \frac{3}{6} =$ _____   2. $\frac{9}{11} - \frac{4}{11} =$ _____

3. $\frac{6}{7} - \frac{2}{7} =$ _____   4. $\frac{3}{12} + \frac{8}{12} =$ _____

5. $\frac{8}{9} - \frac{5}{9} =$ _____   6. $\frac{1}{10} + \frac{8}{10} =$ _____

7. $\frac{4}{15} + \frac{11}{15} =$ _____   8. $\frac{16}{20} - \frac{9}{20} =$ _____

9. **Number Sense** Give an example of two fractions whose sum can be simplified to $\frac{1}{2}$.

_____

_____

10. A quarter has a diameter of $\frac{15}{16}$ in. A dime has a diameter of $\frac{11}{16}$ in., and a nickel has a diameter of $\frac{13}{16}$ in. If you put each coin side by side, what is the combined width of the three coins?

_____

Use with Lesson 4-1.

Name _____

Adding and Subtracting Fractions with Like Denominators

P 4-1

Find each sum or difference. Simplify your answer.

1. $\frac{6}{11} + \frac{4}{11} =$ _____
2. $\frac{5}{9} - \frac{2}{9} =$ _____
3. $\frac{5}{3} + \frac{4}{3} =$ _____

4. $\frac{9}{20} + \frac{7}{20} =$ _____
5. $\frac{15}{16} + \frac{6}{16} =$ _____
6. $\frac{9}{10} - \frac{4}{10} =$ _____

7. $\frac{7}{8} - \frac{6}{8} =$ _____
8. $\frac{8}{15} - \frac{5}{15} =$ _____
9. $\frac{3}{13} + \frac{11}{13} + \frac{5}{13} =$ _____

10. $\frac{8}{9} - \frac{2}{9} =$ _____
11. $\frac{6}{11} + \frac{3}{11} + \frac{1}{11} =$ _____
12. $\frac{19}{20} - \frac{11}{20} =$ _____

13. Write the number sentence shown by the picture and solve it.

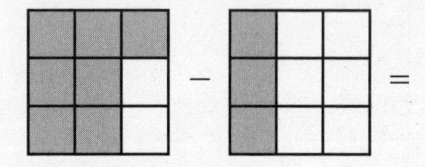

    _____

14. **Number Sense** Which sum is closer to 2, $\frac{11}{12} + \frac{14}{12}$ or $\frac{7}{9} + \frac{8}{9}$?

    _____

15. Max has 13 pairs of socks. Of them, 6 pairs are blue, 3 pairs are brown, 2 pairs are black, and 2 pairs are white. What fraction of Max's socks are either brown or black?

    _____

16. Find two fractions whose difference is $\frac{3}{8}$.

    _____

Test Prep

17. The sum of which two fractions will be in simplest form?

    A. $\frac{4}{8} + \frac{3}{8}$
    B. $\frac{2}{16} + \frac{6}{16}$
    C. $\frac{8}{6} + \frac{10}{6}$
    D. $\frac{5}{15} + \frac{5}{15}$

18. **Writing in Math** Explain how you can add two fractions with denominators of 10 and end up with a sum whose denominator is 5.

    _____

    _____

Use with Lesson 4-1.

Name _____

Adding and Subtracting Fractions with Unlike Denominators

R 4-2

If you are adding or subtracting fractions and the denominators are not the same, the first thing to do is find a common denominator. The best common denominator to use is the least common multiple of the two denominators.

Step 1: Use the LCM to find a common denominator.

Find $\frac{2}{6} + \frac{1}{2}$.
The LCM of 2 and 6 is 6.
The least common denominator (LCD) is 6.

Find $\frac{3}{4} - \frac{1}{3}$.
The LCD of 3 and 4 is 12.

Step 2: Write equivalent fractions.

$\frac{2}{6} = \frac{2}{6}$
$+\frac{1}{2} = +\frac{3}{6}$

$\frac{3}{4} = \frac{9}{12}$
$-\frac{1}{3} = -\frac{4}{12}$

Step 3: Add or subtract. Simplify if possible.

$\frac{2}{6} = \frac{2}{6}$
$+\frac{1}{2} = +\frac{3}{6}$
       $\frac{5}{6}$

$\frac{3}{4} = \frac{9}{12}$
$-\frac{1}{3} = -\frac{4}{12}$
       $\frac{5}{12}$

Find each sum or difference. Simplify your answer.

1. $\frac{3}{4} + \frac{5}{2} =$ _____

2. $\frac{11}{12} - \frac{1}{3} =$ _____

3. $\frac{4}{15} + \frac{4}{5} =$ _____

4. $\frac{5}{6} - \frac{4}{9} =$ _____

5. $\frac{2}{3} + \frac{7}{10} =$ _____

6. $\frac{2}{5} + \frac{2}{3} - \frac{6}{30} =$ _____

7. **Number Sense** The least common denominator for the sum $\frac{3}{8} + \frac{5}{12}$ is 24. Name another common denominator that you could use.

_____

8. A recipe calls for $\frac{1}{2}$ cup of milk and $\frac{1}{3}$ cup of water. What is the total amount of liquid in the recipe?

_____

46 Use with Lesson 4-2.

Name _____

Adding and Subtracting Fractions with Unlike Denominators

P 4-2

Find each sum or difference. Simplify your answer.

1. $\frac{5}{6} + \frac{4}{12} =$ _____
2. $\frac{4}{5} - \frac{1}{10} =$ _____
3. $\frac{5}{12} + \frac{2}{3} =$ _____

4. $\frac{9}{20} + \frac{3}{5} =$ _____
5. $\frac{6}{16} - \frac{1}{4} =$ _____
6. $\frac{19}{21} - \frac{2}{7} =$ _____

7. $\frac{2}{5} + \frac{5}{20} =$ _____
8. $\frac{8}{9} - \frac{5}{12} =$ _____
9. $\frac{7}{8} + \frac{11}{24} - \frac{5}{6} =$ _____

10. **Number Sense** Is $\frac{7}{8}$ or $\frac{11}{10}$ closer to 1? How did you decide?

_____

_____

Emma has a small garden. Emma's garden is $\frac{1}{5}$ beans, $\frac{1}{8}$ peas, and $\frac{1}{2}$ corn. The rest is planted with flowers.

11. What fraction of Emma's garden is planted with vegetables?

_____

_____

12. Are there more flowers or peas in Emma's garden?

_____

_____

Test Prep

13. To solve the subtraction sentence $\frac{17}{10} - \frac{2}{5} = ?$, which common denominator is the best choice?

    A. 10   B. 15   C. 20   D. 50

14. **Writing in Math** To find the sum of $\frac{4}{9}$ and $\frac{7}{12}$, Mario rewrites the fractions as $\frac{8}{36}$ and $\frac{21}{36}$. His answer is $\frac{29}{36}$. Is Mario right? If not, show his error and correct it.

_____

_____

46 Use with Lesson 4-2.

PROBLEM-SOLVING STRATEGY
Look for a Pattern

R 4-3

Sometimes you can solve a problem by identifying a pattern. Here are some different types of patterns.

Patterns in sets of numbers
1, 3, 6, 10, 15, 21

Ask yourself: Are the numbers increasing? Are they decreasing? Do they change by the same amount each time?

Patterns in groups of figures

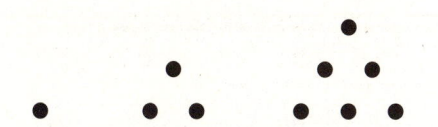

•   • •   • • •
     •   •   •   •   •

Ask yourself: How is the first figure modified to make the second? How is the second modified to make the third?

Patterns in everyday life
Chris tells three friends a secret. Each friend tells three more people, and so on.

Ask yourself: What is happening at each stage of the activity? How can I use numbers to help me understand the pattern?

Name the missing numbers or draw the next three figures. Describe each pattern.

1. 89, 78, 67, _____, _____, _____

2. ○● ○●○ ○●○●

3.
a	1	2	3	4	5	6
b	1	4		16	25	

4. **Number Sense** Certain cells can reproduce in only $\frac{1}{2}$ hr. Starting with 1 cell, how many would there be at the end of 4 hr? _____

Use with Lesson 4-3. **47**

Name _____

PROBLEM-SOLVING STRATEGY   P 4-3

Look for a Pattern

Name the missing numbers or draw the next three figures.

1.

2. 4, 9, 15, _____, _____, _____

4. 90, 81, 72, _____, _____, _____

5. $\frac{1}{2}, \frac{2}{8}, \frac{3}{32}$, _____, _____, _____

6. $\frac{1}{3}, \frac{1}{9}, \frac{1}{27}$, _____, _____, _____

3.
a	b	c
3	9	45
12	36	180
7		
		15

7. **Number Sense** In the figure, the sum of each line forms a pattern. What should be the sum of the seventh row?

    _____

    ```
            1
           2 2
          3 3 3
         4 4 4 4
        5 5 5 5 5
    ```

8. Fran is training for a mile race. Each day she runs a mile in 15 sec less time than the day before. If she starts out running a mile in 10 min, how fast can she complete a mile on her fifth day of training?

    _____

9. **Writing in Math** List the multiples of 9, starting with 9 and ending with 90. What do you notice?

    _____
    _____
    _____

Use with Lesson 4-3. **47**

Estimating Sums and Differences of Fractions and Mixed Numbers

R 4-4

You can use rounding to estimate sums and differences of fractions and mixed numbers.

How to round fractions:

If the fractional part is greater than or equal to $\frac{1}{2}$, round up to the next whole number.

Example: Round $3\frac{5}{7}$ to the nearest whole number.

$\frac{5}{7}$ is greater than $\frac{1}{2}$, so $3\frac{5}{7}$ rounds up to 4.

If the fractional part is less than $\frac{1}{2}$, drop the fraction and use the whole number you already have.

Example: Round $6\frac{1}{3}$ to the nearest whole number.

$\frac{1}{3}$ is less than $\frac{1}{2}$, so drop $\frac{1}{3}$ and round down to 6.

How to estimate sums and differences of fractions and mixed numbers:

Round both numbers to the nearest whole number. Then add or subtract.

Example: Estimate $4\frac{1}{8} + 7\frac{2}{3}$.

$4\frac{1}{8}$ rounds down to 4.

$7\frac{2}{3}$ rounds up to 8.

$4 + 8 = 12$

So, $4\frac{1}{8} + 7\frac{2}{3}$ is about 12.

Round to the nearest whole number.

1. $8\frac{6}{7}$ _____
2. $14\frac{2}{9}$ _____
3. $42\frac{4}{7}$ _____
4. $6\frac{51}{100}$ _____
5. $29\frac{4}{5}$ _____
6. $88\frac{2}{4}$ _____
7. $19\frac{3}{44}$ _____
8. $63\frac{41}{49}$ _____

Estimate each sum or difference.

9. $7\frac{2}{5} + 8\frac{1}{9}$ _____
10. $13\frac{5}{8} - 2\frac{7}{10}$ _____
11. $2\frac{1}{4} + 5\frac{1}{2} + 10\frac{3}{4}$ _____
12. $11\frac{3}{5} - 4\frac{1}{12}$ _____
13. $8 + 4\frac{11}{14} + 5\frac{1}{9}$ _____
14. $15\frac{6}{7} - 12\frac{2}{10}$ _____

Use with Lesson 4-4.

Name _____

Estimating Sums and Differences of Fractions and Mixed Numbers

P 4-4

Round to the nearest whole number.

1. $3\frac{4}{9}$ _____
2. $5\frac{6}{7}$ _____
3. $2\frac{2}{5}$ _____
4. $11\frac{12}{15}$ _____

Estimate each sum or difference.

5. $2\frac{1}{4} + 3\frac{5}{6}$ _____
6. $5\frac{6}{9} - 1\frac{3}{4}$ _____
7. $8\frac{5}{13} + 5\frac{3}{5}$ _____
8. $11 - 6\frac{3}{7} + 2\frac{2}{5}$ _____

Rodrigo and Mel are competing in a track meet. The table at the right shows the results of their events.

9. Rodrigo claims his best jump was about 1 ft longer than Mel's best jump. Is he correct?

   _____

   _____

Participant	Event	Results/Distance
Rodrigo	Long jump	1. $6\frac{3}{8}$ ft 2. $5\frac{5}{6}$ ft
Rodrigo	Softball throw	$62\frac{1}{5}$ ft
Mel	Long jump	1. $4\frac{7}{10}$ ft 2. $4\frac{3}{4}$ ft
Mel	Softball throw	$71\frac{7}{8}$ ft

Test Prep

10. Use the table above. If the school record for the softball throw is 78 ft, about how much farther must Rodrigo throw the ball to match the record?

    A. 15 ft   **B.** 16 ft   **C.** 18 ft   **D.** 20 ft

11. **Writing in Math** Consider the sum of $\frac{3}{5} + \frac{3}{4}$. Round each fraction and estimate the sum. Add the two fractions using a common denominator and then round the result. Which estimate is closest to the actual answer?

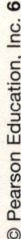

    _____

    _____

    _____

    _____

48 Use with Lesson 4-4.

Adding Mixed Numbers

R 4-5

To add mixed numbers, you can add the fractional parts to the whole number parts, and then simplify.

Find $2\frac{2}{4} + 3\frac{1}{4}$.
The fractions have a common denominator. Add the fractions. Then add the whole numbers.

$$\begin{array}{r} 2\frac{2}{4} \\ +3\frac{1}{4} \\ \hline 5\frac{3}{4} \end{array}$$

Find $3\frac{2}{3} + 4\frac{1}{9}$.
Write equivalent fractions with the LCD.

$$3\frac{2}{3} = 3\frac{6}{9}$$
$$+4\frac{1}{9} = 4\frac{1}{9}$$

Add the whole numbers. Add the fractions. Simplify if possible.

$$\begin{array}{r} 3\frac{6}{9} \\ +4\frac{1}{9} \\ \hline 7\frac{7}{9} \end{array}$$

Find $4 + 3\frac{3}{5}$.
Add the whole numbers; then add the fraction.

$$\begin{array}{r} 4 \\ +3\frac{3}{5} \\ \hline 7\frac{3}{5} \end{array}$$

Find each sum. Simplify your answer.

1. $2\frac{1}{5} + 2\frac{3}{5} =$ _____

2. $4\frac{2}{3} + 1\frac{1}{6} =$ _____

3. $5\frac{3}{5} + \frac{3}{10} =$ _____

4. $8\frac{5}{8} + 1\frac{5}{12} =$ _____

5. $6\frac{1}{4} + 11\frac{3}{8} =$ _____

6. $7 + 8\frac{1}{3} =$ _____

7. In 2001, the men's indoor pole vault record was $20\frac{1}{6}$ ft. The women's record for the indoor pole vault was $15\frac{5}{12}$ ft. What is the combined height of the two records? _____

8. **Writing in Math** How high is a stack of library books if one book is $1\frac{3}{8}$ in. high, the second book is $1\frac{5}{6}$ in. high, and the third is $2\frac{1}{3}$ in. high? Explain how you solved this problem.

_____

_____

_____

Use with Lesson 4-5.

Adding Mixed Numbers

P 4-5

Find each sum. Simplify your answer.

1. $5 + 3\frac{1}{6} =$ _____

2. $4\frac{4}{5} + 8\frac{1}{10} =$ _____

3. $1\frac{5}{8} + \frac{15}{16} =$ _____

4. $6\frac{2}{3} + \frac{5}{4} =$ _____

5. $2\frac{7}{8} + 4 =$ _____

6. $7\frac{6}{10} + 1\frac{9}{20} =$ _____

7. $\frac{7}{8} + 3\frac{3}{5} + 2 =$ _____

8. $9 + 3\frac{2}{3} + \frac{5}{6} =$ _____

9. **Number Sense** Give an example of two mixed numbers whose sum is a whole number.

_____

_____

10. An ostrich egg is $6\frac{4}{5}$ in. long. A California condor's egg is $4\frac{3}{10}$ in. long, and an albatross egg is $5\frac{7}{10}$ in. long. If the three eggs are placed end to end, what is the total length in inches? _____

11. Shanda can travel 10 mi on her electric scooter before she has to recharge the batteries. If it is $4\frac{5}{8}$ mi to the library and $5\frac{2}{5}$ mi to her friend's house, can she make both trips before she needs to recharge the batteries?

_____

_____

Test Prep

12. Which is the fractional portion of the solution to $5\frac{3}{8} + 2\frac{3}{12}$?

    A. $\frac{6}{12}$ B. $\frac{15}{24}$ C. $\frac{6}{8}$ D. $\frac{15}{8}$

13. **Writing in Math** Explain the steps to adding mixed numbers. What must you do first?

_____

_____

Use with Lesson 4-5. **49**

Name _____

Subtracting Mixed Numbers

R 4-6

To subtract mixed numbers, the fractional parts must have the same denominator.

	Step 1	**Step 2**	**Step 3**
Find $9\frac{1}{12} - 4\frac{5}{8}$.	Estimate. $9 - 4 = 5$ Write equivalent fractions for the LCD. $9\frac{1}{12} = 9\frac{2}{24}$ $-4\frac{5}{8} = -4\frac{15}{24}$	Before you can subtract, rename $9\frac{2}{24}$ to show more twenty-fourths. $9\frac{2}{24} = 8 + \frac{24}{24} + \frac{2}{24} = 8\frac{26}{24}$ $-4\frac{15}{24} \qquad\qquad\qquad -4\frac{15}{24}$	Subtract and simplify if possible. $8\frac{26}{24}$ $-4\frac{15}{24}$ $\overline{4\frac{11}{24}}$
Find $10 - 4\frac{2}{5}$.	There is no fraction from which to subtract $\frac{2}{5}$.	Rename 10 to show fifths. $10 = 9 + \frac{5}{5} = 9\frac{5}{5}$	Subtract. Simplify if possible. $9\frac{5}{5}$ $-4\frac{2}{5}$ $\overline{5\frac{3}{5}}$

Find each difference. Simplify if possible.

1. $5\frac{9}{10} - 2\frac{3}{5} =$ _____
2. $11\frac{7}{16} - 8\frac{3}{8} =$ _____
3. $9\frac{2}{3} - 9\frac{1}{6} =$ _____

4. $4\frac{2}{3} - 2 =$ _____
5. $4\frac{1}{4} - \frac{7}{12} =$ _____
6. $5\frac{6}{7} - 2\frac{13}{14} =$ _____

7. **Number Sense** How do you know if you need to rename the first number in a subtraction problem involving mixed numbers?

_____

_____

_____

Use with Lesson 4-6.

Subtracting Mixed Numbers

Find each difference. Simplify if possible.

1. $2\frac{3}{5} - 1\frac{1}{5} =$ _____
2. $1\frac{4}{9} - \frac{8}{9} =$ _____
3. $5\frac{5}{8} - 1\frac{9}{16} =$ _____
4. $12 - 4\frac{5}{6} =$ _____
5. $6\frac{15}{16} - 4 =$ _____
6. $3\frac{7}{12} - 2\frac{3}{4} =$ _____
7. $9 - 7\frac{5}{8} =$ _____
8. $15\frac{1}{6} - 8\frac{2}{3} =$ _____
9. $6\frac{8}{9} - 1\frac{2}{3} =$ _____
10. $2\frac{3}{7} - 1\frac{5}{14} =$ _____

11. In which of the exercises above do you have to rename the first mixed number to show more fractional parts before subtracting?

_____

The table at the right shows the lengths of various carpentry nails.

12. How much longer is a 30d nail than a 5d nail?

_____

13. How much longer is a 12d nail than a 9d nail?

_____

Carpentry Nails

Size	Length (inches)
5d	$1\frac{3}{4}$
9d	$2\frac{3}{4}$
12d	$3\frac{1}{4}$
30d	$4\frac{1}{2}$

Test Prep

14. To subtract $4\frac{5}{6}$ from $10\frac{1}{3}$, which of the following must the mixed number $10\frac{1}{3}$ first be renamed as?

    A. $9\frac{2}{3}$ **B.** $9\frac{4}{6}$ **C.** $9\frac{8}{6}$ **D.** $10\frac{2}{6}$

15. **Writing in Math** Jack says that once you have a common denominator you are ready to subtract two mixed numbers. What other step might be necessary before you can subtract? Give an example.

_____

_____

_____

Choose a Computation Method

R 4-7

Depending on the type of problem, you can use different methods to find the solution. Your goal should be to use the most accurate and efficient method. The different choices are:

Mental Math Think: Are the numbers easy to work with? If there are fractions, is there already a common denominator? Will an estimate solve the problem?

Example: Find $4\frac{1}{5} + 2\frac{2}{5}$.

Paper and Pencil Think: Can I easily convert the fractions to a common denominator? Are the calculations fairly straightforward?

Example: Find $6\frac{1}{4} - 2\frac{1}{2}$.

Calculator Think: Are there many steps needed to find the solution? Would using pencil and paper take too long? Would the numbers be too cumbersome?

Example: Find $3\frac{2}{12} + 4\frac{1}{3} + 9\frac{3}{4} + 7\frac{2}{6}$.

Find each sum or difference. Tell which computation method you used.

1. $8\frac{4}{5} - 1\frac{2}{5} =$ _____

2. $\frac{11}{16} + 4\frac{15}{32} =$ _____

3. $14 - 12\frac{5}{9} + \frac{2}{3} =$ _____

4. $3\frac{9}{16} - 2 =$ _____

5. $7\frac{1}{3} + 7\frac{8}{14} =$ _____

6. $2\frac{1}{9} + 2\frac{1}{9} =$ _____

7. A dog had three puppies. One puppy weighed $2\frac{1}{8}$ lb, one weighed $2\frac{3}{4}$ lb, and the third weighed 3 lb. What is the combined weight of the puppies? What method did you use?

_____

8. **Writing in Math** Why would it be faster to use mental math rather than a calculator to find $4\frac{1}{14} + 2\frac{2}{7}$? Explain.

_____

Use with Lesson 4-7. **51**

Name _____

Choose a Computation Method

P 4-7

Find each sum or difference. Tell what computation method you used.

1. $2\frac{1}{5} + 4\frac{3}{5} =$ _____   _____

2. $12 - 7\frac{5}{6} =$ _____   _____

3. $6\frac{3}{8} + 2\frac{1}{4} =$ _____   _____

4. $15\frac{1}{2} - 9 =$ _____   _____

5. $4\frac{4}{9} - 2\frac{8}{9} =$ _____   _____

6. $6\frac{1}{7} + 6\frac{4}{7} =$ _____   _____

7. $8\frac{3}{4} + 1\frac{5}{16} =$ _____   _____

8. $3\frac{4}{5} - 2\frac{8}{15} =$ _____   _____

9. $\frac{11}{12} + 4\frac{4}{15} =$ _____   _____

10. $\frac{5}{6} + \frac{2}{3} - \frac{1}{15} =$ _____   _____

11. Jon's dog weighs $49\frac{1}{4}$ lb and his cat weighs $11\frac{15}{16}$ lb. Find the combined weight of the two pets. _____

12. A croquet ball has a diameter of $3\frac{5}{8}$ in. If the wicket the ball passes through is 4 in. wide, how much room is there to spare? Use mental math to find the answer. _____

Test Prep

13. For which of the following sums or differences would mental math be most efficient?

    A. $4\frac{1}{3} + 5\frac{2}{5}$ **B.** $6\frac{7}{8} - 3\frac{5}{8}$ **C.** $4\frac{1}{6} - 2\frac{5}{6}$ **D.** $\frac{5}{7} + \frac{1}{14} + \frac{1}{2}$

14. **Writing in Math** Describe a problem that could be easily solved using mental math. Explain why this method works best.

_____

_____

Use with Lesson 4-7.

Name _____

PROBLEM-SOLVING SKILL

R 4-8

Exact Answer or Estimate?

Estimates

Phrases such as "will there be enough" and "more or less than" mean that an estimate will give you enough information to answer the problem.

Ted biked 14 mi on Monday, 11 mi on Tuesday, and 15 mi on Wednesday. Tom averaged 12 mi per day over the same three days. Did Tom bike a longer or shorter distance than Ted?

Read and Understand

Step 1: What do you know?

The four distances are 14, 11, 15, and 12.

Step 2: What are you trying to find?

The problem asks who biked the longer distance. You don't have to add Ted's miles to see that he biked a longer distance. An estimate is all that is needed.

Exact Answers

If the problem asks "what is the total" or "how many" or "how much," calculate the exact amount.

A room is $12\frac{1}{2}$ ft wide and $14\frac{1}{3}$ ft long. What is the area of the room in square feet?

Read and Understand

Step 1: What do you know?

A room is $12\frac{1}{2}$ ft wide and $14\frac{1}{3}$ ft long.

Step 2: What are you trying to find?

The problem asks for the area of the room. You need an exact answer.

Tell whether an exact answer or an estimate is needed. Then solve.

1. Shelly's class made a quilt. The materials cost $65.75. They sold raffle tickets for the quilt and collected $128.00. How much profit did they make after they paid for the materials?

2. The school garden is divided into 4 different sections. $\frac{1}{6}$ of the garden is roses, $\frac{1}{4}$ of the garden is tomatoes, $\frac{1}{12}$ of the garden is lilies, and $\frac{1}{2}$ of the garden is peas. Are there more flowers or vegetables in the garden?

3. **Reasonableness** Maura has to contribute 10 hr to a service project to receive a special award. She has already put in 4 hr. She claims that if she can work on the project for $\frac{3}{4}$ hr each week she will meet her goal in 7 weeks. Is she correct?

52 Use with Lesson 4-8.

Name _____

PROBLEM-SOLVING SKILL   P 4-8

Exact Answer or Estimate?

Tell whether an exact answer or an estimate is needed. Then solve.

1. The maximum weight allowed on an elevator is 1,800 lb. If there are 9 people on the elevator and the average weight of each person is 175 lb, is the total weight over or under the limit?

   _____

   _____

2. In 1970, the U.S. dollar was worth $3\frac{3}{5}$ German marks. In 2000, the dollar was worth only 2 German marks. How much did the value of the dollar decline?

   _____

   _____

3. A cell phone company is giving away 500 free minutes per month with each new phone. If the average person talks 15 min per day on their cell phone, will they have to pay for any calls during the month of June? (Remember: There are 30 days in June.)

   _____

   _____

Katya has a lemonade stand. She sells lemonade for $0.15 per glass. Her pitcher holds 8 servings.

4. After one hour the pitcher is $\frac{1}{4}$ full. How much money has she made?

   _____

5. **Reasonableness** Katya says that if she can sell 4 pitchers of lemonade she will earn more than $5.00. Is she correct? How do you know?

   _____

   _____

   _____

52   Use with Lesson 4-8.

Name _____

PROBLEM-SOLVING APPLICATIONS   R 4-9

Building Square

Peter is building two shelves. One shelf needs to be $2\frac{1}{2}$ ft long. The other shelf needs to be $3\frac{2}{5}$ ft long. How much wood will Peter need for these shelves?

Use the LCM to find a common denominator. The LCM of 2 and 5 is 10.

$$2\frac{1}{2} = 2\frac{5}{10}$$
$$+3\frac{2}{5} = 3\frac{4}{10}$$
$$\overline{\phantom{+3\frac{2}{5}=}\ 5\frac{9}{10}}$$

So, Peter will need $5\frac{9}{10}$ ft of wood.

Use the data file to answer the following questions.

Data File

Board	Length (in feet)
A	$1\frac{3}{4}$
B	$3\frac{5}{8}$
C	$10\frac{1}{2}$
D	$8\frac{2}{3}$

1. Peter needs four of Board A to make a picture frame. How many total feet of wood is that?

   _____

2. What is the difference in lengths of Board B and Board C?

   _____

3. Peter wants to place a shelf all the way across the wall of his kitchen. The wall is 23 ft long. If Peter uses two of Board C, will he have enough wood to go across the wall? Would you use mental math or paper and pencil to find this answer?

   _____

   _____

4. How long would Board B be if Peter cut $2\frac{1}{2}$ ft. from it? _____

5. **Estimation** Peter has five of Board D. About how many feet of wood is that in total?

   _____

Use with Lesson 4-9. **53**

Name _____

PROBLEM-SOLVING APPLICATIONS   P 4-9
Studying Growth

Solve. Simplify your answers.

Studies of humans over the past three centuries have led to some surprising discoveries about the average heights of people from different parts of the world.

1. A recent study revealed that the height of the average American male in 1750 was about $67\frac{7}{10}$ in. By 1800, the average height had changed to about $68\frac{1}{10}$ in. By how much did the average American male height increase? _____

2. The height of the average British male in 1750 was about $64\frac{19}{20}$ in. How much less was this than the height of the average American male whose average height was about $67\frac{7}{10}$ in. in 1750? _____

3. In 1850, the average height of a male from France was about $64\frac{3}{20}$ in. The average male from Norway in 1850 was about $1\frac{1}{5}$ in. taller than this. How tall was the average Norwegian male in 1850? _____

4. Between 1750 and 1950, the average height of a man from Norway increased by about $5\frac{1}{6}$ in. If the height of an average Norwegian male in 1750 was $64\frac{19}{20}$ in., what was the average height of a Norwegian male in 1950? (Hint: the least common multiple of 6 and 20 is 60.) _____

5. In 1750, the average Austrian male's height was about $65\frac{7}{20}$ in. By 1800, the average height had decreased by about $1\frac{1}{5}$ in. How tall was the average Austrian male in 1800? _____

6. How much taller was the average Austrian male in 1750 than the average Norwegian male in 1750? (Hint: Look in Exercises 4 and 5 for the information.) _____

Use with Lesson 4-9.

Name _____

Multiplying a Fraction and a Whole Number

R 5-1

Find $12 \times \frac{1}{4}$.

$12 \times \frac{1}{4}$ is the same as dividing 12 by 4.

$12 \div 4 = 3$

$12 \times \frac{1}{4} = 3$

Find $\frac{3}{5}$ of 15, or $\frac{3}{5} \times 15$.

$15 \div 5 = 3$, so $\frac{1}{5} \times 15 = 3$.

Since $\frac{3}{5}$ is 3 times $\frac{1}{5}$,

$\frac{3}{5} \times 15 = 3 \times \left(\frac{1}{5} \times 15\right) = 3 \times 3 = 9$.

$\frac{3}{5} \times 15 = 9$

Find each product.

1. $\frac{4}{5} \times 20 =$ _____
2. $\frac{6}{7}$ of $14 =$ _____
3. $24 \times \frac{3}{4} =$ _____
4. $\frac{2}{5}$ of $15 =$ _____
5. $400 \times \frac{3}{8} =$ _____
6. $\frac{7}{10}$ of $80 =$ _____

7. **Reasoning** Can you use division and mental math to find $\frac{2}{3}$ of 24? Why or why not?

_____

_____

_____

The chart shows the average high temperatures for different months in Phoenix, Arizona.

Phoenix Weather

Month	Average High
February	70°F
May	93°F
July	105°F

8. What is $\frac{4}{5}$ the average temperature in July? _____

9. What is $\frac{1}{2}$ the average temperature in February? _____

10. What is $\frac{2}{3}$ the average temperature in May? _____

Use with Lesson 5-1.

Name _____

Multiplying a Fraction and a Whole Number

P 5-1

Find each product.

1. $\frac{3}{4} \times 16 =$ _____
2. $\frac{5}{6} \times 30 =$ _____
3. $42 \times \frac{5}{6} =$ _____
4. $\frac{1}{8}$ of $72 =$ _____
5. $900 \times \frac{2}{3} =$ _____
6. $\frac{13}{20}$ of $100 =$ _____

7. **Reasoning** Without multiplying, tell which is greater, $\frac{5}{6}$ of 81 or $\frac{9}{10}$ of 81. Explain.

Driving Distances

Departure City	Destination City	Distance
Pittsfield, Massachusetts	Providence, Rhode Island	132 mi
Reno, Nevada	Wendover, Utah	400 mi

8. Mike drove $\frac{1}{3}$ of the distance between Pittsfield, Massachusetts, and Providence, Rhode Island. How far did he drive? _____

9. Bimal drove $\frac{3}{5}$ of the distance between Reno, Nevada, and Wendover, Utah. How far did he drive? _____

10. **Estimation** How many more miles does Bimal have to drive to get to Wendover, Utah? _____

Test Prep

11. There are 25 students in Mr. Fitch's sixth-grade class. If $\frac{3}{5}$ of the students are girls, how many girls are in Mr. Fitch's class?

    A. 5 girls
    B. 10 girls
    C. 15 girls
    D. 20 girls

12. **Writing in Math** Explain how you would find the product of 36 and $\frac{2}{3}$.

_____

_____

Use with Lesson 5-1.

Multiplying Fractions

R 5-2

Find $\frac{3}{4} \times \frac{2}{7}$.

One Way
Draw a picture. Simplify if possible.

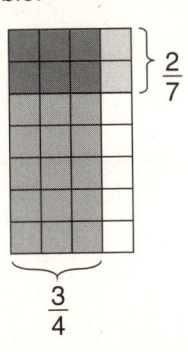

6 of the 28 squares have overlapping shading.

So, $\frac{3}{4} \times \frac{2}{7} = \frac{6}{28}$.

Simplify $\frac{6}{28}$ to $\frac{3}{14}$.

Another Way
Multiply the numerators and denominators. Simplify if possible.

$$\frac{3}{4} \times \frac{2}{7}$$
$$= \frac{3 \times 2}{4 \times 7} = \frac{6}{28}$$
$$= \frac{3}{14}$$

Simplify First
Find the GCF of any numerator and any denominator.

The GCF of 2 and 4 is 2. Divide 2 and 4 by the GCF.

$$\frac{\cancel{3}}{\cancel{4}_2} \times \frac{\cancel{2}^1}{7} = \frac{3}{14}$$

Write an equation for each picture.

1. _____

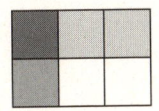

2. _____

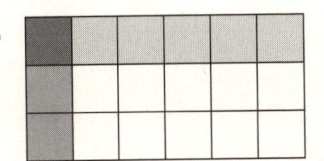

Find each product. Simplify if possible.

3. $\frac{6}{8} \times \frac{1}{3} =$ _____

4. $\frac{5}{6} \times \frac{7}{10} =$ _____

5. $\frac{4}{5} \times \frac{3}{8} =$ _____

6. $\frac{1}{2} \times \frac{4}{9} =$ _____

7. **Number Sense** Can you simplify before multiplying $14 \times \frac{25}{27}$? Explain.

_____

_____

Use with Lesson 5-2. **55**

Name _____

Multiplying Fractions

P 5-2

Write an equation for each picture.

1. 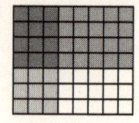 _____   2. _____

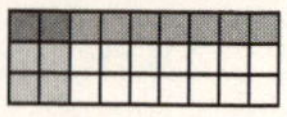

Find each product. Simplify if possible.

3. $\frac{7}{10} \times \frac{13}{14} =$ _____   4. $\frac{4}{5} \times \frac{7}{8} =$ _____

5. $\frac{3}{7} \times \frac{4}{9} =$ _____   6. $\frac{2}{5} \times \frac{3}{10} =$ _____

7. $\frac{5}{9} \times \frac{24}{25} =$ _____   8. $\frac{18}{21} \times 15 =$ _____

9. $\frac{3}{5} \times \frac{17}{21} =$ _____   10. $\frac{11}{12} \times \frac{30}{33} =$ _____

11. **Reasoning** Which is the lesser product, $\frac{5}{6} \times \frac{9}{10}$ or $\frac{5}{6} \times \frac{1}{5}$? Explain how you know.

_____

Pamela spent $\frac{2}{3}$ of one hour doing homework. She solved math problems for $\frac{2}{5}$ of that time and read her science book for $\frac{3}{5}$ of that time. What fraction of one hour did Pamela spend

12. solving math problems? _____

13. reading her science book? _____

Test Prep

14. Find $\frac{7}{13} \times \frac{4}{7}$.

    A. $\frac{3}{13}$ B. $\frac{4}{13}$ C. $\frac{3}{15}$ D. $\frac{4}{15}$

15. **Writing in Math** Explain how you would find the product of $\frac{8}{15}$ and $\frac{9}{16}$.

_____

_____

Use with Lesson 5-2.

Estimating with Fractions and Mixed Numbers

R 5-3

Estimate $5\frac{1}{8} \times 23\frac{5}{6}$ using rounding and compatible numbers.

$5\frac{1}{8} \times 23\frac{5}{6}$ Round each mixed number to the nearest whole number.

$\downarrow$ $\downarrow$

5×24 4×25 is easier to multiply than 5×24.

$\downarrow$ $\downarrow$

$4 \times 25 = 100$

$5\frac{1}{8} \times 23\frac{5}{6} \approx 100$

Estimate $17\frac{1}{7} \div 3\frac{8}{9}$ using rounding and compatible numbers.

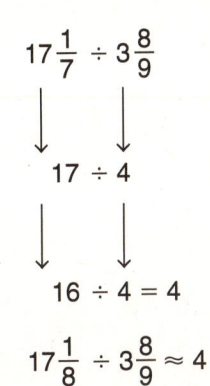

$17\frac{1}{7} \div 3\frac{8}{9}$ Round each mixed number to the nearest whole number.

$\downarrow$ $\downarrow$

$17 \div 4$ Use compatible numbers to divide.

$\downarrow$ $\downarrow$

$16 \div 4 = 4$

$17\frac{1}{8} \div 3\frac{8}{9} \approx 4$

Estimate each product or quotient.

1. $\frac{6}{7} \times 12$ _____

2. $25 \div 4\frac{2}{3}$ _____

3. $3\frac{8}{9} \times 7\frac{3}{4}$ _____

4. $19\frac{12}{15} \div 5\frac{1}{4}$ _____

5. $2\frac{1}{5} \times 36$ _____

6. $39 \div 7\frac{2}{3}$ _____

7. $12\frac{1}{8} \times 2\frac{9}{10}$ _____

8. $35\frac{4}{5} \div 5\frac{7}{8}$ _____

9. $\frac{15}{16} \times 62$ _____

10. $48\frac{7}{9} \div 9\frac{2}{3}$ _____

11. **Writing in Math** Explain how you would estimate $3\frac{5}{6} \times 29\frac{4}{5}$ using compatible numbers.

_____

_____

_____

Estimating with Fractions and Mixed Numbers

P 5-3

Estimate each product or quotient.

1. $\frac{4}{5} \times 21$ _____
2. $2\frac{7}{8} \times 9\frac{1}{4}$ _____
3. $\frac{12}{13} \times 82$ _____

4. $18\frac{7}{8} \times 6\frac{1}{16}$ _____
5. $30 \div 6\frac{3}{4}$ _____
6. $24\frac{3}{16} \div 7\frac{2}{3}$ _____

7. $37 \div 5\frac{2}{3}$ _____
8. $27\frac{4}{9} \div 8\frac{3}{4}$ _____
9. $16\frac{11}{12} \times 3\frac{4}{5}$ _____

10. $90\frac{1}{10} \div 9\frac{9}{10}$ _____
11. $11\frac{3}{8} \times \frac{18}{19}$ _____
12. $12\frac{1}{4} \div 4\frac{3}{10}$ _____

About how much flour is needed to make

13. 2 loaves of zucchini bread?

_____

14. 2 dozen bran muffins?

_____

15. 8 batches of wheat rolls?

_____

Recipe	Cups of Flour
Zucchini bread (1 loaf)	$2\frac{1}{2}$
Bran muffins ($\frac{1}{2}$ dozen)	$1\frac{1}{3}$
Wheat rolls (2 batches)	$2\frac{1}{4}$

16. **Number Sense** What benchmark fraction could you use to estimate the product of 54 and $\frac{7}{16}$? _____

Test Prep

17. Estimate $31\frac{1}{8} \times 5\frac{1}{4}$.

    A. 150   **B.** 170   **C.** 180   **D.** 190

18. **Writing in Math** Explain how you would estimate $16\frac{5}{9} \div 3\frac{7}{8}$.

_____

_____

_____

Use with Lesson 5-3.

Multiplying Mixed Numbers

R 5-4

How to find the product of two mixed numbers:

Find $3\frac{2}{3} \times 4\frac{1}{2}$.

Step 1
Estimate by rounding.

$3\frac{2}{3} \times 4\frac{1}{2}$
$\downarrow \quad\quad \downarrow$
$4 \times 5 = 20$

Then write each mixed number as an improper fraction.

$3\frac{2}{3} \times 4\frac{1}{2}$
$\downarrow \quad\quad \downarrow$
$\frac{11}{3} \times \frac{9}{2}$

Step 2
Look for common factors and simplify.

$\frac{11}{\cancel{3}_1} \times \frac{\cancel{9}^3}{2} = \frac{11}{1} \times \frac{3}{2}$

Step 3
Multiply. Write the product as a mixed number.

$\frac{11}{1} \times \frac{3}{2} = \frac{33}{2} = 16\frac{1}{2}$

$16\frac{1}{2}$ is close to 20, so the answer is reasonable.

Find each product. Simplify if possible.

1. $2\frac{3}{4} \times 3\frac{1}{2} =$ _____
2. $2\frac{1}{5} \times 2\frac{2}{3} =$ _____
3. $6 \times 3\frac{1}{4} =$ _____
4. $1\frac{2}{5} \times 3\frac{1}{4} =$ _____
5. $4\frac{1}{2} \times 16 =$ _____
6. $1\frac{3}{8} \times 2\frac{1}{2} =$ _____

7. **Number Sense** Is $2 \times 17\frac{5}{6}$ greater than or less than 36? Explain.

_____

_____

_____

_____

Use with Lesson 5-4.

Name _____

Multiplying Mixed Numbers

P 5-4

Find each product. Simplify if possible.

1. $3\frac{1}{2} \times 1\frac{2}{3} =$ _____
2. $1\frac{1}{8} \times 2\frac{1}{3} =$ _____
3. $7 \times 1\frac{1}{4} =$ _____

4. $2\frac{1}{6} \times 1\frac{1}{5} =$ _____
5. $3\frac{1}{6} \times 18 =$ _____
6. $1\frac{1}{8} \times 2\frac{1}{2} =$ _____

7. $1\frac{2}{3} \times 2\frac{1}{4} =$ _____
8. $10 \times 1\frac{1}{3} =$ _____
9. $2\frac{4}{5} \times 3\frac{1}{3} =$ _____

10. **Number Sense** Is $6\frac{1}{4} \times 3$ greater than or less than 18? Explain.

_____

_____

Average Precipitation in Boston

Month	Precipitation (in inches)
March	$3\frac{7}{10}$
July	$2\frac{4}{5}$
November	$4\frac{1}{5}$

11. If Boston receives $\frac{5}{7}$ of its average July precipitation, how much precipitation will it receive? _____

12. How much precipitation will Boston receive if it receives half of the March average? _____

13. If Boston receives $1\frac{1}{3}$ of its average November precipitation, how much precipitation will it receive? _____

Test Prep

14. Clarice is making a recipe that requires $1\frac{1}{3}$ c of raisins for 1 batch. How many cups of raisins does she need to make $3\frac{1}{2}$ batches?

   A. $3\frac{3}{4}$ c
   B. $4\frac{1}{3}$ c
   C. $4\frac{2}{3}$ c
   D. $5\frac{1}{2}$ c

15. **Writing in Math** Explain how you would find the product of $1\frac{2}{3}$ and $3\frac{1}{2}$.

_____

_____

Use with Lesson 5-4. **57**

Name _____

PROBLEM-SOLVING STRATEGY   R 5-5
Make an Organized List

Standing in Line How many different ways can Jose, Sumi, and Tina be arranged in a straight line?

Read and Understand

Step 1: What do you know?

There are 3 different people who must be arranged in a straight line: Jose, Sumi, and Tina.

Step 2: What are you trying to find?

How many different ways they can be arranged?

Plan and Solve

Step 3: What strategy will you use?

Strategy: Make an organized list

Jose first
Jose, Sumi, Tina
Jose, Tina, Sumi

Sumi first
Sumi, Jose, Tina
Sumi, Tina, Jose

Tina first
Tina, Jose, Sumi
Tina, Sumi, Jose

Answer: The students can be arranged 6 different ways.

Look Back and Check

Is your answer reasonable? Yes, no combinations are repeated.

---

1. How many different four-digit combinations can be made using the digits 2, 3, 6, and 9? No digit combinations can be repeated. Complete the chart.

2	3	6	9
2369	3269	6239	9236
2396			
2_93			
263_			

58 Use with Lesson 5-5.

Name _____

PROBLEM-SOLVING STRATEGY

Make an Organized List

P 5-5

Solve by making an organized list.

1. Ernest is planting flowers, four to a row. He is planting red, purple, yellow, and white flowers. Each row must contain all four colors and be in a different order from right to left. How many rows can Ernest plant?

2. Sandra is buying tickets for a play. There are shows on Friday, Saturday, and Sunday. Each day has a show at 6:00 P.M., 8:00 P.M., and 10:00 P.M. How many possible choices for a day and a time are there?

3. Tanya has to wear a cap and a T-shirt for her job at the amusement park. She can wear a red, blue, or yellow cap and a red or green shirt. How many different shirt and hat combinations can Tanya wear?

4. **Writing in Math** Explain how you would find the number of three-letter arrangements that can be made with the letters L, G, and F if no repetition of letters is allowed.

Name _____

Dividing Fractions

R 5-6

Dividing by a fraction is the same as multiplying by its reciprocal.
The product of a number and its reciprocal is 1. For example:

Number	×	Reciprocal	=	Product
3	×	$\frac{1}{3}$	=	1
$\frac{1}{8}$	×	$\frac{8}{1}$	=	1
$\frac{2}{3}$	×	$\frac{3}{2}$	=	1

Find $\frac{4}{5} \div \frac{3}{10}$.

Step 1	Step 2
Rewrite the problem as a multiplication problem. Rewrite the divisor as its reciprocal.	Simplify if possible. Multiply. If your answer is an improper fraction, change it to a mixed number.
The reciprocal of $\frac{3}{10}$ is $\frac{10}{3}$. $\frac{4}{5} \times \frac{10}{3}$	$\frac{4}{\cancel{5}_1} \times \frac{\cancel{10}^2}{3} = \frac{8}{3}$ $\frac{8}{3} = 2\frac{2}{3}$

Write the reciprocal of each fraction or number.

1. $\frac{2}{5}$ _____   2. $\frac{1}{7}$ _____

3. 9 _____   4. 15 _____

Find each quotient. Simplify if possible.

5. $6 \div \frac{1}{4} =$ _____   6. $\frac{2}{3} \div \frac{1}{2} =$ _____

7. $\frac{4}{5} \div 10 =$ _____   8. $\frac{1}{3} \div \frac{8}{9} =$ _____

9. $12 \div \frac{3}{8} =$ _____   10. $\frac{7}{10} \div \frac{3}{4} =$ _____

11. $\frac{11}{12} \div \frac{1}{3} =$ _____   12. $\frac{5}{8} \div 6 =$ _____

13. Marcus is making tea for his friends. He has 6 tbsp of honey. If he puts $\frac{1}{2}$ tbsp of honey in each cup of tea, how many cups can he make?

Use with Lesson 5-6.

Name _____

Dividing Fractions

P 5-6

Write the reciprocal for each fraction or number.

1. 5 _____
2. $\frac{7}{12}$ _____
3. $\frac{16}{20}$ _____

Find each quotient. Simplify if possible.

4. $8 \div \frac{1}{5}$ = _____
5. $\frac{1}{2} \div \frac{1}{3}$ = _____
6. $\frac{3}{4} \div 12$ = _____

7. $\frac{3}{5} \div \frac{7}{8}$ = _____
8. $20 \div \frac{4}{9}$ = _____
9. $\frac{9}{10} \div \frac{5}{6}$ = _____

10. $\frac{13}{16} \div \frac{1}{4}$ = _____
11. $\frac{4}{7} \div 8$ = _____
12. $3 \div \frac{1}{5}$ = _____

13. **Reasoning** Will the quotient of $5 \div \frac{7}{8}$ be greater than 5? Explain.

_____

_____

_____

14. Louis has $7\frac{1}{2}$ ft of red ribbon. How many red bows can he make using $\frac{3}{4}$ ft pieces of ribbon for each bow? _____

15. Debra has 14 ft of silver ribbon. How many silver bows can she make using $\frac{2}{3}$ ft pieces of ribbon for each bow? _____

Test Prep

16. Find $\frac{1}{2} \div \frac{7}{8}$.

   A. $\frac{3}{5}$
   B. $\frac{3}{7}$
   C. $\frac{4}{5}$
   D. $\frac{4}{7}$

17. **Writing in Math** Explain how you would find the quotient of $\frac{2}{3}$ and $\frac{3}{4}$.

_____

_____

_____

Use with Lesson 5-6. **59**

Dividing Mixed Numbers

R 5-7

You can follow these steps to find $5\frac{1}{3} \div 1\frac{1}{3}$ and $21 \div 2\frac{1}{3}$.

Step 1	Step 2	Step 3
First estimate. Then write each number as an improper fraction.	Find the reciprocal of the divisor. Rewrite as a multiplication problem.	Look for common factors. Simplify, then multiply.
Find $5\frac{1}{3} \div 1\frac{1}{3}$. Estimate $5 \div 1 = 5$. $5\frac{1}{3} \div 1\frac{1}{3} =$ $\downarrow \quad \downarrow$ $\frac{16}{3} \div \frac{4}{3}$	$\frac{16}{3} \div \frac{4}{3} =$ $\frac{16}{3} \times \frac{3}{4}$	$\frac{16}{3} \times \frac{3}{4} =$ $\frac{\overset{4}{\cancel{16}}}{\underset{1}{\cancel{3}}} \times \frac{\overset{1}{\cancel{3}}}{\underset{1}{\cancel{4}}} = \frac{4}{1} = 4$ 4 is close to 5, so the answer is reasonable.
Find $21 \div 2\frac{1}{3}$. Estimate $21 \div 2 = 10\frac{1}{2}$. $21 \div 2\frac{1}{3}$ $\downarrow \quad \downarrow$ $\frac{21}{1} \div \frac{7}{3}$	$\frac{21}{1} \div \frac{7}{3} =$ $\frac{21}{1} \times \frac{3}{7}$	$\frac{21}{1} \times \frac{3}{7} =$ $\frac{\overset{3}{\cancel{21}}}{1} \times \frac{3}{\underset{1}{\cancel{7}}} = \frac{9}{1} = 9$ 9 is close to $10\frac{1}{2}$, so the answer is reasonable.

Find each quotient. Simplify if possible.

1. $2\frac{2}{3} \div 3\frac{1}{4} =$ _____
2. $1\frac{3}{4} \div 4\frac{1}{8} =$ _____
3. $2\frac{1}{5} \div 2\frac{1}{3} =$ _____
4. $5\frac{1}{4} \div 3 =$ _____
5. $10 \div 3\frac{1}{4} =$ _____
6. $7\frac{1}{4} \div 2\frac{1}{8} =$ _____

7. **Writing in Math** Paper needs to be cut for voting ballots. Each piece of paper is $10\frac{1}{2}$ in. long. Each ballot should be $1\frac{3}{4}$ in. long. How many ballots can be cut from one piece of paper?

Use with Lesson 5-7.

Name _____

Dividing Mixed Numbers

P 5-7

Find each quotient. Simplify if possible.

1. $1\frac{1}{2} \div 2\frac{1}{3} =$ _____
2. $4\frac{1}{4} \div 3\frac{1}{8} =$ _____
3. $2\frac{1}{4} \div 5\frac{1}{2} =$ _____

4. $3\frac{1}{2} \div 2\frac{1}{4} =$ _____
5. $3\frac{3}{4} \div 2 =$ _____
6. $1\frac{1}{2} \div 2\frac{1}{4} =$ _____

7. $8 \div 2\frac{3}{4} =$ _____
8. $2\frac{1}{2} \div 1\frac{3}{8} =$ _____
9. $4\frac{2}{3} \div 1\frac{3}{4} =$ _____

10. **Reasoning** Is it possible to divide 15 by a mixed number and get a quotient that is greater than 15? Explain.

_____

_____

Room	Gallons of Paint
Kitchen	$2\frac{1}{2}$
Bedroom	$3\frac{3}{4}$
Living room	$4\frac{1}{3}$

Max is painting the inside of an apartment complex. The table shows how many gallons of paint are needed to paint each type of room.

11. How many kitchens can Max paint with 20 gal? _____

12. How many living rooms can Max paint with 26 gal? _____

13. How many bedrooms can Max paint with 60 gal? _____

Test Prep

14. Find $4\frac{1}{2} \div 2\frac{1}{4}$.

    A. 1
    B. 2
    C. 3
    D. 4

15. **Writing in Math** Explain how you would find $4\frac{1}{5} \div 2\frac{1}{3}$.

_____

_____

Use with Lesson 5-7.

Expressions with Fractions

R 5-8

Writing an Algebraic Expression

Yesterday the temperature in Portland, Oregon, was 10° more than half the temperature in Phoenix, Arizona. Write an algebraic expression for the temperature in Portland.

Let m = the temperature in Phoenix.

The temperature in Portland was $\frac{1}{2}m + 10$.

Evaluating an Algebraic Expression

If the temperature in Phoenix was 80° yesterday, what was the temperature in Portland?

Substitute 80 for m.

Use order of operations to simplify.

$\frac{1}{2}(80) + 10$

$40 + 10 = 50$

It was 50° in Portland.

Write each word phrase as an algebraic expression.

1. 1 more than $\frac{3}{5}f$ _____

2. $\frac{2}{3}$ Tom's weight _____

3. 5 fewer than $\frac{5}{6}$ the amount _____

4. **Number Sense** Write a word phrase that represents $\frac{1}{2}n + 4$.

   _____

   _____

Evaluate each expression for $n = \frac{1}{3}$ and $n = 1\frac{1}{4}$.

5. $\frac{7}{8}n$ _____

6. $2\frac{1}{3}n$ _____

7. $3 + \frac{1}{2}n$ _____

8. $10n - 3$ _____

Use with Lesson 5-8. **61**

Expressions with Fractions

P 5-8

Write each word phrase as an algebraic expression.

1. 2 more than $\frac{2}{3}d$ _____

2. $\frac{7}{8}$ Amanda's age _____

3. 10 fewer than $\frac{1}{2}$ the number _____

4. **Number Sense** How do the word phrases representing $\frac{5}{6}x + 4$ and $\frac{5}{6}x - 4$ differ?

_____

_____

_____

Evaluate each expression for $n = \frac{1}{4}$ and $n = 1\frac{5}{6}$.

5. $\frac{9}{10}n$ _____ 6. $4\frac{1}{8}n$ _____

Evaluate each expression for $n = 2\frac{1}{3}$ and $n = 3\frac{3}{4}$.

7. $\frac{3}{5}n$ _____ 8. $5\frac{1}{2}n$ _____

9. You can calculate Aaron's age using the expression $\frac{1}{2}n + 5$. If n = Beth's age and Beth is 16, how old is Aaron? _____

Test Prep

10. Evaluate $5\frac{1}{4}n$ for $n = \frac{2}{3}$.

    A. $1\frac{1}{2}$ B. $2\frac{1}{5}$ C. $2\frac{3}{4}$ D. $3\frac{1}{2}$

11. **Writing in Math** Martha's teacher gave her a phrase and asked her to write an expression for the phrase. The expression Martha wrote was $\frac{3}{8}n$. What could the phrase have been? Explain how you know.

_____

_____

Use with Lesson 5-8. **61**

Solving Equations with Fractions

R 5-9

Here is how to solve addition, subtraction, multiplication, and division equations with fractions.

Addition

Solve $n + \frac{3}{5} = 9$.

$n + \frac{3}{5} = 9$

$n + \frac{3}{5} - \frac{3}{5} = 9 - \frac{3}{5}$

$n = 8\frac{2}{5}$

Subtraction

Solve $x - 2\frac{1}{3} = 6\frac{1}{9}$.

$x - 2\frac{1}{3} = 6\frac{1}{9}$

$x - 2\frac{1}{3} + 2\frac{1}{3} = 6\frac{1}{9} + 2\frac{1}{3}$

$x = 6\frac{1}{9} + 2\frac{3}{9}$

$x = 8\frac{4}{9}$

Multiplication

Solve $\frac{5}{8}y = 1\frac{2}{3}$.

$\frac{5}{8}y = 1\frac{2}{3}$

$\left(\frac{8}{5}\right)\frac{5}{8}y = \frac{5}{3}\left(\frac{8}{5}\right)$

$y = \frac{5}{3} \times \frac{8}{5}$

$y = \frac{8}{3} = 2\frac{2}{3}$

Division

Solve $a \div \frac{1}{4} = 3\frac{1}{2}$.

$a \div \frac{1}{4} = 3\frac{1}{2}$

$a \times \frac{4}{1} = 3\frac{1}{2}$

$a \times \frac{4}{1}\left(\frac{1}{4}\right) = \frac{7}{2}\left(\frac{1}{4}\right)$

$a = \frac{7}{8}$

Solve each equation and check your answer.

1. $z + 2\frac{1}{3} = 3\frac{1}{6}$ _____

2. $6n = \frac{3}{4}$ _____

3. $x - 1 = 4\frac{2}{3}$ _____

4. $y \div \frac{1}{2} = 2\frac{1}{8}$ _____

5. $\frac{3}{8} + n = 10$ _____

6. $2\frac{2}{9} \div 5 = x$ _____

7. **Algebra** The rainfall total for June is $4\frac{9}{10}$ in. Yesterday it rained $2\frac{1}{10}$ in. Use the equation $n + 2\frac{1}{10} = 4\frac{9}{10}$ to calculate how much rainfall was received before yesterday.

_____

62 Use with Lesson 5-9.

Solving Equations with Fractions

P 5-9

Solve each equation and check your answer.

1. $y + 1\frac{1}{4} = 2\frac{3}{8}$ _____

2. $w - 2 = 3\frac{1}{2}$ _____

3. $z \div \frac{3}{4} = 4\frac{1}{4}$ _____

4. $\frac{1}{3} = \frac{7}{8}q$ _____

5. $6\frac{1}{2} = \frac{5}{6}b$ _____

6. $2\frac{1}{4} = p - \frac{3}{8}$ _____

7. $2\frac{1}{4} = x \div \frac{1}{2}$ _____

8. **Number Sense** Is the solution of $m \div \frac{2}{3} = 9$ greater than or less than the solution of $m \div \frac{1}{4} = 9$? Explain.

_____

_____

9. The bakery used $42\frac{1}{3}$ c of flour. There were $10\frac{1}{3}$ c left in the flour bin. Use the equation $x - 42\frac{1}{3} = 10\frac{1}{3}$ to find out how many cups of flour the bakery had to start with. _____

10. Alex had a ball of string. He cut the string into 26 equal pieces. Each piece measured $3\frac{1}{4}$ in. Use the equation $m \div 26 = 3\frac{1}{4}$ to find the length of the ball of string. _____

Test Prep

11. Solve $12y = 2\frac{1}{4}$.

    A. $1\frac{1}{2}$ B. $1\frac{1}{8}$ C. $\frac{7}{36}$ D. $\frac{9}{48}$

12. **Writing in Math** Write the steps you would use to solve the equation $z + 3\frac{1}{5} = 6\frac{3}{5}$. Solve.

_____

_____

_____

62 Use with Lesson 5-9.

PROBLEM-SOLVING SKILL
Writing to Explain

R 5-10

Stanley and Mary are growing plants in science class. Stanley's plant is $1\frac{3}{8}$ in. tall. Mary's plant is 4 times as tall. How tall is Mary's plant?

When you are writing to explain your solution,
- include the work you did that led to that solution.
- describe the steps and operations you used in the order you used them.
- refer to any diagrams or data that provide important information or supporting details.

To find the height of Mary's plant, I multiplied the height of Stanley's plant by 4.

Before multiplying I estimated

$1\frac{3}{8} \times 4 \rightarrow 1 \times 4 = 4$

$1\frac{3}{8} \times 4 = \frac{11}{\underset{2}{\cancel{8}}} \times \frac{\overset{1}{\cancel{4}}}{1} = \frac{11}{2} = 5\frac{1}{2}$

$5\frac{1}{2}$ is close to 4, so my answer is reasonable.

So Mary's plant is $5\frac{1}{2}$ in. tall.

Explain your solution and show your work.

1. Paula is 12 years old. Tess is 4 more than $\frac{3}{4}$ Paula's age. How old is Tess?

_____
_____
_____
_____
_____
_____

PROBLEM-SOLVING SKILL

Writing to Explain

P 5-10

Explain your solution and show your work.

1. Rita is riding in an 18 mi bike race. She takes a break every $4\frac{1}{2}$ mi. How many breaks will she take?

2. Frederick makes toy rocking horses. He needs $7\frac{1}{2}$ ft of wood to make a small horse and $9\frac{3}{4}$ ft of wood to make a large horse. How many feet of wood does he need to make 5 small horses and 7 large horses?

3. Sephina is baking bread for the school bake sale. She is planning on baking 15 small loaves and 5 large loaves. For each of the small loaves, she needs $1\frac{2}{3}$ c of flour. For each of the large loaves, she needs $4\frac{1}{5}$ c of flour. How many cups of flour does she need altogether?

Use with Lesson 5-10.

PROBLEM-SOLVING APPLICATIONS

The Bridge

R 5-11

The Golden Gate Bridge in California is approximately $1\frac{7}{10}$ mi long and crosses the Golden Gate Strait.

How long would $2\frac{1}{2}$ times the length of the Golden Gate Bridge be?

$1\frac{7}{10} \times 2\frac{1}{2}$

$\frac{\cancel{17}^{\,}}{\cancel{10}_{2}} \times \frac{\cancel{5}^{1}}{2}$ Write the mixed numbers as improper fractions. Simplify if possible.

$\frac{17}{2} \times \frac{1}{2} = \frac{17}{4} = 4\frac{1}{4}$ Multiply. Write the product as a mixed number.

The bridge would be $4\frac{1}{4}$ mi long.

1. If you rode your bike halfway across the Golden Gate Bridge, how far would you have ridden? _____

2. If a man jogged from one end of the Golden Gate Bridge and back, how many miles would he have jogged? _____

3. Suppose the first $\frac{5}{8}$ of the Golden Gate Bridge was repainted. How many miles of the bridge were repainted? _____

4. Suppose a different bridge in California were $\frac{1}{3}$ the length of the Golden Gate Bridge. Write an algebraic expression for the length of this other bridge. Let d equal the length of the Golden Gate Bridge. _____

5. If the Golden Gate Bridge were divided into 5 equal sections, how long would each section be? _____

6. How long would 5 times the length of the Golden Gate Bridge be? _____

Use with Lesson 5-11.

PROBLEM-SOLVING APPLICATION P 5-11

Black Walnut Tree

The Institute of Agriculture and Natural Resources at the University of Nebraska published a study of the black walnut tree. The information in the published report is used by farmers and forestry experts to monitor and improve the growth of the black walnut tree in the Nebraska area.

Part of the study examined the growth of 10 different black walnut trees on 2 different sites. Site 1 was a shallow, hilly area that had some clay in the soil. Site 2 was a deep, well-drained area.

Tree 1 on Site 1 grew at a rate of about $1\frac{3}{4}$ ft per year.

1. At this rate, how tall would the tree be after $\frac{1}{3}$ year? _____

2. At this rate, how tall would the tree be after 6 years? After 8 years? _____

Suppose the black walnut tree's growth changes every $3\frac{5}{12}$ years. As a result, the researchers make records of the tree's growth every $3\frac{5}{12}$ years. For the study, the researchers called every $3\frac{5}{12}$ years a "period." At a growth rate of $1\frac{3}{4}$ ft per year, the black walnut tree would grow about $5\frac{19}{20}$ ft every period of $3\frac{5}{12}$ years.

3. To find an estimate for how much the tree would grow in 3 periods, first round $5\frac{19}{20}$ to a compatible whole number. Then multiply your answer by 3 to get the estimate.

_____

_____

4. Now find exactly how much the tree would grow in 3 periods, based on the data given. _____

5. How much would the tree grow in 12 periods? _____

6. Suppose researchers found that Tree 7 on Site 2 grew $2\frac{1}{7}$ ft per year. How much would Tree 7 grow in 1 period of $3\frac{5}{12}$ years? _____

7. How much would Tree 7 grow in 4 periods? _____

Name _____

Understanding Ratios

R 6-1

Ratios are used to compare quantities or amounts. What ratio could be used to compare the number of circles to the number of squares?

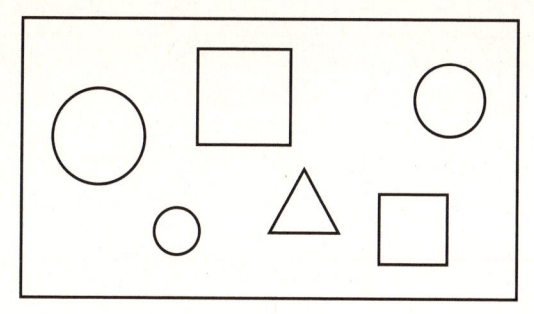

The quantities in the ratio are called terms. Which quantity is mentioned first? Circles

The first term is the number of circles.
Which quantity is mentioned second? Squares

The second term is the number of squares.
number of circles : number of squares

    3   2

The ratio is 3:2.

This ratio can also be written as $\frac{3}{2}$, or 3 to 2.

Use the picture above for 1–6. Write a ratio for each comparison in three ways.

1. the number of squares to the number of triangles _____

2. the number of squares to the number of circles _____

3. the number of triangles to the number of circles _____

4. the number of triangles to the number of squares _____

5. the number of circles to the total number of shapes _____

6. **Number Sense** Is a ratio of 3:1 the same as a ratio of 1:3? Explain.

Use with Lesson 6-1. **65**

Understanding Ratios

P 6-1

A string quartet consists of 2 violins, 1 viola, and 1 cello. Write a ratio for each comparison in three ways.

1. violins to cellos _____

2. cellos to violas _____

3. violins to all instruments _____

4. **Number Sense** How are the ratios in Exercises 1 and 2 different from the ratio in Exercise 3?

_____

_____

_____

Midland Orchards grows a large variety of apples. The orchard contains 12 rows of Granny Smith trees, 10 rows of Fuji trees, 15 rows of Gala trees, 2 rows of Golden Delicious trees, and 2 rows of Jonathan trees. Write each ratio in three ways.

5. rows of Granny Smith trees to rows of Golden Delicious trees _____

6. rows of Fuji trees to the total number of rows of trees _____

Test Prep

7. A grade school has 45 students who walk to school and 150 students who ride the bus. The other 50 students are driven to school. Which shows the ratio of students who walk to school to the total number of students in the school?

   A. 45:50   **B.** 45:195   **C.** 45:150   **D.** 45:245

8. **Writing in Math** Steve said it does not matter which term is first and which term is second in a ratio, since ratios are different than fractions. Is he correct? Explain why or why not.

_____

_____

Use with Lesson 6-1. **65**

Equal Ratios

R 6-2

Find 3 ratios that are equal to $\frac{30}{40}$.

Use multiplication.	Use division.
Multiply both terms by the same nonzero number.	Divide both terms by the same nonzero number.
$\frac{30 \times 2}{40 \times 2} = \frac{60}{80}$	$\frac{30 \div 2}{40 \div 2} = \frac{15}{20}$
$\frac{30 \times 3}{40 \times 3} = \frac{90}{120}$	$\frac{30 \div 5}{40 \div 5} = \frac{6}{8}$
$\frac{30 \times 5}{40 \times 5} = \frac{150}{200}$	$\frac{30 \div 10}{40 \div 10} = \frac{3}{4}$

So $\frac{30}{40}, \frac{3}{4}, \frac{6}{8}, \frac{15}{20}, \frac{60}{80}, \frac{90}{120}$, and $\frac{150}{200}$ are all equal ratios.

Decide if 12:16 and 6:9 are equal.

$\frac{12}{16} = \frac{12 \div 4}{16 \div 4} = \frac{3}{4}$ $\frac{6}{9} = \frac{6 \div 3}{9 \div 3} = \frac{2}{3}$

Divide by the GCF of 12 and 16.   Divide by the GCF of 6 and 9.

Since $\frac{3}{4} \neq \frac{2}{3}$, 12:16 is not equal to 6:9.

Write the ratio 84:40 in simplest form.

$\frac{84}{40} = \frac{84 \div 2}{40 \div 2} = \frac{42}{20}$ Divide each number by a common factor. Continue until the only common factor is 1.

$\frac{42}{20} = \frac{42 \div 2}{20 \div 2} = \frac{21}{10}$

21:10 is simplest form, because the only number that divides both 21 and 10 is 1.

Give three ratios that are equal to each ratio.

1. 5:3 _____

2. 8:10 _____

3. $\frac{4}{2}$ _____

Tell whether the ratios in each pair are equal.

4. $\frac{5}{6}$ and $\frac{25}{30}$ _____

5. 9:5 and 5 to 9 _____

6. **Number Sense** Dale says that the ratios 3:5 and 2:10 are equal. Is he correct? Explain.

_____

_____

Name _____

Equal Ratios

P 6-2

Give three ratios that are equal to each ratio.

1. 3 to 9 _____

2. 1:2.5 _____

3. $\frac{18}{9}$ _____

Tell whether the ratios in each pair are equal.

4. $\frac{5}{6}$ and $\frac{12}{10}$ _____

5. 7:7 and 100:100 _____

6. 1:9 and 0.5:4.5 _____

Write each ratio in simplest form.

7. 51:17 _____

8. $\frac{1.2}{8.4}$ _____

9. 5:25 _____

10. 14 to 35 _____

11. **Number Sense** What operations can be used to find equal ratios? What operations cannot be used to find equal ratios?

_____
_____
_____
_____

Test Prep

12. Which ratio is equal to 95:100?

    A. $\frac{9.5}{1.0}$
    B. 100:95
    C. 180:200
    D. $\frac{285}{300}$

13. **Writing in Math** Find a ratio equal to 55:11. Tell what operation you used to find your answer.

_____
_____

66 Use with Lesson 6-2.

Rates and Unit Rates

R 6-3

A rate is a ratio in which the two terms use different units of measurement.

For example:

2 <u>sandwiches</u> for 5 <u>dollars</u>   150 <u>mi</u> in 3 <u>hr</u>

A unit rate is a rate in which the second term is 1.

For example: 50 mi in 1 hr

This is a unit rate because the units are different for the first and second term, and the second term is 1.

How to write rates as unit rates	How to use unit rates to make comparisons
Give the unit rate for 20 yards in 4 minutes. **Example A:** Find an equal ratio. $\frac{20 \text{ yds}}{4 \text{ min}} = \frac{? \text{ yds}}{1 \text{ min}}$ $\frac{20 \div 4}{4 \div 4} = \frac{5}{1}$ Unit Rate: $\frac{5 \text{ yds}}{1 \text{ min}}$ **Example B:** Find the quotient of the terms. Rate = $\frac{20 \text{ yds}}{4 \text{ min}}$ $20 \div 4 = 5$ Unit Rate: $\frac{5 \text{ yds}}{1 \text{ min}}$ The unit rate is 5 yards per minute.	Dan painted 9 planks in 6 minutes. Bill painted 22 planks in 11 minutes. Which boy painted at a faster rate? Dan's Rate $\qquad$ Bill's Rate $\frac{9 \text{ planks}}{6 \text{ min}}$ $\qquad$ $\frac{22 \text{ planks}}{11 \text{ min}}$ Unit Rate: $\frac{1.5 \text{ planks}}{1 \text{ min}}$ $\quad$ Unit Rate: $\frac{2 \text{ planks}}{1 \text{ min}}$ Bill painted at a faster rate.

Write each as a unit rate.

1. 25 goals in 5 games _____

2. 48 mi in 8 days _____

3. 30 books in 15 days _____

4. 120 oz in 20 min _____

Which is the faster rate?

5. 3 mi in 12 hr or 8 mi in 18 hr? _____

6. 32 ft in 45 min or 50 ft in 60 min? _____

7. **Number Sense** If a car goes 350 mi in 5 hr, what is its rate per hour? _____

Use with Lesson 6-3. **67**

Name _____

Rates and Unit Rates

P 6-3

Write each as a unit rate.

1. 120 mi to 10 gal of gas

2. 45 pages in 30 min

3. 500 mi in 25 hr

4. $12.00 for 3 lb

Which is the better buy?

5. 1 lb of apples for $1.98 or
   3 lb for $6.95

6. 5 lb of flour for $0.90 or
   8 lb for $1.25

Which is the lower rate?

7. 44 people in 4 theaters or 100 people in 10 theaters

8. 8 cashiers for 96 people or 2 cashiers for 20 people

9. **Number Sense** What makes a unit rate different from other rates?

10. NASA's space shuttle orbits Earth 1 time in 90 minutes. How many times would the space shuttle orbit Earth in 6 hours?

Test Prep

11. Which is the unit rate for 39 people in 3 vans?

    A. 39 people per van
    B. 13 vans per person
    C. 13 people per van
    D. 3 people per van

12. **Writing in Math** Explain how you could convert a rate of miles per hour to a rate of miles per second.

Use with Lesson 6-3. **67**

Name _____

PROBLEM-SOLVING STRATEGY
Use Objects

R 6-4

Food Tasting The Parkline School's languages club held an international food-tasting event. Each of the 21 club members brought in a dish of food. Out of every 7 dishes brought to the event, 2 were Mexican dishes. How many Mexican dishes were brought to the international food-tasting event?

Read and Understand

Step 1: What do you know?

There were a total of 21 dishes. Out of every 7 dishes, 2 were Mexican.

Step 2: What are you trying to find out?

How many out of the 21 dishes were Mexican dishes?

Plan and Solve

Step 3: What strategy should you use?   **Strategy:** Use objects

Step 1

Use two different counters.
- ● = Mexican dish
- ○ = Non-Mexican dish

Step 2

Two out of every seven dishes were Mexican. Show this with counters.

● ● ○ ○ ○ ○ ○
● ● ○ ○ ○ ○ ○
● ● ○ ○ ○ ○ ○

2 Mexican dishes   The other 5 were non-Mexican dishes.

Step 3

Count how many dishes were Mexican.

● ● ○ ○ ○ ○ ○
● ● ○ ○ ○ ○ ○
● ● ○ ○ ○ ○ ○

There were 6 counters for Mexican dishes.

Answer: There were 6 Mexican dishes at the international food-tasting event.

Look Back and Check

Is your work correct?

Yes, the counters show 21 dishes, and 2 out of every 7 were Mexican dishes.

Solve the problem. Give the answer in a complete sentence.

1. At the international food-tasting event, 1 out of every 9 people who attended was a teacher. There were 63 people at the event. How many teachers attended the event? Think: How can you use a model to show the data?

---

68 Use with Lesson 6-4.

Name _____

PROBLEM-SOLVING STRATEGY

P 6-4

Use Objects

Solve each problem. Give the answer in a complete sentence.

1. Of the 150 items at the bake sale, 3 out of 5 are muffins. How many muffins are for sale at the bake sale?

   _____
   _____

2. The school orchestra plays 24 different pieces of music. Of the 24 pieces, 18 are folk songs and the rest are classical pieces. What is the ratio of classical pieces to the total number of pieces played by the orchestra?

   _____
   _____

3. The ratio of students to teachers at a high school is 18:1. The school has 12 teachers. How many students attend the school?

   _____
   _____

4. A farmer planted 60 acres of wheat. The ratio of acres planted with wheat to total acres is 3:5. How many total acres does the farmer have?

   _____
   _____

5. **Writing in Math** Kara kept track of how she spent her time for one full week. She found that the ratio of hours spent sleeping to total number of hours in a week was 1:3. How many hours did Kara sleep during the week? Explain how you found your answer.

   _____
   _____
   _____

Use with Lesson 6-4.

Understanding Proportions

R 6-5

Do the ratios $\frac{20 \text{ mi}}{5 \text{ days}}$ and $\frac{40 \text{ mi}}{10 \text{ days}}$ form a proportion?

First, check that the units are the same across the top and bottom.

$$\frac{20 \text{ mi}}{5 \text{ days}} \stackrel{?}{=} \frac{40 \text{ mi}}{10 \text{ days}}$$

The units are the same.

Then look at the cross products.

$\frac{20}{5} = \frac{40}{10}$ Multiply the denominator of one fraction by the numerator of the other fraction.

$\frac{20}{5} \times \frac{40}{10}$ $20 \times 10 = 40 \times 5$
$200 = 200$

The cross products are equal.

Since the units are the same and the cross products are equal, the ratios form a proportion.

Decide if the ratios form a proportion.

1. $\frac{5 \text{ min}}{30 \text{ ft}}, \frac{20 \text{ min}}{120 \text{ ft}}$ _____

2. $\frac{20 \text{ mi}}{2 \text{ gal}}, \frac{25 \text{ mi}}{2.5 \text{ gal}}$ _____

3. $10.00: 2 \text{ hr}; \$400.00: 40 \text{ hr}$ _____

4. $\frac{20 \text{ ft}}{1 \text{ sec}}, \frac{80 \text{ ft}}{4 \text{ sec}}$ _____

5. $\frac{64 \text{ mi}}{4 \text{ sec}}, \frac{64 \text{ sec}}{4 \text{ mi}}$ _____

6. $\frac{22 \text{ gal}}{5 \text{ c}}, \frac{44 \text{ gal}}{15 \text{ c}}$ _____

7. **Reasoning** How can you tell that $\frac{\$10.25}{5 \text{ hr}}$ and $\frac{11 \text{ gal}}{10 \text{ hr}}$ do not form a proportion?

_____

_____

_____

Use with Lesson 6-5.

Name _____

Understanding Proportions

P 6-5

Decide if the ratios form a proportion.

1. $\frac{12 \text{ min.}}{30 \text{ min}}, \frac{36 \text{ ft}}{90 \text{ min}}$ _____

2. $\frac{15 \text{ mi.}}{1 \text{ gal}}, \frac{25 \text{ mi}}{1 \text{ gal}}$ _____

3. $5.00:1 hr; $200.00:40 hr _____

4. $\frac{200 \text{ ft.}}{1 \text{ sec}}, \frac{4,000 \text{ ft}}{20 \text{ sec}}$ _____

5. $\frac{32 \text{ gal.}}{2 \text{ sec}}, \frac{64 \text{ sec}}{4 \text{ gal}}$ _____

6. $18.75:10 lb; $56.25: 30 lb _____

7. **Number Sense** Explain how you could write $\frac{12 \text{ mi}}{30 \text{ min}}$ and $\frac{24 \text{ mi}}{1 \text{ hr}}$ as a proportion.

_____

_____

8. **Algebra** What value of x would form a proportion?
$\frac{32 \text{ mi}}{x} = \frac{160 \text{ mi}}{50 \text{ min}}$ _____

9. Which two fruit stands' apple to orange ratios are equal?

_____

_____

Fruit Stand	Apples	Oranges
Kendra	32	4
Chloe	10	25
Hillary	7	21
Bethany	16	2

10. Write a ratio equal to Chloe's apple to orange ratio.

_____

Test Prep

11. Which of the following ratios forms a proportion with $\frac{45 \text{ mi}}{1 \text{ hr}}$?

    A. $\frac{21 \text{ mi}}{30 \text{ sec}}$ B. $\frac{4.5 \text{ mi}}{1 \text{ min}}$ C. $\frac{450 \text{ mi}}{10 \text{ hr}}$ D. $\frac{45 \text{ hr}}{1 \text{ mi}}$

12. **Writing in Math** Write a ratio that is proportional with $\frac{5 \text{ mi}}{20 \text{ min}}$. Explain how you found this ratio.

_____

_____

_____

Use with Lesson 6-5.

Name _____

Solving Proportions

R 6-6

The Deejay A radio deejay plays 2 min of commercials for every 10 min of music he plays. If he has played 60 min of music, how many minutes of commercials does he need to play?

First, make a table.

Minutes of Music	10	20	30	40	50	60
Minutes of Commercials	2	?	?	?	?	?

Then look for a pattern.

Minutes of Music	10	20	30	40	50	60
Minutes of Commercials	2	4	6	8	10	(12)

The deejay would have to play 12 minutes of commercials.

Find the unit rate.

Rate = $\frac{10 \text{ min of music}}{2 \text{ min of commercials}}$

$10 \div 2 = 5$

Unit rate = $\frac{5 \text{ min of music}}{1 \text{ min of commercials}}$

5 min of music × 12 = 60 min of music

1 min of commercials × 12 = 12 min of commercials

The deejay would play 12 min of commercials.

Determine how to get from $\frac{10 \text{ min of music}}{2 \text{ min of commercials}}$ to $\frac{60 \text{ min of music}}{? \text{ min of commercials}}$

Think of equal ratios.

$\frac{10}{2} = \frac{60}{?}$

What is 10 multiplied by to get 60? 6
So multiply 2 by 6 to find x.

$10 \times 6 = 60$, so $2 \times 6 = 12$

The deejay would play 12 min of commercials.

Solve each proportion using any method.

1. $\frac{2 \text{ ft}}{6 \text{ hr}} = \frac{x \text{ ft}}{18 \text{ hr}}$ _____

2. $\frac{15 \text{ ft}}{t \text{ hr}} = \frac{60 \text{ ft}}{4 \text{ hr}}$ _____

3. $\frac{5 \text{ in.}}{2 \text{ weeks}} = \frac{b \text{ in.}}{1 \text{ week}}$ _____

4. $\frac{65 \text{ mi}}{\text{hr}} = \frac{455 \text{ mi}}{r \text{ hr}}$ _____

5. $\frac{w \text{ ft}}{2 \text{ hr}} = \frac{600 \text{ ft}}{10 \text{ hr}}$ _____

6. $\frac{\$125}{\text{week}} = \frac{\$1{,}000}{s \text{ weeks}}$ _____

7. **Number Sense** Movies are filmed as a series of pictures called frames. Usually movies are shown at a rate of 24 frames, or pictures, per second. How many frames are in 8 sec of a movie? _____

Name _____

Solving Proportions

P 6-6

Solve each proportion using any method.

1. $\frac{12 \text{ ft}}{t \text{ hr}} = \frac{20 \text{ ft}}{4 \text{ hr}}$ _____

2. $\frac{\$45.00}{2 \text{ wk}} = \frac{b}{1 \text{ wk}}$ _____

3. $\frac{65 \text{ mi}}{1 \text{ hr}} = \frac{715 \text{ mi}}{r \text{ hr}}$ _____

4. $\frac{w \text{ km}}{3 \text{ hr}} = \frac{900 \text{ km}}{30 \text{ hr}}$ _____

5. **Number Sense** Explain how you can tell that $\frac{35 \text{ mi}}{30 \text{ min}} = \frac{350 \text{ mi}}{300 \text{ min}}$ using mental math.

_____

_____

6. How many cups of sand would you use to make 66 c of potting soil?

_____

7. How many cups of humus would you use to make 11 c of potting soil?

_____

8. If you made an amount of potting soil that called for 78 c of sand, how many cups of humus would you need?

_____

Potting Soil for Ferns (Makes 22 c)

6 c sand
6 c loam
6 c peat moss
3 c humus
1 c dried cow manure

Test Prep

9. Which is the correct value for *y*?

$\frac{45 \text{ mi}}{y \text{ min}} = \frac{135 \text{ mi}}{12 \text{ min}}$

A. 4 mi   B. 36 mi   C. 4 min   D. 36 min

10. **Writing in Math** Find a set of values for *x* and *y* to make $\frac{x}{y} = \frac{4 \text{ mi}}{32 \text{ min}}$ a proportion. Explain how you found the values.

_____

_____

_____

Solving Proportions Using Cross Products

R 6-7

Costumes Gena is making costumes for the school play. She knows that 4 costumes will require 16 yd of fabric. How many yards of fabric will she need for 10 costumes?

Step 1	**Step 2**	**Step 3**
Set up the proportion with the information in the problem. $\frac{4}{16} = \frac{10}{y}$	Write the cross products. $\frac{4}{16} \times \frac{10}{y}$ $4 \times y = 16 \times 10$ Then multiply: $4y = 160$	Solve for the variable. $4y = 160$ $\frac{4y}{4} = \frac{160}{4}$ $y = 40$ Gena will need 40 yards of fabric for 10 costumes.

Solve each proportion using cross products. Round to the nearest hundredth as needed.

1. $\frac{r}{50} = \frac{20}{80}$ _____

2. $\frac{54}{h} = \frac{10.5}{21}$ _____

3. $\frac{50}{60} = \frac{90}{g}$ _____

4. $\frac{20}{y} = \frac{10}{100}$ _____

5. $\frac{15}{w} = \frac{45}{120}$ _____

6. $\frac{80}{75} = \frac{p}{90}$ _____

7. **Number Sense** How can you tell that n is greater than 100 without solving $\frac{85}{150} = \frac{n}{375}$?

© Pearson Education, Inc. 6

Use with Lesson 6-7.

Name _____

Solving Proportions Using Cross Products

P 6-7

Solve each proportion using cross products. Round to the nearest hundredth as needed.

1. $\frac{r}{45} = \frac{90}{270}$ _____

2. $\frac{32}{h} = \frac{5.9}{12}$ _____

3. $\frac{45}{60} = \frac{81}{g}$ _____

4. $\frac{78}{y} = \frac{98}{100}$ _____

5. **Number Sense** Are the two ratios that make up a proportion always, sometimes, or never equivalent? _____

The weight of objects on Earth would vary on other planets. This is due to the different gravitational force on each planet. The weight of objects on other planets can be determined by solving proportions.

6. An object that weighs 10 lb on Earth weighs 9 lb on Venus. What would an object that weighs 90 lb on Earth weigh on Venus? _____

7. An object that weighs 100 lb on Earth weighs 112.5 lb on Neptune. What would an object that weighs 50 lb on Earth weigh on Neptune? _____

8. An object that weighs 234 lb on Jupiter weighs 100 lb on Earth. What would an object that weighs 400 lb on Jupiter weigh on Earth? (Round your answer to the nearest hundredth.) _____

Test Prep

9. Cecelia has read 12 books this summer and has collected 72 tokens from the library's summer reading program. Which of the following shows how to solve for the number of tokens rewarded for each book?

   A. $\frac{12}{72} = \frac{t}{1}$ B. $\frac{12}{1} = \frac{t}{72}$ C. $\frac{12}{72} = \frac{1}{t}$ D. $\frac{1}{12} = \frac{72}{t}$

10. **Writing in Math** Explain how you would use mental math to solve the proportion $\frac{75}{w} = \frac{1}{2}$.

_____

_____

_____

Use with Lesson 6-7. **71**

PROBLEM-SOLVING SKILL
Writing to Explain

R 6-8

Chess Club The chess club has 16 members. Out of every 4 members, 1 is a fifth grader and the other members are sixth graders. How many of the chess-club members are fifth graders?

Gerry's explanation:

There are 4 fifth graders. Here is how I found out.

There are 16 members in the group. I drew a circle for each member. Since 1 out of every 4 is a fifth grader, I drew 16 circles in groups of 4. Then I colored in 1 circle out of each group of 4.

● ○ ○ ○   ● = fifth graders
● ○ ○ ○   ○ = other students
● ○ ○ ○
● ○ ○ ○

Then I counted up the number of dark circles. There are 4, so I know there are 4 fifth graders in the club.

To write a good explanation, you should write the steps in order and explain any symbols or drawings you used.

---

1. Ms. Chin's class recorded the weather conditions for 14 days. Out of every 7 days for which they recorded the data, 3 days were cloudy. Ms. Jensen's class recorded the weather for the next 10 days. Out of every 5 days for which they recorded the data, 4 days were cloudy. Which class recorded more cloudy days? Write and explain how you decided. Remember the steps for a good written explanation.

   _____
   _____
   _____
   _____
   _____
   _____

Use with Lesson 6-8.

PROBLEM-SOLVING SKILL
Writing to Explain

P 6-8

1. A school fundraiser was held to raise money for a new school playground. Of every $20.00 raised, $16.00 will be spent on playground equipment, $2.00 on new walkways, and $2.00 on a new fence. The fundraiser provided $500.00 for playground equipment. What was the total amount of money raised? Explain how you found the answer.

2. Stephan planned a hiking trip at a national park. He planned to hike 22.5 mi per day and camp at night. After the fourth day of the trip, he had hiked a total of 90.5 mi. Is Stephan ahead of schedule, behind schedule, or right on schedule? Explain how you found the answer.

3. Marcos has a new odometer on his bike that records the distance he traveled in both miles and kilometers. After his bike ride, the odometer read 15 mi, or 24.15 km. How could Marcos use this information to find the number of kilometers equal to 1 mi?

4. Kara can run 3 mi in 25.5 min. At this pace, how long would it take her to run 2 mi? Explain how you found the answer.

Use with Lesson 6-8.

Using Formulas

R 6-9

A formula is an equation that shows the way quantities relate to one another.

For example:

The formula $0.45p = k$ relates pounds to kilograms. The variable p stands for pounds and the variable k stands for kilograms.

How many kilograms does a 100 lb person measure?

First, substitute the information you know:

$0.45\ p = k$
$0.45\ (100\ \text{lb}) = k$

Then, solve the equation to find the answer.

$0.45 \times 100 = 45\ \text{kg}$

Use the formula *total cost = unit price × ounces* to solve the exercises.

1. Orange juice costs $0.13 per ounce. How much do 8 oz of orange juice cost? _____

2. Cranberry juice costs $0.18 per ounce. How much do 6 oz of cranberry juice cost? _____

3. Grape juice costs $0.25 per ounce. How much do 7 oz of grape juice cost? _____

4. **Estimation** Carrot juice costs $0.32 per ounce. Durango purchased $1.92 worth of carrot juice. How many ounces of carrot juice did he purchase? _____

Use the formula *distance = rate × time* to solve the problems.

5. A car travels at a rate of 50 mi per hour. How far will the car travel in 4 hr? _____

6. A train travels at a rate of 110 mi per hour. How far will the train travel in 9 hr? _____

7. A truck traveled a total distance of 180 mi. It drove at a rate of 30 mi per hour. For how many hours did the truck travel? _____

Use with Lesson 6-9.

Using Formulas

P 6-9

Use the formulas to solve the problems.

Area Conversion

$a = \dfrac{s}{43.56}$
$s = 43.56 \times a$

a = acres
s = square feet

1. If the area is 5 acres, what is the area in square feet?

   _____

2. If the area is 500.94 ft², what is the area in acres?

   _____

3. If the area is 1,359.072 ft², what is the area in acres?

   _____

4. **Estimation** José says that a quick way to estimate the area in square feet is to multiply the number of acres by 40. Does his method make sense? Is it a good way to estimate?

   _____

   _____

5. Elise's science teacher had the students count their pulse for 10 seconds. They then used the formula *beats in 10 sec × 6 = beats per minute*. If Elise counted 12 beats in 10 sec, how many beats would she have in 1 minute? _____

Test Prep

6. If there are about 28.35 g in 1 oz, about how many grams are equal to 16 ounces?

   A. 0.56 g **B.** 1.77 g **C.** 453.6 g **D.** 4,356 g

7. **Writing in Math** Explain how you would use the data in Exercise 6 to find the number of ounces in a certain number of grams.

   _____

   _____

   _____

Use with Lesson 6-9. **73**

Name _____

Scale Drawings and Maps

R 6-10

On the drawing at the right, the scale tells us that 1 cm = 2 ft.

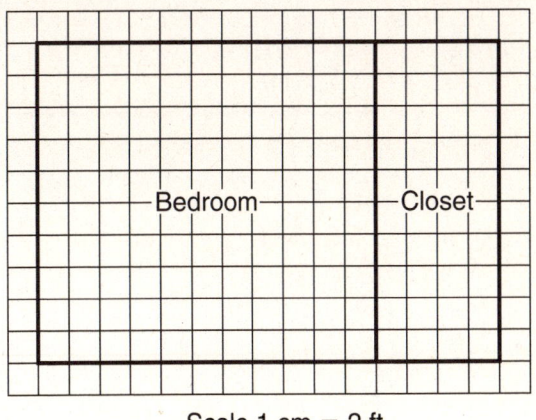

What is the actual length of the bedroom?

Let y be the actual length of the bedroom in feet. Use the scale to set up a proportion. Write the scale as the first ratio. The bedroom is 11 cm on the map. Use this information for the second ratio:

$$\frac{1 \text{ cm}}{2 \text{ ft}} = \frac{11 \text{ cm}}{y \text{ ft}} \quad \leftarrow \text{ scale length} \\ \leftarrow \text{ actual length}$$

Scale 1 cm = 2 ft

Solve the proportion to find the actual length of the bedroom. Use cross products.

$$\frac{1 \text{ cm}}{2 \text{ ft}} = \frac{11 \text{ cm}}{y \text{ ft}}$$

$$\frac{1y}{1} = \frac{22}{1}$$

$$y = 22 \text{ ft}$$

The actual length of the bedroom is 22 ft.

Use the scale drawing to answer 1–3.

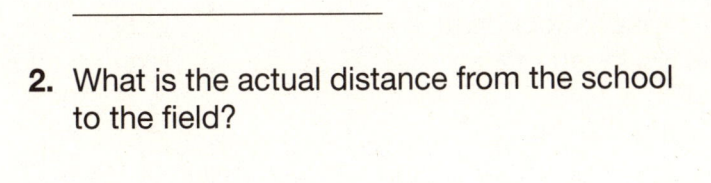

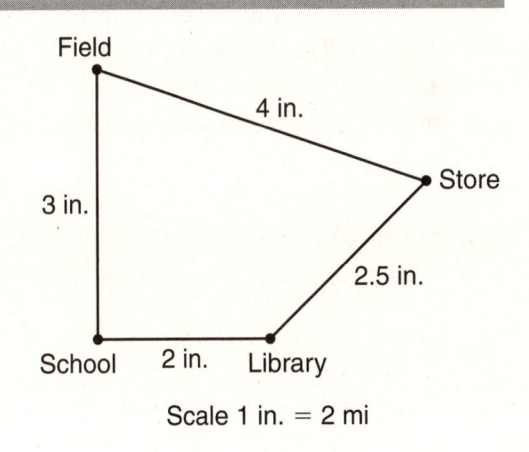

1. What is the actual distance from the school to the library?

   _____

2. What is the actual distance from the school to the field?

   _____

3. What is the actual distance from the field to the store?

   _____

Scale 1 in. = 2 mi

4. **Reasoning** If a scale on a map is 1 in. = 300 mi, what would the map distance be if the actual distance between two places is 600 mi? Explain.

74 Use with Lesson 6-10.

Name _____

Scale Drawings and Maps

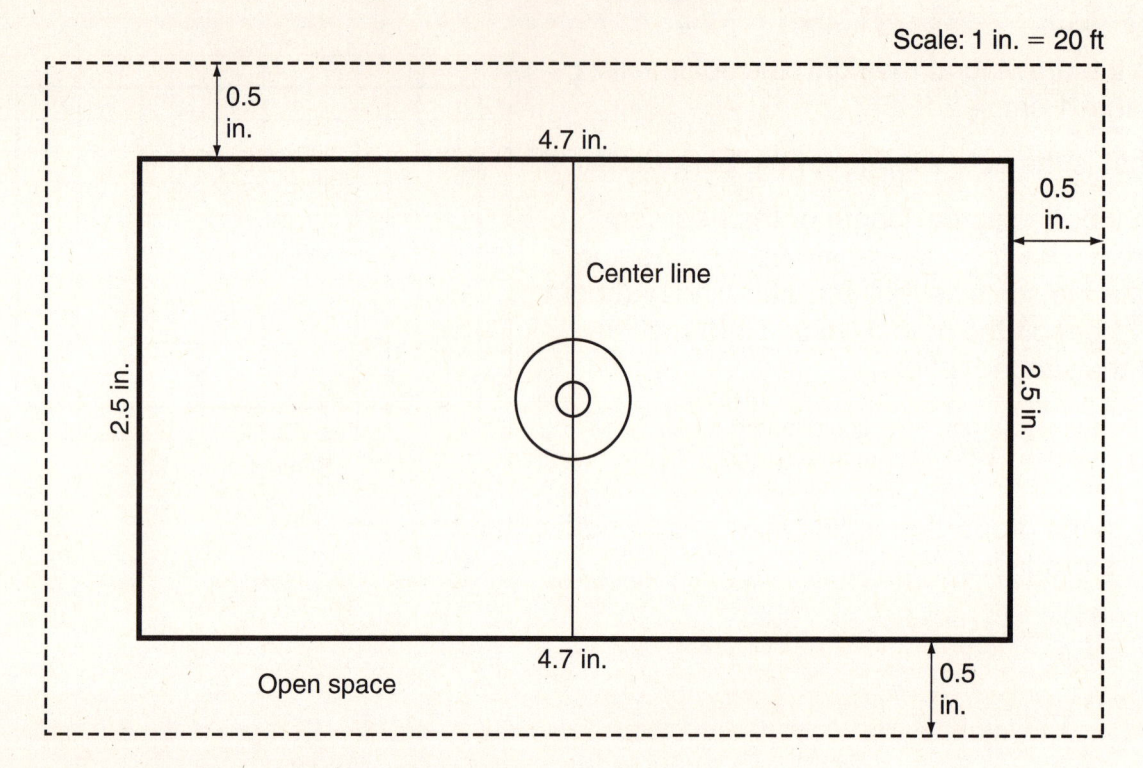

P 6-10

Scale: 1 in. = 20 ft

[Diagram of basketball court: 4.7 in. by 2.5 in., with 0.5 in. open space on all sides, center line dividing court, Open space labeled]

1. What is the actual length and width of a college basketball court? _____

2. How far should open space extend from each side of the court? _____

3. What is the actual measurement from the end of the court to the center line? _____

4. **Reasoning** What is the scale on a map that shows two cities that are 400 mi apart as 2.5 in. apart? _____

Test Prep

5. If the scale of a drawing is 1 in. = 2.5 ft, which is the actual size of an object that is 2 in. long in the drawing?

   A. 1 in.　　**B.** 5 in.　　**C.** 2.5 ft　　**D.** 5 ft

6. **Writing in Math** Explain how you would choose a scale to use for a map. What things would you need to consider?

_____

_____

_____

74　Use with Lesson 6-10.

PROBLEM-SOLVING APPLICATIONS   R 6-11

Outer Space

Data File

Distance from Earth to the moon:	238,900 mi
Time for Earth to rotate once:	24 hr
Number of planets that rotate clockwise:	1
Number of planets that rotate counterclockwise:	8

How many times does Earth rotate in 144 hr?

I know that Earth rotates 1 time in 24 hr. I can make a table to solve this problem. By looking for a pattern and filling in the table, I can see that in 144 hr, Earth will rotate 6 times.

Number of Hours	24	48	72	96	120	144
Number of Rotations	1	2	3	4	5	6

1. Write a ratio that compares the number of planets that rotate clockwise to the total number of planets.

2. It takes the planet Mercury 88 days to revolve around the sun. The ratio for revolutions to days is 1:88. Write two other ratios that are equal to 1:88.

3. Venus rotates on its axis once every 243 days. How many days would it take to rotate 4 times?

4. Jason needed to make a scale drawing to show the distance between Earth and the moon. If the scale of his drawing was 1 in. = 60,000 mi, about how many inches apart would Earth and the moon be in Jason's drawing?

PROBLEM-SOLVING APPLICATIONS
Sandwich Shop Hours

P 6-11

FRANK'S SANDWICH SHOP
Schedule — Week of Aug. 12

Name	Mon.	Tues.	Wed.	Thurs.	Fri.	Sat.	Sun.
Sasha	9–5	9–5	12–6	X	9–5	9–5	X
Miguel	5–8	5–8	X	5–8	X	X	X
Eric	X	X	5–8	X	5–8	5–8	12–6
Jen	10–6	X	9–12	9–5	X	X	12–6
Frank	9–6	9–6	9–6	X	12–5	9–6	12–4

1. What ratio describes the number of hours that Eric worked to the number of hours that Frank worked? _____

2. What ratio describes the number of hours that Miguel worked to the number of hours that Frank worked? _____

3. What ratio describes the number of hours that Jen worked to the number of hours all of the employees worked? _____

4. Since everyone at the sandwich shop gets paid by the hour, the amount of pay is proportionate to the amount of work. If Sasha got paid $304.00 for the week of August 12, what would she have gotten paid for a week she worked 30 hr? _____

5. Using the information in Exercise 4, express Sasha's pay as a unit rate. _____

6. Frank gets paid twice as much as the other workers. Express Frank's pay as a unit rate. _____

7. If Miguel gets paid $9.00 per hour, how much did he earn the week of August 12? _____

8. Jen made $212.50 the week of August 12. Express her pay as a unit rate. _____

Name _____

Understanding Percent

R 7-1

A percent is always a comparison to 100. The whole of something is divided into 100 equal parts called hundredths. One hundredth is written as $\frac{1}{100}$. One percent is written as 1%. They are equivalent to each other.

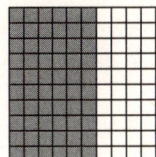

The grid to the right has 100 squares, and 60 of them are shaded. We can say that 60% are shaded. $\frac{60}{100}$ is the same as 60%.

Write the percent of each figure that is shaded.

1.

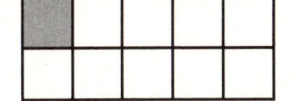

2.

3.

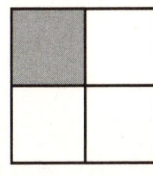

4.

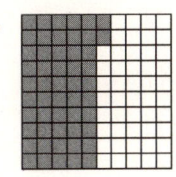

5.

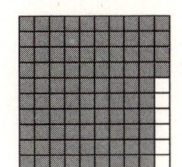

6.

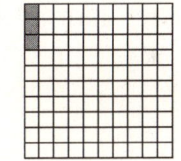

7. **Number Sense** Jana divided a piece of paper into 5 equal sections and colored 2 of them. What percent of the paper is now colored? _____

76 Use with Lesson 7-1.

Understanding Percent

P 7-1

Write the percent of each figure that is shaded.

1.

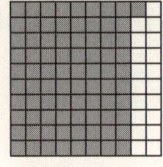

2.

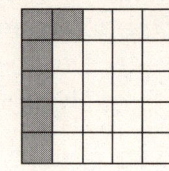

3.

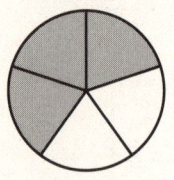

4.

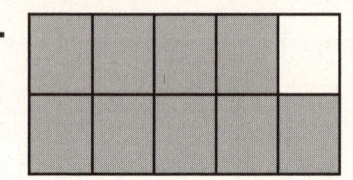

5. **Number Sense** What percent of line segment AB is equal to 50% of line segment CD?

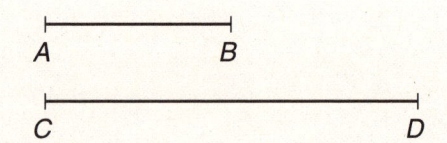

6. The line segment below shows 100%. Show 25%, 50%, and 75% of the segment.

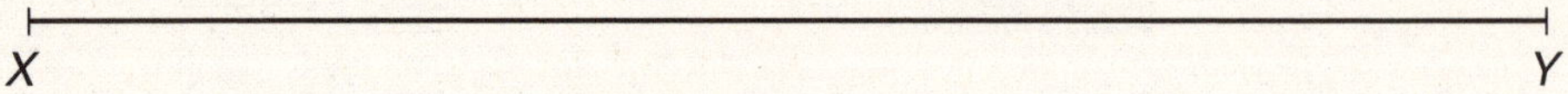

X ——————————————— Y

Test Prep

7. Which of the following figures is 60% shaded?

   A. 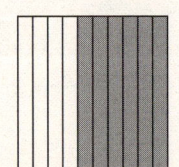   B. 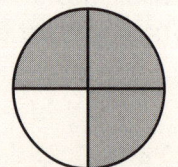   C. 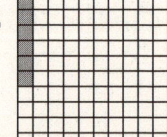   D.

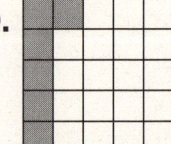

8. **Writing in Math** You are thirsty, so a friend has offered to give you 50% of his water. What information must you have in order to find out how much water your friend will give you?

76 Use with Lesson 7-1.

Fractions, Decimals, and Percents   R 7-2

Fractions, decimals, and percents all name parts of a whole. The grid to the right has 72 out of 100 squares shaded.

72 out of 100 are shaded. As a fraction, that is $\frac{72}{100}$. As a decimal, that is 0.72. As a percent, that is 72%.

Write 40% as a fraction and decimal.

40% = $\frac{40}{100}$ = 0.40

The decimal point moves two places to the left.

Write 0.3% as a fraction and decimal.

0.3% = $\frac{0.3}{100}$ = 0.003

The decimal point moves two places to the left. Fill in any spaces with zeros.

Write 0.47 as a fraction and percent.

0.47 = $\frac{47}{100}$ = 47%

Write $\frac{3}{4}$ as a decimal and percent.

You can use a proportion:

$\frac{3}{4} = \frac{n}{100}$

$\frac{4n}{4} = \frac{300}{4}$

$n = 75$

So, $\frac{3}{4}$ = 0.75 = 75%.

Write each in two other ways.

1. $\frac{2}{10}$ _____ ; _____
2. $\frac{23}{100}$ _____ ; _____
3. $\frac{7}{10}$ _____ ; _____
4. 97% _____ ; _____
5. 16% _____ ; _____
6. 52% _____ ; _____
7. 0.04 _____ ; _____
8. 0.35 _____ ; _____

9. **Number Sense** Sheila got 87% of the problem correct. Patrick got $\frac{91}{100}$ correct. Who scored higher? _____

Use with Lesson 7-2. **77**

Name _____

Fractions, Decimals, and Percents   P 7-2

Describe the shaded portion of each as a fraction, decimal, and percent.

1. 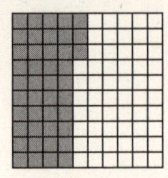   2.

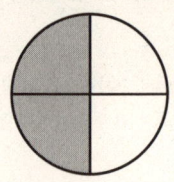

   _____   _____

Write each in two other ways.

3. 64%   4. 0.09   5. $\frac{12}{50}$ 6. 37%

_____   _____   _____   _____

7. $\frac{4}{250}$ 8. 0.023

_____   _____

The table at the right shows the number of states in the United States at different times in history. There are currently 50 states in the United States. Use the information to answer the questions.

Year	States
1792	15
1817	20
1836	25
1848	30
1863	35
1889	40
1896	45
1959	50

9. In what year were there 0.5 as many states as today?

_____

10. What percent of the current number of states had joined the United States by the year 1863?

_____

11. In what year were there about $\frac{2}{3}$ as many states as in 1896? _____

Test Prep

12. Which of the following is equivalent to 98%?

   A. 0.49   B. $\frac{100}{98}$ C. 0.98   D. $\frac{49}{100}$

13. **Writing in Math** Explain how you would write $\frac{5}{6}$ as a percent.

_____

Use with Lesson 7-2.   **77**

Name _____

PROBLEM-SOLVING SKILL
Writing to Explain

R 7-3

The Store The Clothes Shoppe advertised a sale of 10% off the regular prices. Julio wants to buy a shirt that normally costs $15.00. Julio has $13.00. Does Julio have enough money to buy the shirt at the sale price? Explain.

Tips for Writing Good Explanations

Just as you need to break this problem into two parts to solve, you can break explanations into parts to make them easier to follow.

Use specific numbers for examples to explain why something works or does not work.

Give alternate explanations if appropriate.

Example:

The regular price of the shirt is $15.00. 10% of $15.00 is $1.50.

The sale price of the shirt is $15.00 − $1.50, or $13.50.

Julio needs $13.50 − $13.00 = $0.50 more to be able to buy the shirt at the sale price.

Suppose the Clothes Shoppe has a 20% off sale next week. Will Julio have enough money then? Twenty percent of $15 is $3. This means that the new sale price is $15 − $3 = $12. Thus, Julio has $1 dollar more than he needs to buy the shirt at the new sale price.

Solve. Explain your answers.

1. James got 48 out of 50 answers correct on a science test. He got 22 out of 25 answers correct on a history test. On which test did James get a greater portion of the problems correct?

   _____

   _____

2. Giovanni ate 25% of a pizza, while Glynis ate 30% of a different pizza. Can you tell who ate more pizza? Explain.

   _____

   _____

Name _____

PROBLEM-SOLVING SKILL   P 7-3
Writing to Explain

1. Does the circle graph make sense? Write a good explanation of your answer.

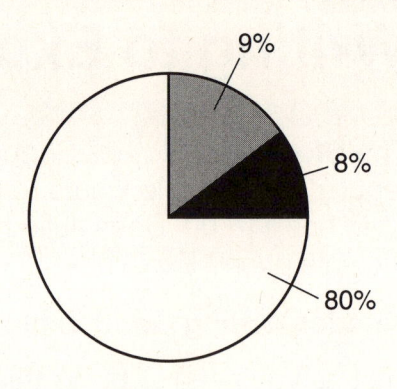

   _____

   _____

   (Circle graph shows: 9%, 8%, 80%)

2. Of the students in a history club, 23% are fifth graders and 45% are sixth graders. Is this possible? Explain.

   _____

   _____

   _____

   _____

3. Could 67% of the students at Middledale School ride the bus each day, and 57% walk to school each day? Explain.

   _____

   _____

4. At the football game, 72% of the fans were cheering for the home team. What percent of the fans were cheering for the visiting team? Explain.

   _____

   _____

5. Tim is saving for a new CD player. He has 60% of the money he needs. How much more money does he need? Can you solve this problem? Explain.

   _____

   _____

Name _____

Mental Math: Finding a Percent of a Number

R 7-4

You can use fractions to find the percent of a number. The chart below shows some common percents and their equivalent fractions.

Percent	10%	20%	25%	$33\frac{1}{3}$%	40%	50%	60%	$66\frac{2}{3}$%	75%	80%
Fraction	$\frac{1}{10}$	$\frac{1}{5}$	$\frac{1}{4}$	$\frac{1}{3}$	$\frac{2}{5}$	$\frac{1}{2}$	$\frac{3}{5}$	$\frac{2}{3}$	$\frac{3}{4}$	$\frac{4}{5}$

Find 20% of 60.
One Way

Think: 20% is $\frac{2}{10}$.

Multiply $\frac{2}{10}$ by 60.

$\frac{2}{10} \times 60$

$\frac{2}{\cancel{10}} \times \frac{\cancel{60}^{6}}{1}$

$2 \times 6 = 12$

So, 20% of 60 = 12.

Find 20% of 60.
Another Way

Think: 20% is 2 × 10%.

10% of 60 is 6.

2 × 6 = 12

So, 20% of 60 = 12.

Find the percent of each number mentally.

1. 10% of 50 _____
2. 20% of 90 _____
3. 30% of 70 _____

4. 25% of 24 _____
5. 40% of 120 _____
6. 75% of 16 _____

7. 50% of 36 _____
8. 60% of 60 _____
9. 80% of 70 _____

10. **Number Sense** If 10% of 250 is 25, what is 30% of 250? Explain how you know.

_____
_____
_____
_____

Use with Lesson 7-4. **79**

Name _____

Mental Math: Finding a Percent of a Number

P 7-4

Find the percent of each number mentally.

1. 20% of 50 _____
2. 25% of 60 _____
3. 40% of 200 _____

4. 90% of 20 _____
5. 80% of 300 _____
6. $33\frac{1}{3}$% of 72 _____

7. 30% of 100 _____
8. $66\frac{2}{3}$% of 21 _____
9. 75% of 48 _____

10. **Number Sense** What is 50% of 1,000? Of 10,000? _____ ; _____

The number of air miles between some U.S. cities is shown in the table.

11. Tom and his family have flown 50% of the way from Detroit to Cleveland. How many miles have they flown?

From → To	Miles
Boston → Buffalo	400
Detroit → Cleveland	90
Denver → Minneapolis	700

_____

12. Mike's family is 60% of the way from Boston to Buffalo. How many miles is this?

_____

13. Which is further, 90% of the way from Detroit to Cleveland or 20% of the way from Denver to Minneapolis?

_____

_____

Test Prep

14. Which of the following is 45% of 2,000?

    A. 90   **B.** 450   **C.** 900   **D.** 4,500

15. **Writing in Math** Explain how you would find 40% of 60.

_____

_____

_____

Use with Lesson 7-4. **79**

Name _____

Estimating with Percents

R 7-5

Here are some ways to estimate with percents.

Estimate 8% of 500,000.

8% is close to 10%, so find 10% of 500,000.

10% of 500,000 = $\frac{1}{10}$ × 500,000 = 0.1 × 500,000.

When you multiply a number by 0.1, you can just move the decimal point one space to the left.

0.1 × 500,000 = 50,000

So, 8% of 500,000 is about 50,000.

Estimate 46% of 378,491.

46% is close to 50%, so use 50%.

378,491 is close to 400,000, so use 400,000 in your estimate.

50% is the same as $\frac{1}{2}$.

$\frac{1}{2}$ of 400,000 is 200,000.

So, 46% of 378,491 is about 200,000.

Estimate.

1. 9% of 20 _____   2. 21% of 31 _____   3. 31% of 37 _____

4. 38% of 49 _____   5. 49% of 101 _____   6. 61% of 19 _____

7. 59% of 30 _____   8. 70% of 71 _____   9. 80% of 149 _____

10. **Number Sense** Explain how to estimate 51% of 42.

_____

_____

_____

_____

_____

_____

80 Use with Lesson 7-5.

Name _____

Estimating with Percents

P 7-5

Estimate.

1. 35% of 102 _____
2. 42% of 307 _____
3. 79% of 13 _____

4. 84% of 897 _____
5. 13% of 97 _____
6. 28% of 95 _____

7. 61% of 211 _____
8. 19% of 489 _____
9. 48% of 641 _____

10. 21% of 411 _____
11. 77% of 164 _____
12. 51% of 894 _____

13. 39% of 306 _____
14. 62% of 522 _____
15. 48% of 341 _____

16. **Number Sense** Which would you need to estimate to find an answer, 45% of 200 or 46% of 97? _____

17. The school store sold 48 items on Monday. Of those items, 60% were pens. About how many pens were sold on Monday? _____

18. The school cafeteria workers cooked 52 lb of pasta on Thursday. Of that, 90% was sold on Thursday, and 10% was stored in the refrigerator. About how much pasta was stored in the refrigerator? _____

19. On a rainy day, 76% of the students in the school brought umbrellas. There are 600 students in the school. About how many students brought umbrellas? _____

Test Prep

20. Which of the following is the best estimate for 68% of 251?

    A. 150   B. 175   C. 204   D. 210

21. **Writing in Math** Explain how you would estimate 79% of 389.

_____

_____

_____

_____

Use with Lesson 7-5.

Finding a Percent of a Number

R 7-6

Suppose there were 240 secondary schools in Delaware County in 1996. If these schools were typical of U.S. schools, about how many would have had Internet access?

Percentage of U.S. Schools with Internet Access

	1994	1996	1998
Elementary	30%	61%	88%
Secondary	49%	77%	94%

Find 77% of 240.

First estimate: 77% is close to 75%, and 75% is $\frac{3}{4}$. $\frac{3}{4} \times 240 = 180$

One Way

Write the percent as a decimal.

77% of 240

$0.77 \times 240 = 184.8$

So, about 185 schools had Internet access.

Another Way

Write a proportion.

$\frac{part}{whole} = \frac{percent\ value}{100}$

$\frac{x}{240} = \frac{77}{100}$

$100x = 18,480$

$\frac{100x}{100} = \frac{18,480}{100}$

$x = 184.8$

With a Calculator

Press: 0.77 [×] 240 [ENTER =]

Display: 184.8

OR

Press: 77 [▸%] [×]

240 [ENTER =]

Display: 184.8

40% of what number is 30?

1. Let x represent the unknown total or whole.

2. Write a proportion: $\frac{percent\ value}{100} = \frac{known\ part}{unknown\ whole}$; $\frac{40}{100} = \frac{30}{x}$

3. Find cross products: $40x = 3,000$

4. Divide to solve for x: $\frac{40x}{40} = \frac{3,000}{40}$; $x = 75$

Find the percent of each number.

1. 25% of 24 _____
2. 50% of 72 _____
3. 72% of 88 _____

Find the total amount.

4. 60% of _____ is 45
5. 25% of _____ is 22
6. 6% of _____ is 1.5

7. **Estimation** Is 49% of 32 greater than or less than 17?

_____

_____

Use with Lesson 7-6. **81**

Name _____

Finding a Percent of a Number

P 7-6

Find the percent of each number.

1. 42% of 800 _____ 2. 5.6% of 425 _____ 3. 85% of 15 _____

4. $33\frac{1}{3}$% of 678 _____ 5. 12% of 65 _____ 6. 58% of 324 _____

Find the total amount.

7. 98% of _____ is 245   8. 32% of _____ is 57.6

9. 78% of _____ is 319.8   10. 10% of _____ is 65

11. 24% of _____ is $0.36   12. 3.5% of _____ is 5.6

13. 20% of _____ is 28   14. 28% of _____ is 43.4

15. 64% of _____ is 208   16. 72% of _____ is 615.6

17. **Estimation** Give an estimate and an exact answer for 68% of 32. Which answer is greater?

_____

For 18 and 19, round to the nearest whole number.

18. An adult has 206 bones. Of those, about 2.9% are found in the inner ear. How many bones in the human body are found in the inner ear? _____

19. About 12.6% of the bones are vertebrae in the human back. How many bones in the human body are vertebrae? _____

Test Prep

20. 45 is 12% of which number?

    A. 540   **B.** 450   **C.** 375   **D.** 5.4

21. **Writing in Math** Which is greater, 52% of 3,400 or 98% of 1,500? Explain.

_____
_____
_____

Use with Lesson 7-6.

PROBLEM-SOLVING STRATEGY
Solve a Simpler Problem

R 7-7

How can you solve a complex problem by solving a simpler problem?

The Dinner Gibran and Hector have had dinner in a restaurant. Their total bill was $35.00. Gibran and Hector want to leave the server a 15% tip. How much should they leave?

Read and Understand

Step 1: What do you know? The total bill is $35.00. Gibran and Hector want to leave a 15% tip.

Step 2: What are you trying to find? The amount of the tip

Plan and Solve

Step 3: What strategy will you use?

Strategy: Solve a simpler problem

You know it is easy to find 10% of a number, so break apart 15% into 10% and 5%.

10% of $35 = $3.50

5% of $35 = $\frac{1}{2} \times $3.50 = $1.75

So, 15% of $35 is $3.50 + $1.75 = $5.25.

Answer: They should leave a tip of $5.25.

Look Back and Check

Step 4: Is your work correct? Yes, 15% of $35 is $5.25.

Solve the simpler problem. Then use your solution to help you solve the original problem.

1. Joan hits the cymbals 3 times after each measure of the band's song. The song has 5 verses, and each verse has 7 measures. How many times will Joan hit the cymbals in the song?

   _____

   _____

   Simpler Problem: How many times will Joan hit the cymbals in 1 verse?

   _____

   _____

Use with Lesson 7-7.

Name _____

PROBLEM-SOLVING STRATEGY   P 7-7
Solve a Simpler Problem

Solve the simpler problems. Then use your solutions to help solve the original problem.

1. Matt's mother has agreed to pay 20% of the price of a CD player if Matt pays the other 80%. If the CD player that Matt buys costs $200.00, how much will his mother contribute? _____

   Simpler Problem: What is 10% of the price? _____

2. Hannah walks 3 mi each afternoon when the weather is nice. In rainy weather, she walks 50% as far. In the past 7 days, 4 have been rainy. How many total miles has Hannah walked in the past 7 days? _____

   Simpler Problems: How far did Hannah walk on the 4 rainy days? _____

   How far did Hannah walk on the 3 nice days? _____

For each problem, first solve the simpler problems.

3. Alexandra went to the sandwich shop for lunch. There were 3 types of soup and 2 types of salad. How many different soup and salad combinations could Alexandra order?

   _____

   _____

4. Jared has a rectangular garden with a length of 20 ft and a width of 15 ft. Mike also has a rectangular garden. Mike's garden is 60% as long as Jared's garden and 50% as wide as Jared's garden. What is the perimeter of Mike's garden?

   _____

   _____

5. There are usually 90 fifth graders and 100 sixth graders at Washington Elementary School. On February 12, some of the students were ill and stayed home. 20% of the fifth graders were absent, and 10% of the sixth graders were absent. How many fifth- and sixth-grade students attended school on February 12?

   _____

   _____

Use with Lesson 7-7.

Sales Tax and Discount

R 7-8

Book Sale A bookstore sells hardcover best-selling books at a 30% discount. The book Billie wants to buy is regularly priced at $24.00. What is the sale price of the book?

One Way

Find the discount amount and subtract it from the original price.

The discount is 30% of $24.00.

Estimate: $\frac{1}{3} \times \$24 = \$8.00$

30% of 24 = 0.30 × 24 = $7.20

sale price = regular price − discount

$24.00 − $7.20 = $16.80

So the sale price of the book Billie wants to buy is $16.80.

Since $7.20 is close to $8.00, the answer is reasonable.

Another Way

The discount is 30%. So the sale price is 100% − 30%, or 70% of the regular price.

Estimate: $\frac{3}{4} \times \$24.00 = \$18.00$

Find 70% of $24.00.

0.70 × $24.00 = $16.80

Since $16.80 is close to $18.00, the answer is reasonable.

Billie will also have to pay 5% sales tax.

How do you calculate sales tax?

Find the sales tax and add it to the price of the book.

The sales tax is 5% of $16.80.

Estimate: 5% of 15 = $0.75

5% of $16.80 = 0.05 × $16.80 = $0.84

Then add the tax amount to the price of the book (or the subtotal).

$16.80 + $0.84 = $17.64

Billie will pay a total of $17.64.

Find the sale price or total cost.

1. Regular price: $100.00

   Discount: 10%

   Sale price: _____

2. Regular price: $200.00

   Discount: 15%

   Sale price: _____

3. Regular price: $65.00

   Discount: 25%

   Sale price: _____

4. Subtotal: $60.00

   Tax: 5%

   Total cost: _____

5. Subtotal: $24.95

   Tax: 6%

   Total cost: _____

6. Subtotal: $242.00

   Tax: 8%

   Total cost: _____

Use with Lesson 7-8.

Name _____

Sales Tax and Discount

P 7-8

Find the sale price or total cost.

1. Regular Price: $125.00

    Discount: 15%

    Sale Price: _____

2. Regular Price: $98.00

    Discount: 12%

    Sale Price: _____

3. Subtotal: $135.00

    Sales Tax: 8%

    Total Cost: _____

4. Regular Price: $50.00

    Discount: 8%

    Sale Price: _____

5. Subtotal: $60.00

    Sales Tax: 4%

    Total Cost: _____

6. Regular Price: $30.00

    Discount: 20%

    Sale Price: _____

7. **Number Sense** Would $50.00 be enough to buy a radio that usually costs $65.00 and is discounted 12%?

    _____

8. What percent discount is indicated on the price tag of the football?

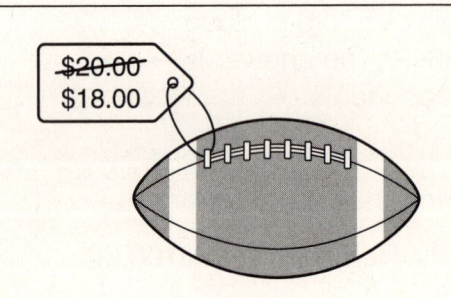

    $20.00
    $18.00

    _____

Test Prep

9. Which is the total cost of a $75.00 item after 5% sales tax is added?

    A. $80.00 **B.** $78.75 **C.** $71.25 **D.** $70.00

10. **Writing in Math** Explain how to find the sale price when you know the regular price and the percent discount.

    _____

    _____

    _____

Use with Lesson 7-8. **83**

Percent of Increase and Decrease

R 7-9

Bike Riders The number of students riding bikes to school has changed over the years. By what percent did bike riding increase or decrease?

Students Riding Bikes to School

	1996	2004
Third grade	320	400
Sixth grade	500	425

Third Grade

Step 1
Subtract to find the amount of increase or decrease.

Amount of increase:
$400 - 320 = 80$

Step 2
Write and solve a proportion to find the percent of increase or decrease.

$$\frac{\text{percent change}}{100} = \frac{\text{increase amount}}{\text{original amount}}$$

$$\frac{x}{100} = \frac{80}{320}$$

$$x = \frac{80}{320} \times 100$$

$$x = 0.25 \times 100$$

$$x = 25$$

The number of third grade bike riders increased by 25%.

Sixth Grade

Amount of decrease:
$500 - 425 = 75$

$$\frac{\text{percent change}}{100} = \frac{\text{decrease amount}}{\text{original amount}}$$

$$\frac{x}{100} = \frac{75}{500}$$

$$500x = 7,500$$

$$x = 15$$

The number of sixth grade bike riders decreased by 15%.

Find the percent of increase or decrease. If necessary, round answers to the nearest tenth of a percent.

1. Last year the book for required summer reading cost $5. This year the same paperback book cost $6. _____

2. At Windsor School last year, there were 125 students enrolled in the sixth grade. This year, there are 180 students in the sixth grade. _____

3. The Windsor School library purchased 200 new books in 2002. In 2003, the school library purchased only 180 new books. _____

4. **Reasoning** Using mental math only, tell by what percent the price decreased: Year 1: $40, Year 2: $30. _____

84 Use with Lesson 7-9.

Name _____

Percent of Increase and Decrease   P 7-9

Find the percent of increase or decrease. If necessary, round answers to the nearest tenth of a percent.

1. 390 students rode the bus last year; 300 students ride the bus this year.

   _____

2. A large veggie pizza is usually $12.00; This week, it is only $10.50.

   _____

3. The number of spelling words increased from 20 last week to 25 this week.

   _____

4. The number of books in the library last year was 12,790; This year there are 13,000 books.

   _____

The table shows how the prices of some types of foods have changed over the years. Use the information to answer the questions.

Year	Dozen Eggs	Loaf of Bread	Quart of Milk
1914	$0.35	$0.06	$0.09
1924	$0.48	$0.09	$0.14
1976	$0.75	$0.35	$0.60
2002	$0.89	$1.49	$1.49

5. What is the percent change in the price of a loaf of bread from 1914 to 1924?

   _____

6. What is the percent change in the price of a dozen eggs from 1914 to 2002?

   _____

7. What is the percent change in the price of a quart of milk from 1976 to 2002?

   _____

8. **Reasoning** Does a 15% decrease in the price of pencils result in the same final price for each customer? Explain.

   _____

Test Prep

9. The number of students in choir was 50 last year and is 60 this year. Which is the percent change in choir membership?

   A. 10% increase   **B.** 10% decrease   **C.** 20% decrease   **D.** 20% increase

10. **Writing in Math** Explain the steps you would use to find the percent of increase from 90 to 200.

    _____

Simple Interest

R 7-10

$I = p \times r \times t$

I stands for the interest.

p stands for the principal, the amount originally deposited.

r stands for the interest rate to be paid.

t stands for the time period over which the interest is earned.

Roberto deposits $1,000 at the bank. He plans to leave the money in deposit for 4 years. The bank will pay him a 6% interest rate per year. How much money will Roberto have at the end of 4 years?

Step 1: Find the simple interest.

I need to find the amount of interest on $1,000 invested at 6% for 4 years.

$I = p \times r \times t$

$I = \$1,000 \times 6\% \times 4$

$I = \$1,000 \times 0.06 \times 4$

$I = \$240$

Step 2: Find the total.

Roberto will still have his principal, or original deposit. Now he will have the earned interest as well. To find the total amount Roberto has at the end of 4 years, I need to add the principal and the amount of earned interest.

Let *T* represent the total.

$T = p + I$

$T = \$1,000 + 240$

$T = \$1,240$

So, Roberto will have a total of $1,240 at the end of 4 years.

Find the amount of interest and the total amount.

1. $300 for 2 years at a simple interest rate of 5% per year

2. $400 for 4 years at a simple interest rate of 4% per year

3. $700 for 3 years at a simple interest rate of 5% per year

4. $550 for 5 years at a simple interest rate of 7% per year

5. **Mental Math** At which of the following would you prefer to invest your money: 3%, 10%, or 35%? Why?

Use with Lesson 7-10. **85**

Name _____

Simple Interest

P 7-10

Find the amount of interest and the total amount.

1. $1,200 for 5 years at a simple interest rate of 10% per year

    _____

2. $300 for 10 years at a simple interest rate of 4% per year

    _____

3. $700 for 4 years at a simple interest rate of 8% per year

    _____

4. $4,000 for 10 years at a simple interest rate of 2% per year

    _____

5. Sam bought a video game system for $250.00. He used the store credit plan to borrow the money for the purchase at an 8.5% simple interest rate per year. What amount of money would Sam need to pay for the system if he took one year to pay for it?

    _____

6. Jackie's parents have agreed to lend her money for a new bike. Her parents will charge Jackie 1% simple interest per year. How much does Jackie need to repay them, if she borrowed $120.00 for one year?

    _____

7. **Algebra** Tara's bank account contains $250.00. She made only one deposit exactly one year ago. The bank account pays a simple interest rate of 8%. How much money did Tara deposit in the account one year ago?

    _____

Test Prep

8. Jen deposited $200.00. How much interest would she get in one year, if the simple interest rate on the account is 6%?

    A. $212.00   **B.** $206.00   **C.** $12.00   **D.** $6.00

9. **Writing in Math** Joy put $150.00 in a bank account that pays a simple interest rate of 5% a year. Explain how to find how much will be in the account in 5 years.

    _____

    _____

    _____

    _____

Use with Lesson 7-10.

PROBLEM-SOLVING APPLICATIONS

Going Shopping

R 7-11

Reza Goes Shopping Reza has $50.00 to buy a large picture frame. At the Wall Art Shop, the frame is regularly priced at $60.00. This week, the picture frame is now selling at a 20% discount. Sales tax in Reza's state is 8%. Does Reza have enough money to buy the picture frame?

Step 1: Find the amount of the discount.

$60.00 × 20% = $60.00 × 0.20 = $12.00

Step 2: Find the discounted price.

$60.00 − $12.00 = $48.00. This is Reza's subtotal.

Step 3: Find the amount of sales tax.

$48.00 × 8% = $48.00 × 0.08 = $3.84

Step 4: Find the total bill for the picture frame.

$48.00 + 3.84 = $51.84

Since $51.84 is greater than $50.00, Reza does not have enough money for the frame.

Solve.

1. Jeff buys 2 books. One book costs $22.00 and the other costs $18.00. Sales tax is 4%. What is the total amount Jeff pays? _____

2. Reba and Ciara have dinner in a restaurant. Their total bill is for $24.95. They want to leave at least a 15% tip for the server. Estimate the amount they need to leave for a tip. _____

3. In 1990, the population of Chillville was 12,750. The 2000 census showed that the population of Chillville had changed to 15,600. Find the percent of increase or decrease.

4. Juan deposits $800 in the bank. The bank will pay him simple interest of 7.5% per year. How much will Juan have at the end of 10 years?

Use with Lesson 7-11.

Name _____

PROBLEM-SOLVING APPLICATION   P 7-11
Bicycle Repair

Solve. Write your answer in a complete sentence.

1. Tina and Hector have decided to open a bicycle repair shop in Tina's garage. Each contributed 40% of the start-up costs. Hector's dad contributed the rest of the money. Tina and Hector contributed $50.00 toward starting the business. How much did Hector's dad contribute?

   _____

   _____

2. The first month, the bicycle repair shop had 10 customers. Tina and Hector decided to run a newspaper ad. The shop had 26 customers the second month. What was the percent change in the number of customers?

   _____

   _____

3. Tina and Hector purchased some tools that had a regular price of $28.00. The tools were on sale for 15% off. What was their cost after the discount?

   _____

   _____

4. Tina took some of her profits from the business and deposited them into a savings account with a 4% simple interest rate. If Tina put $200.00 in the bank, how much would she have after 3 years?

   _____

   _____

5. Of the shop's customers, 34% needed repairs on their bicycles' brakes. If Tina and Hector had 50 customers in the first 3 months, how many customers had their brakes fixed?

   _____

86   Use with Lesson 7-11.

Understanding Integers

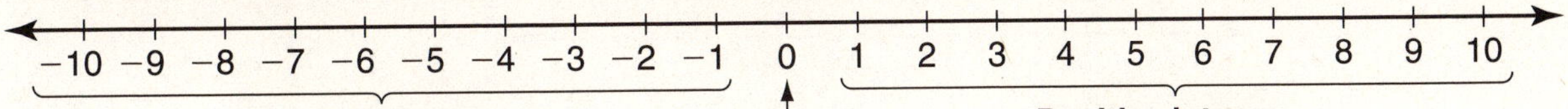

R 8-1

Number line from −10 to 10.

Negative integers — These are the opposites of positive integers.

Zero is neither positive nor negative. The opposite of 0 is 0.

Positive integers — These are also called the counting numbers.

The absolute value of an integer is its distance from zero. Absolute value is always positive. The absolute value of −6 is written like this: $|-6|$.

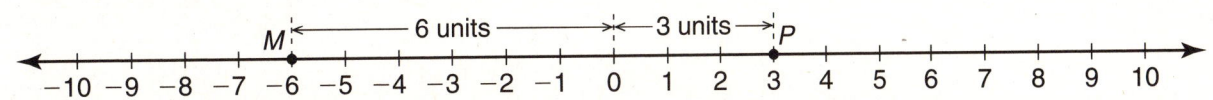

Number line showing point M at −6 (6 units from 0) and point P at 3 (3 units from 0).

On the number line above, point M is located at −6. Because it is 6 units from 0, its absolute value is 6.

Point P is located at 3 on the number line. Because it is 3 units from 0, its absolute value is 3.

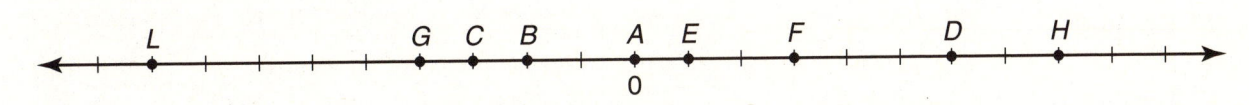

Number line with points: L, G, C, B, A, E, F, D, H (A is at 0).

For 1–9, use the number line above. Write the integer for each point. Then give its opposite and absolute values.

1. B _____ 2. H _____

3. C _____ 4. F _____

5. A _____ 6. E _____

7. G _____ 8. D _____

9. L _____

10. **Number Sense** John borrowed $6 from Adam. The next week John borrowed $15 more from Adam. Write an integer that represents John's total debt to Adam. _____

Use with Lesson 8-1.

Understanding Integers

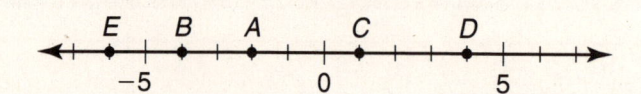

P 8-1

Use the number line. Write the integer for each point. Then give its opposite and absolute value.

1. A _____
2. B _____
3. C _____
4. D _____
5. E _____

6. On the number line, graph the points −8, 3, −4, 2, and −1.

The table gives the highest and lowest temperatures for some states in the United States. Use integers to describe the two temperatures for each state.

7. Delaware _____
8. Hawaii _____
9. Colorado _____
10. Alabama _____

Record Temperatures (in degrees, relative to zero)

State	Highest	Lowest
Alabama	112 above	27 below
Delaware	110 above	17 below
Hawaii	100 above	12 above
Colorado	118 above	61 below

Test Prep

11. Which is an integer?

    A. −0.5   B. −5   C. 5.5   D. $5\frac{4}{5}$

12. **Writing in Math** In your own words, tell what is meant by "the absolute value of an integer."

_____

_____

Use with Lesson 8-1.

Comparing and Ordering Integers

R 8-2

When comparing two integers on a number line, the integer that is farther to the right is greater. The integer that is farther to the left is less.

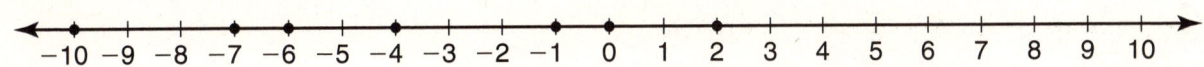

```
←—+—+—+—+—+—+—+—+—+—+—+—+—+—+—+—+—+—+—+—+—→
 -10 -9 -8 -7 -6 -5 -4 -3 -2 -1  0  1  2  3  4  5  6  7  8  9  10
```

Compare −6 and −10.	Compare −1 and 2.	Order −4, 0, −7 from least to greatest.
Because −6 is farther to the right than −10, it is greater. So −6 > −10.	Because 2 is farther to the right than −1, it is greater. So 2 > −1.	Because −7 is the farthest to the left, it is the least. 0 is farther to the right than −4, so −4 is the next least. So, the numbers in order from least to greatest are −7, −4, and 0.

Use >, <, or = to compare.

1. −5 ◯ 3
2. 15 ◯ −4
3. 13 ◯ 27
4. 52 ◯ |−52|
5. −9 ◯ |−9|
6. −6 ◯ −7
7. 123 ◯ 132
8. 267 ◯ 227
9. −9 ◯ −9

10. **Reasoning** Write three integers less than −27.

_____

_____

11. Order 15, −7, −12, 0, and 5 from least to greatest.

_____

_____

_____

12. Order −19, −24, 17, −28, 19, and −17 from least to greatest.

_____

_____

_____

Use with Lesson 8-2.

Name _____

Comparing and Ordering Integers   P 8-2

Use <, >, or = to compare.

1. 6 ◯ −8   2. −12 ◯ −11   3. 2 ◯ |−2|
4. 12 ◯ −11   5. 11 ◯ −1   6. |−3| ◯ 4

Order from least to greatest.

7. −6, 4, 7, 0, −9   _____

8. −1, −5, 5, 7, −8   _____

9. −7, −8, −2, 6, |−11|, −11, −9, 4, 5

_____

10. **Reasoning** Can any negative integer be greater than a positive integer? Explain.

_____
_____
_____

Kyle kept track of the number of points he scored each time he played a video game. Sometimes the score is less than zero.

Kyle's Scores	
Play 1:	Gained 5 points
Play 2:	Lost 15 points
Play 3:	Gained 32 points
Play 4:	Gained 10 points
Play 5:	Lost 12 points
Play 6:	Lost 8 points

11. Order the negative plays from least to greatest.

_____

12. Order the positive plays from greatest to least.

_____

Test Prep

13. Which integer is greatest?

    A. 1   B. −10   C. 9   D. 3

14. **Writing in Math** Explain how to find the greatest integer on a number line.

_____
_____

Use with Lesson 8-2.

Understanding Rational Numbers

R 8-3

How would you graph $-1\frac{1}{2}$, 2.75, and -2.5 on the same number line?

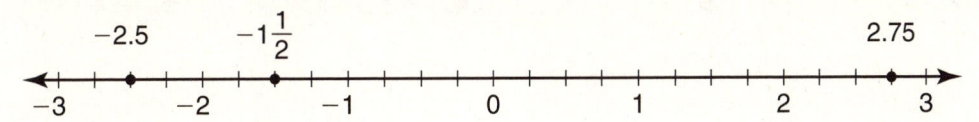

-2.5 is the same as $-2\frac{1}{2}$.

2.75 is the same as $2\frac{3}{4}$.

When comparing and ordering rational numbers, it sometimes helps to change all of the numbers into fractions. Other times it is easier to change all of the numbers into decimals.

How do you compare rational numbers?	**How do you order rational numbers?**
Compare $-2\frac{1}{4}$ and -1.75.	Order $\frac{1}{4}$, 0.3, -0.27 from greatest to least.
-1.75 is the same as $-1\frac{3}{4}$. On a number line, $-2\frac{1}{4}$ is to the left of $-1\frac{3}{4}$. Therefore, $-2\frac{1}{4}$ is less than $-1\frac{3}{4}$. So, $-2\frac{1}{4} < -1\frac{3}{4}$.	You can rewrite $\frac{1}{4}$ as 0.25. You can also rewrite 0.3 as 0.30. Now it is easy to see that -0.27 is less than 0.25, and that 0.25 is less than 0.30. So, the numbers in order from least to greatest are -0.27, $\frac{1}{4}$, 0.30.

Graph each rational number on the number line.

1. -1.25
2. $1\frac{3}{4}$
3. $\frac{6}{8}$
4. $-\frac{3}{8}$

Use > or < to compare.

5. $-1\frac{1}{2}$ ◯ 1.75
6. -1.2 ◯ -1.1
7. $-1\frac{3}{4}$ ◯ $-\frac{3}{4}$

Order from least to greatest.

8. 0.15   0.63 -0.2 -0.35

9. $-\frac{1}{2}$ -1 $-\frac{1}{3}$ $\frac{1}{4}$

Use with Lesson 8-3. **89**

Understanding Rational Numbers

P 8-3

Graph each rational number on the same number line.

1. 1.5
2. $\frac{1}{2}$
3. $\frac{2}{8}$
4. −2.5
5. $-\frac{3}{4}$

Use <, >, or = to compare.

6. $-0.2 \bigcirc -\frac{1}{4}$
7. $-2.5 \bigcirc -2\frac{1}{2}$
8. $-\frac{1}{2} \bigcirc -0.42$

Order from least to greatest.

9. $-\frac{6}{10}, \frac{4}{5}, \frac{7}{10}, 0.5, -\frac{4}{5}$ _____

10. −1.2, −5.3, 5.5, −1.5 _____

11. **Reasoning** Explain why $\frac{4}{5}$ is a rational number but is not an integer.

_____

_____

_____

_____

Test Prep

12. Which rational number is least?

    A. −0.2 B. $-\frac{9}{10}$ C. $-\frac{6}{7}$ D. −0.5

13. **Writing in Math** Explain what a *rational number* is in your own words.

_____

_____

_____

_____

Use with Lesson 8-3. **89**

Name _____

PROBLEM-SOLVING SKILL   R 8-4
Choose an Operation

Driving Joe drove from Merrillville to Johnson City. Later that day, he drove from Johnson City to Martin's Ferry. Then he drove from Martin's Ferry back to Merrillville. How many total miles did Joe drive that day?

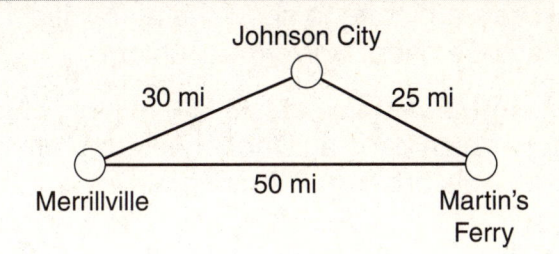

```
              Johnson City
         30 mi  ○  25 mi
        /           \
       ○─────────────○
   Merrillville  50 mi  Martin's
                        Ferry
```

Read and Understand

Show the Main Idea

30	25	50
?

Plan and Solve

Choose an Operation Add to find the total number of miles.

30 + 25 + 50 = 105 mi. So, Joe drove 105 mi.

Draw a picture to show the main idea. Use the picture to choose an operation. Solve the problem.

1. Carol is baking cookies for the school bake sale. She wants to make three times the number of cookies her recipe will make. The recipe calls for 2 c of flour. How many cups of flour will Carol need for her triple batch of cookies?

2. Dieter earned $35 cutting grass. He owed Juan $12. Dieter also wants to buy a gift for his father, which costs $21. Does Dieter have enough money to pay Juan and also buy his father the gift?

90 Use with Lesson 8-4.

Name _____

PROBLEM-SOLVING SKILL P 8-4
Choose an Operation

Draw a picture to show the main idea. Use the picture to choose an operation. Solve the problem.

1. Mount Everest is 8,850 m high. How many meters high does a climber need to go to climb $\frac{1}{5}$ of the distance up the mountain? _____

2. Each week Sara practices violin for 120 min. She reads for $\frac{2}{3}$ hr each week. How many times greater is the length of time she spends practicing violin than the time she spends reading? _____

3. The cross-country team jogged for 30 min the first day of practice. Each day of practice after that they will run 5 min longer than they did at the previous practice. How long will they run on the sixth day of practice? _____

4. Tom studied math for 30 min a night for 5 nights to prepare for a big math test. Damien studied 15 min on one night for the test. How many times greater is Tom's study time than Damien's study time? _____

5. Tara measured the bean seedlings her science class was growing. The seedlings grew an average of 0.5 cm for every 24 hr. At that rate, how much did the bean seedlings grow in 6 days? _____

Adding Integers

R 8-5

You can use the rules below to add integers.

Adding two integers with the same sign

Find $-7 + (-3)$.

Step 1: Find the sum of the absolute values of the two numbers.

$|-7| = 7$

$|-3| = 3$

$7 + 3 = 10$

Step 2: Give the sum the same sign as the addends.

Because -7 and -3 both have negative signs, the sum receives a negative sign.

So, $-7 + (-3) = -10$.

Adding two integers with different signs

Find $2 + (-6)$.

Step 1: Find the difference of the absolute values of the two numbers.

$|-6| - |2| = 4$

Step 2: Give the difference the same sign as the addend with the greater absolute value.

Because -6 has the greater absolute value, the difference receives a negative sign.

So, $2 + (-6) = -4$.

Find each sum.

1. $3 + 10 =$ _____

2. $4 + (-6) =$ _____

3. $(-3) + (-5) =$ _____

4. $9 + (-2) + 1 =$ _____

5. $9 + (-8) =$ _____

6. $(-6) + (-5) =$ _____

7. $13 + (-22) =$ _____

8. $30 + (-16) + 5 =$ _____

9. **Algebra** The rule is Add -8. The input is 9. What is the output? _____

Use with Lesson 8-5.

Name _____

Adding Integers

P 8-5

1. Draw a number line to find 3 + (−4). _____

Draw a number line or use the rules for adding integers to find each sum.

2. 4 + (−12) = _____   3. −12 + (−14) = _____

4. 10 + (−1) = _____   5. −2 + (−1) = _____

6. −50 + (−1) = _____   7. 8 + (−4) = _____

8. −9 + 7 = _____   9. −3 + (−6) = _____

Algebra Use the rule to complete each table.

10. **Rule: Add −6**

Input	Output
5	
3	
−1	

11. **Rule: Add 2**

Input	Output
−7	
−4	
0	

Test Prep

12. Which is the sum of −6 + (−9) + (−9)?

    A. −24   B. −12   C. −6   D. 24

13. **Writing in Math** Explain how you would solve −4 + 4 + 5.

_____

_____

Use with Lesson 8-5. **91**

Subtracting Integers

R 8-6

Here is a rule for subtracting integers:

Add the opposite of the second number to the first number.

$6 - (-8) = ?$	$-9 - 2 = ?$	$-5 - 4 = ?$
The second number is -8. The opposite of -8 is 8. Add this number, 8, to the first number, 6.	The second number is 2. The opposite of 2 is -2. Add this number, -2, to the first number, -9.	The second number is 4. The opposite of 4 is -4. Add this number, -4, to the first number, -5.
$6 + 8 = 14$	$-9 + (-2) = -11$	$-5 + (-4) = -9$
So, $6 - (-8) = 14$.	So, $-9 - 2 = -11$.	So, $-5 - 4 = -9$.

Find each difference.

1. $10 - 12 =$ _____

2. $-3 - 2 =$ _____

3. $8 - (-4) =$ _____

4. $-3 - (-9) =$ _____

5. $15 - (-9) =$ _____

6. $-8 - 7 =$ _____

7. $-30 - 22 =$ _____

8. $45 - (-3) =$ _____

9. **Number Sense** Without computing, how do you know that the answer to $7 - (-15)$ is positive?

_____

_____

_____

_____

Use with Lesson 8-6.

Name _____

Subtracting Integers

P 8-6

Draw a number line or use the rules for subtracting integers to find each difference.

1. $-14 - (-14) =$ _____
2. $-9 - 10 =$ _____
3. $-15 - (-18) =$ _____
4. $-3 - (-12) =$ _____
5. $-5 - (-4) =$ _____
6. $-7 - 2 =$ _____

Algebra Evaluate each expression for $t = -9$.

7. $64 - t =$ _____
8. $t - (-7) =$ _____
9. $4 - t - 10 =$ _____

In football, the number of yards a team carries the ball is sometimes a negative number. The table shows the number of yards the Panthers and Wildcats carried the ball in a game.

Total Yards

Team	1st Quarter	2nd Quarter	3rd Quarter	4th Quarter
Panthers	30	15	−8	−25
Wildcats	−2	−10	102	27

10. What is the difference between the greatest and least number of yards the Panthers carried the ball? _____

11. How many more yards did the Wildcats carry the ball in the 4th quarter than the Panthers?

_____

Test Prep

12. Which is the value of t if $t - (-10) = -8$?

    A. −18   B. −2   C. 2   D. 18

13. **Writing in Math** Explain how you would solve $-8 - (-6)$ using a number line.

_____

_____

_____

92   Use with Lesson 8-6.

Multiplying Integers

R 8-7

Rules for multiplying integers:

• The product of two integers with the same sign is positive.

• The product of two integers with different signs is negative.

Here are some examples:

Find 5 × 6.

5 × 6 = 30

Both integers have the same sign, so the product is positive.

Find 3 × (−2).

3 × (−2) = (−2) + (−2) + (−2) = −6

So, 3 × (−2) = −6.

The integers have different signs, so the product is negative.

1. 6 × 3 = _____
2. 5 × (−6) = _____
3. −4 × 0 = _____
4. 12 × (−5) = _____
5. −4 × (−9) = _____
6. 22 × 4 = _____
7. (−1)(−37) = _____
8. (−7)(−7) = _____
9. (2)(4)(−3) = _____
10. (−8)(−7) = _____

For 11–14, evaluate each expression when $d = 2$.

11. −3d _____
12. $d \times |-3|$ _____
13. −10d − 3 _____
14. $|-9| + d$ _____

15. **Number Sense** Is the product of 4 negative integers positive or negative?

Use with Lesson 8-7. **93**

Name _____

Multiplying Integers

P 8-7

1. $(-8)(-2) =$ _____
2. $7 \times (-10) =$ _____
3. $5 \times 3 =$ _____
4. $(-9)(-6) =$ _____
5. $(-6)(-3) =$ _____
6. $3 \times (-18) =$ _____
7. $-9 \times -41 =$ _____
8. $(-6)(-21) =$ _____

Number Sense Use order of operations to evaluate each expression.

9. $(-3) + 5 + 4 - 9 \times 3 =$ _____
10. $(-6) - 4 \times 8 + 11 \times 2 =$ _____

Algebra Evaluate each expression when $r = 8$.

11. $-12r - 120 =$ _____
12. $7r + -5 =$ _____
13. $(-4r)(-30) - (-8) =$ _____
14. $(-2r)(8) + (-25) =$ _____

15. From 1950 to 1970, the glaciers in Alaska thinned by an average of 1.7 ft per year. What was the change in glacier thickness during this period? _____

16. From 1995 to 2000, the Alaskan glaciers thinned by 6 ft per year. What was the change in glacier thickness during this period? _____

Test Prep

17. Which is the product of $(-4)(-12)$?

    A. -48 B. -36 C. 36   D. 48

18. **Writing in Math** Explain how to evaluate $5p + (-6)$ when $p = -4$.

_____

_____

_____

_____

_____

Name _____

Dividing Integers

R 8-8

Rules for dividing integers:

• The quotient of two integers with the same sign is positive.

• The quotient of two integers with different signs is negative.

$54 \div -6$	$-36 \div -3$
$54 \div 6 = 9$. Because the signs of the two integers are different, the sign of the quotient is negative.	$36 \div 3 = 12$. Because the signs of the two integers are the same, the sign of the quotient is positive.
So, $54 \div -6 = -9$.	So, $-36 \div -3 = 12$.

1. $\frac{30}{6}$ _____

2. $\frac{-15}{3}$ _____

3. $\frac{28}{-4}$ _____

4. $\frac{-50}{-5}$ _____

Use order of operations to evaluate each expression.

5. $(-48 \div 6) + (-8) =$ _____

6. $4^2 + 50 - 33 \div -11 =$ _____

7. $40 - (-18 \div -6) =$ _____

8. $(-64 \div -8) + 6^2 \div -9 =$ _____

For 9–12, evaluate each expression when $n = -4$.

9. $-40 \div n =$ _____

10. $\frac{n}{-2} + 21 =$ _____

11. $n^2 - (-3) =$ _____

12. $\frac{32}{n} - 4 =$ _____

13. **Reasoning** Without computing the answer, how do you know if the quotient $-232 \div 11$ is negative or positive?

_____

_____

_____

_____

Dividing Integers

P 8-8

1. $\frac{80}{-8} =$ _____
2. $\frac{-75}{-5} =$ _____
3. $\frac{-48}{8} =$ _____
4. $\frac{-45}{-9} =$ _____
5. $-64 \div 8 =$ _____
6. $132 \div -12 =$ _____
7. $-72 \div -24 =$ _____
8. $81 \div -3 =$ _____

Number Sense Use order of operations to evaluate each expression.

9. $-75 \div 3 \div (-5) + 25 =$ _____

10. $80 \div (-10) \div (-2) - 15 =$ _____

Algebra Evaluate each expression when $m = -6$.

11. $-78 \div m =$ _____
12. $\frac{60}{m} - 22 =$ _____

13. **Reasoning** Is the quotient of $\frac{120}{-6}$ positive or negative? _____

14. A drop in a roller coaster of 224 ft took 2 sec. What was the change in height per second?

_____

Test Prep

15. Which is the answer for $30 \div (-5) \div (-2) + 3$?

    A. 2.3   B. 6   C. 15   D. 23

16. **Writing in Math** Explain how the rules of multiplying and dividing integers are alike.

_____

_____

_____

_____

Use with Lesson 8-8.

Name _____

Solving Equations with Integers

R 8-9

When solving equations with integers, use inverse operations to "undo" each other. Also, remember to do the same thing to both sides of an equation.

Solve $s + 14 = -12$.

$s + 14 - 14 = -12 - 14$

$s + 0 = -26$

$s = -26$

Solve $-3y = 60$.

$\frac{-3y}{-3} = \frac{60}{-3}$

$y = -20$

Solve $\frac{d}{-10} = 7$.

$(\frac{d}{-10}) \times (-10) = 7 \times (-10)$

$d = -70$

Solve and check each equation.

1. $t + 8 = -20$ _____

2. $b - (-15) = 25$ _____

3. $\frac{k}{5} = 15$ _____

4. $w + (-4) = 9$ _____

5. $\frac{n}{-9} = 7$ _____

6. $2p = -18$ _____

7. $-3d = -27$ _____

8. $\frac{y}{3} = -12$ _____

9. $40r = -280$ _____

10. **Number Sense** Suppose a number was multiplied by -3. What would you do to undo the multiplication?

_____

Use with Lesson 8-9.

Solving Equations with Integers

P 8-9

Solve and check each equation.

1. $y - (-6) = -6$

    $y =$ _____

2. $\frac{-80}{t} = 8$

    $t =$ _____

3. $-4w = -80$

    $w =$ _____

4. $u - (-96) = 2$

    $u =$ _____

5. $55 + h = -7$

    $h =$ _____

6. $n \div -9 = -9$

    $n =$ _____

7. $x + (-8) = -15$

    $x =$ _____

8. $-21c = 21$

    $c =$ _____

Reasoning Without solving, tell whether the variable is greater than, less than, or equal to -15. Tell how you decided.

9. $p + 14 = 2$

_____

_____

10. The temperature at 3:00 P.M. was $-5°F$. The temperature 1 hr later was $-8°F$. Solve the equation $-5 + d = -8$ to find the change in temperature. _____

11. A climber reached 2,500 ft up a mountain. Over the next 3 hr, she descended 600 ft down the mountain. Solve the equation $3y = -600$ to find the number of feet she descended per hour. _____

Test Prep

12. Which is the value of s in $s - (-87) = -120$?

    A. -207 **B.** -33 **C.** 33 **D.** 207

13. **Writing in Math** Write an equation in which the variable g stands for a negative integer. Then solve the equation for g.

_____

Use with Lesson 8-9.

PROBLEM-SOLVING STRATEGY
Work Backward

R 8-10

School At the end of the first quarter, there were 6 fewer students than at the start of the year. At the end of the second quarter, 12 students had been added. At the end of the third quarter there were 8 fewer students. At the end of the year there were 5 more students. If there were 95 students at the end of the year, how many sixth-grade students had been enrolled at the start of the year?

Read and Understand

Step 1: What do you know?

6 students left, 12 students were added, 8 students left, and 5 students were added

Step 2: What are you trying to find?

The number of students enrolled in the sixth grade at the start of the school year

Plan and Solve

Step 3: What strategy will you use?   **Strategy:** Work backward

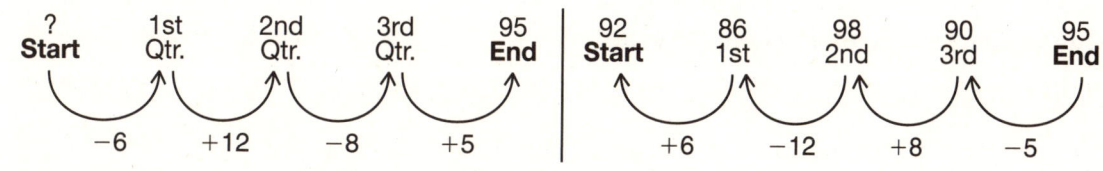

```
  ?     1st   2nd   3rd   95        92    86    98    90    95
Start   Qtr.  Qtr.  Qtr.  End      Start  1st   2nd   3rd   End
   -6    +12   -8    +5              +6    -12   +8    -5
```

Begin with the enrollment at the end of the year, 95.
Then work backward, adding or subtracting each change.

There were 92 students at the start of the year.

Look Back and Check

Step 4: What can you do to check your answer?
Begin at the start of the year and work forward.
$92 - 6 + 12 - 8 + 5 = 95$

---

1. Barton has twice as many people as Adamsville. Carson has 2,000 more people than Barton. Dunbar has $\frac{1}{3}$ the population of Carson. If Dunbar has 4,000 residents, what is the population of Adamsville?

96 Use with Lesson 8-10.

Name _____

PROBLEM-SOLVING STRATEGY   P 8-10
Work Backward

	How to Work Backward
Step 1	Identify what you are trying to find.
Step 2	Draw a diagram to show each change, starting from the unknown.
Step 3	Start at the end. Work backward using the inverse of each change.

For each exercise, solve using the steps in How to Work Backward.

1. Ohio joined the United States 12 years after Vermont. Florida joined the United States 42 years after Ohio. Washington joined the United States 44 years after Florida. Vermont joined the United States in 1791. What year did Washington join the United States? _____

2. Leona left the library at 4:30 P.M. She had been studying at the library for 45 min. It takes her 12 min to walk to the library from her home. At what time did Leona leave home to walk to the library? _____

3. Fruit crops are often measured using the units dry quarts, pecks, and bushels. One bushel equals 4 pecks. One peck equals 8 dry quarts. If a farmer had 30 bushels of apples, how many dry quarts of apples did he have? _____

4. Ms. Thompson's class worked for 45 min on history projects. After that, they spent 30 min at lunch. Then they went outside for 20 min of recess. If recess finished at 1:15 P.M., what time did Ms. Thompson's class start working on their history projects? _____

5. Jeff and Max had hiked for 8 mi when they realized they had dropped their compass. They went back 2 mi and found it. They then hiked 2 mi, rested for 30 min, and hiked another 4 mi. If they hiked on a straight path, how far from their starting point did they hike? _____

96 Use with Lesson 8-10.

Graphing Ordered Pairs

R 8-11

An ordered pair gives the coordinates and location of a point. The first number tells you how far left or right the point is located. The second number tells you how far up or down the point is located.

Point M is located at (−3, 2).

Point L is located at (2, 1).

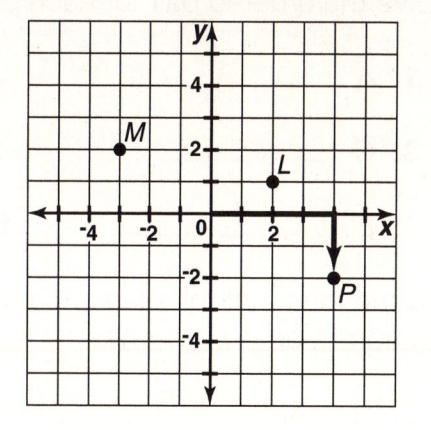

Here is how to graph point P (4, −2):

Step 1: Start at the origin (0, 0). | **Step 2:** Move 4 units to the right. | **Step 3:** Move 2 units down. Draw a point. Label it P.

Give the ordered pair for each point.

1. P _____

2. Q _____

3. R _____

4. S _____

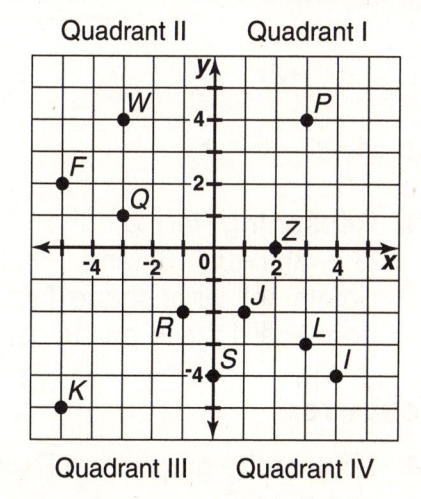

Name the point for each ordered pair and the quadrant or axis on which it lies.

5. (−5, −5) _____

6. (−3, 4) _____

7. (1, −2) _____

8. (3, −3) _____

Graph and label the points on the graph above.

9. B (−4, −2)

10. C (5, 0)

Use with Lesson 8-11.

Name _____

Graphing Ordered Pairs

P 8-11

Give the ordered pair for each point.

1. A _____   2. B _____

3. C _____   4. D _____

5. E _____   6. F _____

Name the point for each ordered pair and the quadrant or axis on which it lies.

7. (1, −4) _____

8. (4, 5) _____

9. (−4, −5) _____

10. (4, −3) _____

11. (−5, −2) _____

12. (1, 3) _____

13. **Reasoning** Tara graphed the following points: (3, 3), (3, −3), (−3, −3), and (−3, 3). Without plotting the points, tell what shape Tara would form if she connected these points using straight lines.

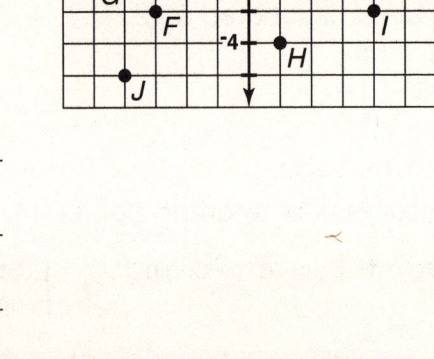

_____

Test Prep

14. Look at the graph from Exercise 1. What are the coordinates of point Q?

    A. (−3, 1)   **B.** (1, −3)   **C.** (−3, −1)   **D.** (−1, −3)

15. **Writing in Math** Explain how, if you know a point is in Quadrant II, you can determine the signs of the coordinates. Give an example.

_____

_____

_____

_____

Use with Lesson 8-11.

Patterns and Tables

R 8-12

Is the relation a function?

In Example A, there is just one *y*-value for each *x*-value. The relation is a function.

In Example B, two *y*-values, 3 and 0, are assigned to the *x*-value, −1. So, the relation is not a function.

Example A

x	y
−3	1
−2	2
−1	3
0	4

Example B

x	y
−1	3
−2	−1
0	1
−1	0

Writing a rule for a function:

x	y
−5	10
−2	4
0	0
3	−6

What can I do to −5 to get 10?
   I can multiply by −2.
Does the rule "multiply by −2" work with other numbers?
   −2 (−2) = 4. Yes
   3 (−2) = −6. Yes
The rule is $y = -2x$.

Tell whether each relation is a function.

1.

x	y
5	2
6	3
7	4
8	5

2.

x	y
0	1
0	2
2	4
4	6

Write a rule and an equation to describe the function.

3.

x	−3	−1	1	6
y	−21	−7	7	42

98   Use with Lesson 8-12.

Name _____

Patterns and Tables

P 8-12

Tell whether each relation is a function.

1.
a	3	5	7	12
b	-2	0	2	7

_____

2.
x	3	3	4	5
y	-1	1	-1	1

_____

3.
m	1	2	3	4
n	11	12	13	14

_____

4.
x	12	9	6	3
y	3	0	-3	-6

_____

Complete each table.

5. $r = 4 + m$

m	r
-2	
0	
2	
4	

6. $y = \frac{x}{2} + 1$

x	y
4	
6	
8	
10	

7. $b = 2a - 7$

a	b
12	
10	
8	
6	

Write a rule and an equation to describe the function.

8.
x	y
5	11
10	21
15	31
20	41

_____

9.
a	b
14	2
10	-2
6	-6
2	-10

_____

Test Prep

10. Which rule describes this table of values?

    A. $y = x - 8$ B. $y = 8 - x$
    C. $y = x - (-8)$ D. $x = y + 8$

x	y
0	8
5	13
10	18
15	23

11. **Writing in Math** Explain in your own words how you can tell if a relation is a function.

_____

_____

Name _____

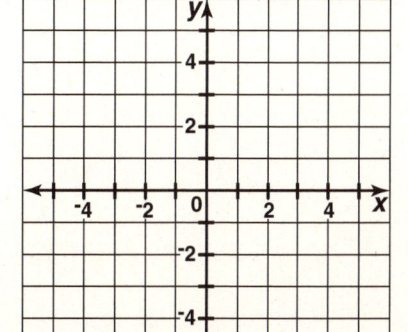

Graphing Equations

R 8-13

How to graph equations:

Graph the equation $y = -3 + x$.

First make a T-table like the one at the right.

Use at least 3 values for x.

x	y
3	0
2	−1
1	−2

Graph each ordered pair onto the coordinate plane, then draw a line connecting the points. Every point on this line meets the condition that $y = -3 + x$.

Because the graph of this equation is a straight line, it is called a linear equation.

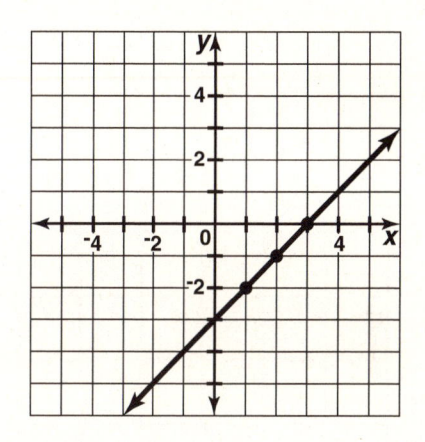

Complete each T-table. Then graph each equation.

1. $y = x + 1$

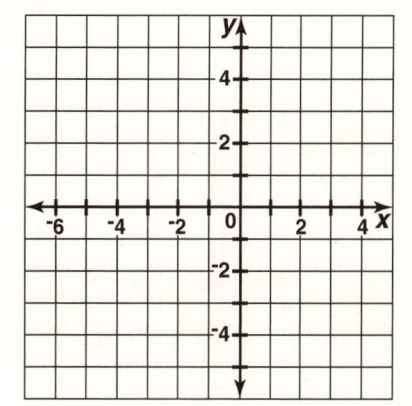

x	y
−5	
−4	
−3	

2. $y = 3 - x$

x	y
4	
3	
2	

Use with Lesson 8-13. **99**

Name _____

Graphing Equations

P 8-13

For 1 and 2, make a T-table. Then graph each equation.

1. $y = x - 3$

2. $y = -2x$

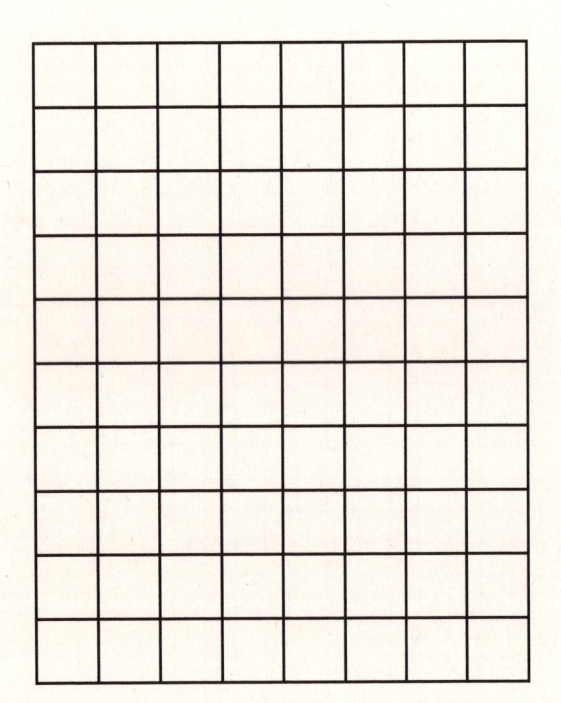

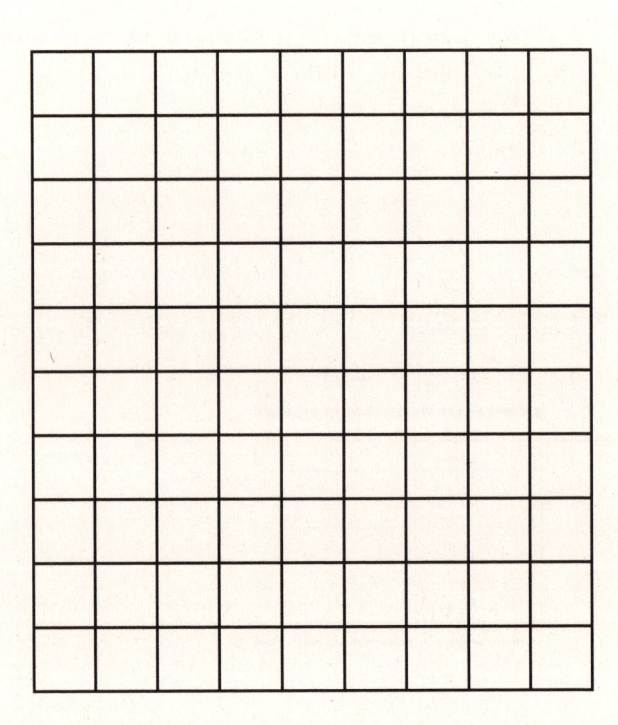

3. **Reasoning** Is the point (5, 6) on the graph for the equation $y = -2x + 5$? _____

Test Prep

4. Which point is on the graph for the equation $y = -14 + x$?

   A. (1, 5)   B. (2, 12)   C. (−2, −16)   D. (−7, 21)

5. **Writing in Math** Explain how making a T-table helps you graph an equation.

_____

_____

Use with Lesson 8-13. 99

Name _____

PROBLEM-SOLVING APPLICATION

The Environment

R 8-14

Fran was on a donkey ride in the Grand Canyon. At one point she was 200 ft below the start of the trail at the top of the canyon. Later she moved up a total of 25 ft. How many feet was she from the top of the canyon?

$-200 + 25 = -175$

So, Fran was 175 ft from the top of the canyon.

1. In 1960, a low temperature of −127°F was recorded at Vostok, Antarctica. In 1922, a high temperature of 136°F was recorded at Al'Aziziyah, Libya. What is the difference between these two temperatures?

2. The highest mountain in the United States is Mount McKinley in Alaska with an elevation of 20,320 ft. The lowest point in the United States is in Death Valley, California, with an elevation of −282 ft. What is the difference between these elevations?

3. One of the coldest cities in North America is Whitehorse in the Yukon Territory of Canada. Over a period of about 30 years it experienced an average temperature of −1.3°C. Over the same period, Fairbanks, Alaska, was about 3 times colder than Whitehorse. What was the average temperature in Fairbanks?

4. Rico recorded the temperature each morning when he woke up. During one week the temperatures were −16°F, −24°F, 18°F, 1°F, 12°F, −13°F, and 0°F. Write the temperatures in order from coldest to warmest.

Name _____

PROBLEM-SOLVING APPLICATION   P 8-14

Family Amusement

Solve. Write your answers in complete sentences.

1. Tim went to an amusement park with his family. The first ride he went on was the roller coaster. At the end of the ride, the speed of the roller coaster went from 50 mi per hour to a stop in 10 sec. If the speed of the roller coaster decreased at an even pace, what was the change in speed per second? Express the speed as a negative integer.

_____

_____

2. The lines for the most popular rides at the amusement park can be quite long. When Tim walked by the tornado coaster, the posted wait time was $1\frac{1}{2}$ hr. After lunch, the posted wait time at the tornado coaster had decreased by $\frac{5}{6}$ hr. What was the wait time at the tornado coaster after lunch?

_____

_____

3. When the family arrived at the amusement park, the temperature was 68°F. The temperature decreased 2 degrees per hour for the first 4 hr the family was there. What was the temperature after the family had been there for 4 hr?

_____

_____

4. Tim went on the water slide, the merry-go-round, and the Ferris wheel. He got to the Ferris wheel at 3:00 P.M. It took him 10 min to ride the water slide, 10 min to walk to the merry-go-round, 15 min to ride the merry-go-round, and 10 min to walk to the Ferris wheel. He waited 5 min for each ride. What time did he start riding the water slide?

_____

_____

Use with Lesson 8-14.

Geometric Ideas

R 9-1

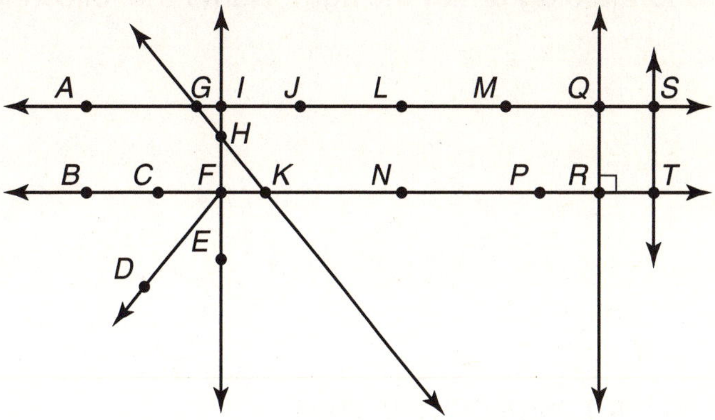

- A **line** is a straight path of points that goes on forever in two directions. Examples: $\overleftrightarrow{AS}$, $\overleftrightarrow{GK}$.

- A **ray** is a part of a line with one endpoint, extending forever in only one direction. Examples: $\overrightarrow{FD}$, $\overrightarrow{FB}$.

- A **line segment** is part of a line with two endpoints. Examples: $\overline{CF}$, $\overline{MQ}$.

- A **midpoint** is the point halfway between the endpoints of a line segment. Example: Point L is halfway between points J and M on $\overline{JM}$.

- **Congruent line segments** are line segments that have the same length. Example: $\overline{QR}$ is congruent to $\overline{ST}$.

- **Parallel lines** are in the same plane but do not intersect. Example: $\overleftrightarrow{AS}$ is parallel to $\overleftrightarrow{BT}$.

Use the diagram at the right. Name the following.

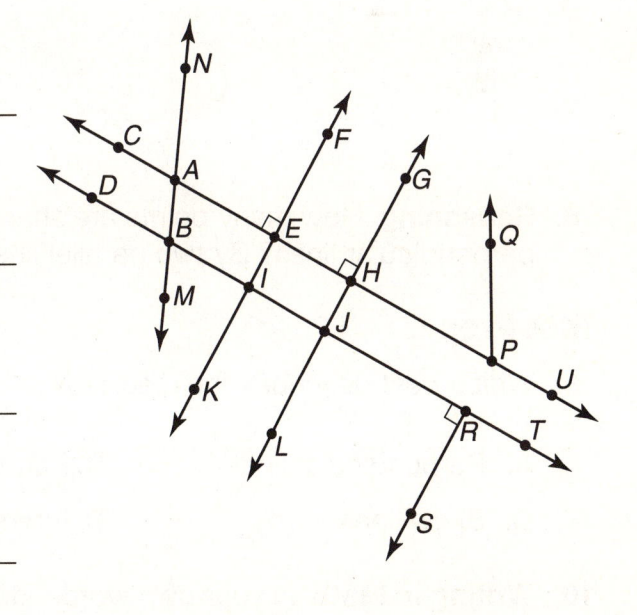

1. three line segments

   _____

2. two parallel lines

   _____

3. two lines that intersect $\overleftrightarrow{DT}$

   _____

4. two congruent line segments

   _____

5. two lines perpendicular to $\overleftrightarrow{BR}$

   _____

6. two midpoints of line segments

Use with Lesson 9-1. **101**

Name _____

Geometric Ideas

P 9-1

Use the diagram at the right. Name the following.

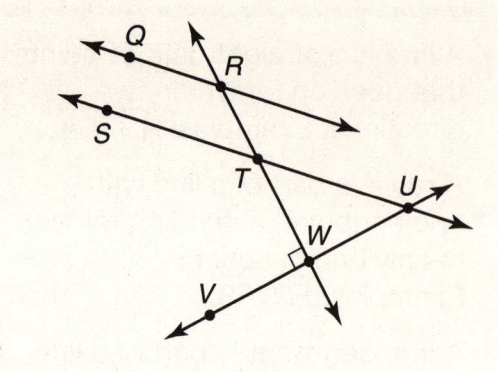

1. two perpendicular lines _____

2. two rays _____

3. two parallel lines _____

4. four line segments _____

5. two lines that intersect _____

Draw a diagram to illustrate each situation.

6. $\overline{XY}$ with midpoint R

7. $\overline{JK}$ perpendicular to $\overline{LM}$

8. **Reasoning** How many points are shared by two perpendicular lines? By two parallel lines?

Test Prep

9. Which best describes the diagram?

   A. Perpendicular lines   B. Parallel lines
   C. Skew lines   D. Intersecting lines

10. **Writing in Math** In your own words, describe a plane.

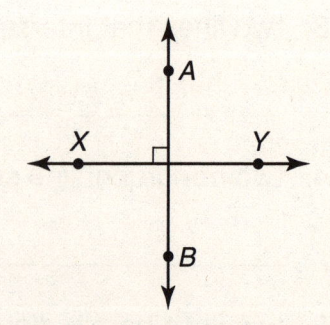

_____

_____

Use with Lesson 9-1. **101**

Measuring and Drawing Angles

How to measure an angle:

Step 1 Place the protractor's center on the angle's vertex.

Step 2 Place the 0° mark on one side of the angle.

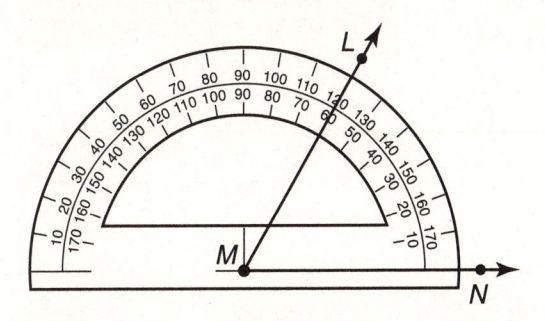

LMN = 60°

Step 3 Use the scale beginning with the 0° mark to read the measurement where the other side of the angle crosses the protractor.

How to draw an angle:

Draw an angle of 52°.

Step 1 Draw a ray.

Step 2 Place the protractor's center on the endpoint. Line up the ray with the 0° mark.

Step 3 Using the scale with the 0° mark, place a point at 52°.

Step 4 Draw the other ray.

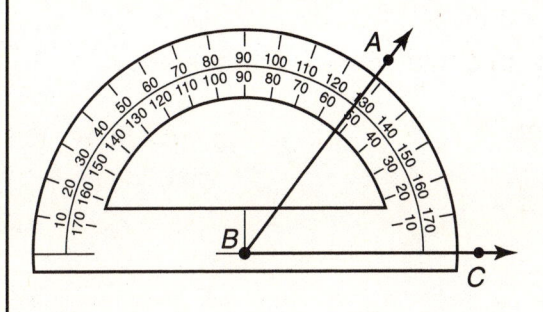

∠ABC = 52°

Classify each angle as acute, right, obtuse, or straight. Then measure the angle.

1.

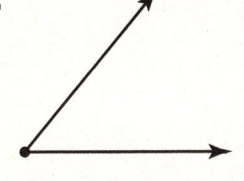

2.

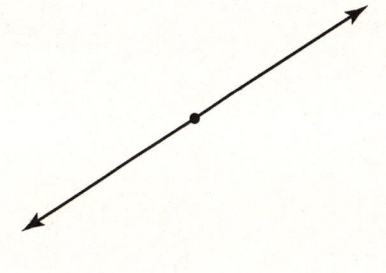

Draw an angle with each measure.

3. 45°

4. 120°

Name _____

Measuring and Drawing Angles

P 9-2

Classify each angle as acute, right, obtuse, or straight. Then measure the angle.

1.

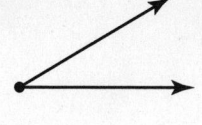

2.

3.

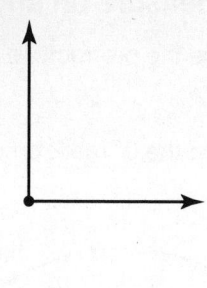

_____   _____   _____

Draw an angle with each measure.

4. 90°   **5.** 50°   **6.** 112°

Estimation Without a protractor, try to sketch an angle with the given measure. Then use a protractor to check your estimate.

7. 120°   **8.** 100°   **9.** 10°

Test Prep

10. Which is a measure of an acute angle?

   A. 40°   **B.** 90°   **C.** 120°   **D.** 180°

11. Writing in Math Explain the steps you use to measure an angle using a protractor.

_____

_____

_____

Use with Lesson 9-2.

Angle Pairs

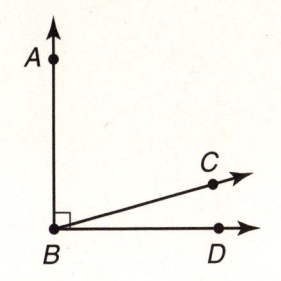

R 9-3

Complementary angles are two angles whose measures add up to 90°. ∠ABC and ∠CBD are complementary. If ∠ABC = 75°, then ∠CBD = 15°, because 75 + 15 = 90.

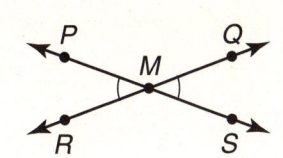

Vertical angles are formed by intersecting lines and are congruent. ∠PMR is congruent to ∠SMQ. Because ∠PMR = 40°, you know that ∠QMS = 40°.

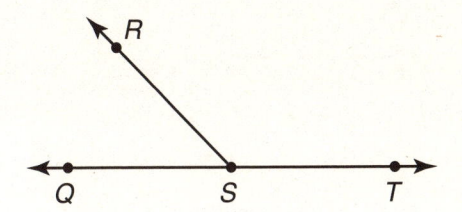

Supplementary angles are two angles whose measures add up to 180°. ∠QSR and ∠RST are supplementary. If ∠QSR = 45°, ∠RST = 135°, because 45 + 135 = 180.

Find x.

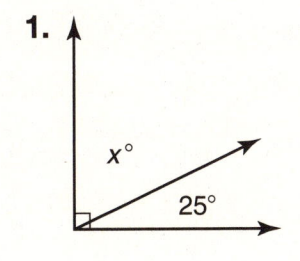

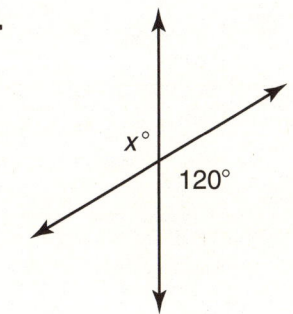

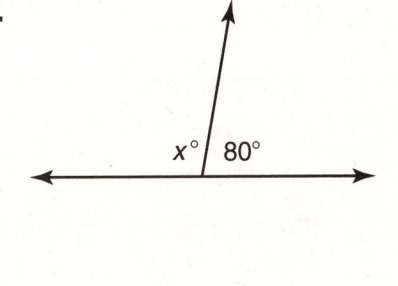

1. $x°$, 25° _____

2. $x°$, 120° _____

3. $x°$, 80° _____

Find the measure of an angle complementary to an angle with each measure.

4. 15° _____ 5. 85° _____ 6. 20° _____ 7. 39° _____

Find the measure of an angle supplementary to an angle with each measure.

8. 15° _____ 9. 75° _____ 10. 90° _____ 11. 115° _____

Use with Lesson 9-3. **103**

Name _____

Angle Pairs

P 9-3

Find x.

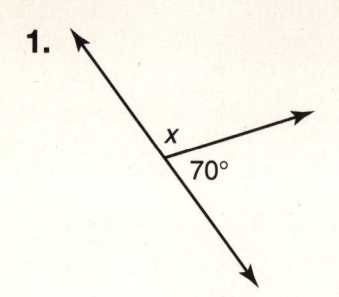

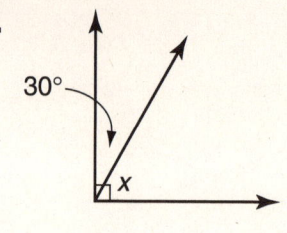

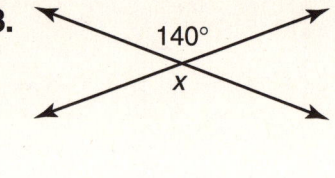

1. [diagram: x, 70°]

2. [diagram: 30°, x with right angle]

3. [diagram: 140°, x]

_____   _____   _____

Find the measure of an angle complementary to an angle with each measure.

4. 30° _____   5. 22° _____   6. 85° _____

Find the measure of an angle supplementary to an angle with each measure.

7. 105° _____   8. 120° _____   9. 92° _____

10. **Reasoning** Are two right angles always supplementary to each other? _____

Find the measure of each angle in the diagram.

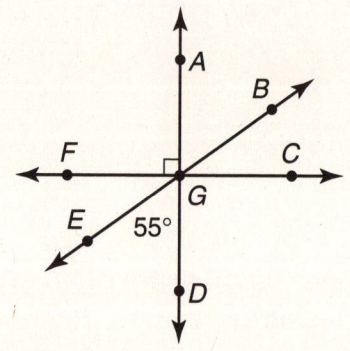

11. ∠AGB _____   12. ∠CGE _____

13. ∠BGC _____   14. ∠DGB _____

[diagram with points A, B, C, D, E, F, G and 55° angle]

Test Prep

15. Which is complementary to a 72° angle?

    A. 108°   B. 72°
    C. 18°   D. 10°

16. **Writing in Math** Explain what is always the same about two congruent angles.

_____

_____

Use with Lesson 9-3. **103**

Constructions

R 9-4

Constructing a congruent segment:

Construct a segment congruent to $\overline{CD}$.

C •————————————• D

Step 1 Draw a line and label point P.

←————•————→
    P

Step 2 Adjust your compass to a setting equal to CD by placing the center of the compass on point C and moving the slider to point D. Tighten the knob.

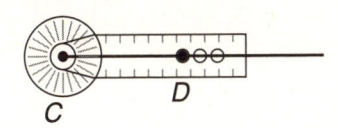

Step 3 Place the center at point P and draw an arc that intersects the line. Label point H, the point of intersection. $\overline{PH} \cong \overline{CD}$.

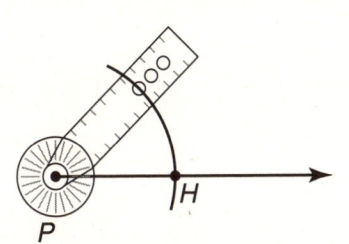

Constructing an angle bisector:

Construct the bisector of $\angle XYZ$.

Step 1 Place the compass center on Y and draw an arc intersecting the sides of $\angle XYZ$. Label the points of intersection Q and R.

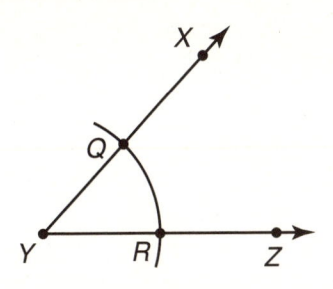

Step 2 Adjust your compass to a setting greater than $\frac{1}{2}$ QR. Place the center on Q and draw an arc. With the same setting, place the center on R and draw an arc.

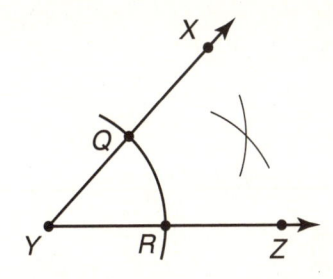

Step 3 Label the point of intersection M. Draw $\overline{YM}$. $\overline{YM}$ is the bisector of $\angle XYZ$.

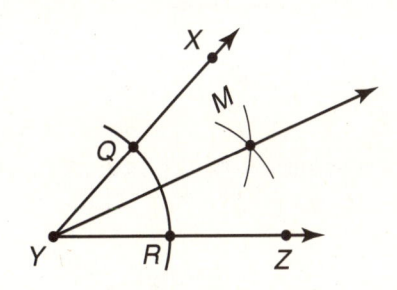

---

1. Construct the angle bisector of $\angle RST$.

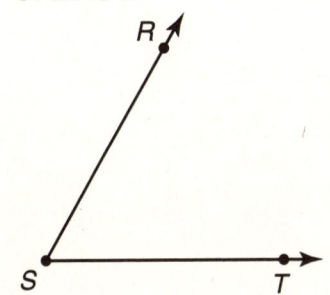

2. Construct a segment congruent to $\overline{JK}$.

J •————————————————• K

Name _____

Constructions

P 9-4

Use $\overline{EF}$ and $\angle T$ for 1 and 2.

1. Construct a segment congruent to $\overline{EF}$.

2. Construct an angle congruent to $\angle T$.

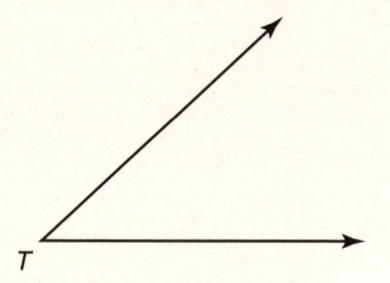

Use $\overline{HJ}$ and $\angle V$ for 3 and 4.

3. Construct a perpendicular bisector of $\overline{HJ}$.

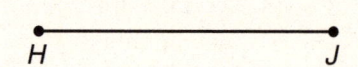

4. Construct a bisector of $\angle V$.

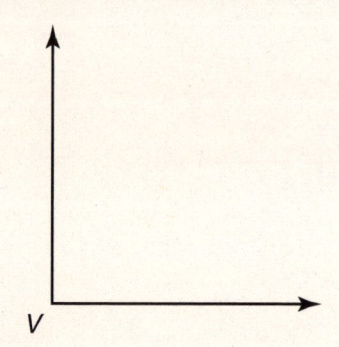

Test Prep

5. If $\overrightarrow{MP}$ is the bisector of $\angle LMN$, and $\angle LMN$ is a right angle, what is the measure of $\angle LMP$?

   A. 30°   B. 45°   C. 65°   D. 90°

6. **Writing in Math** Explain how you would use a compass and a straightedge to draw the perpendicular bisector of a line segment.

_____

_____

_____

_____

Use with Lesson 9-4.

PROBLEM-SOLVING STRATEGY
Draw a Picture

R 9-5

The Fence Bill wants to build a fence around his rectangular yard. The yard is 120 ft wide and 60 ft deep. The fence will enclose the yard except for an 8 ft opening at the back of the yard, where Bill will bring his car in. How much fencing does Bill need?

Read and Understand

Step 1: What do you know?

The yard is a 60 ft × 120 ft rectangle. There will be an 8 ft opening in the back.

Step 2: What are you trying to find?

The total amount of fencing needed

Plan and Solve

Step 3: What strategy will you use?

Strategy: Draw a picture

```
      120 ft
   ┌─────────┐
60 ft│         │
   └───────┘ └┘
            8 ft
```

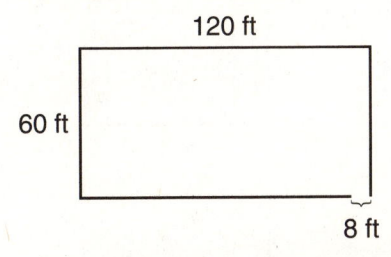

Find the perimeter of the rectangle and then subtract the width of the opening.

120 ft + 120 ft + 60 ft + 60 ft − 8 = 352 ft.
So, 352 ft of fencing is needed.

Look Back and Check

Step 4: Is your answer reasonable?

Yes, I checked. (2 × 120) + (2 × 60) − 8 = 352

Draw a picture to solve the problem.

1. The elevator was found on the 20th floor. The building manager had to trace its movements back. It had just come up 5 floors. Before that it had descended 8 floors. Where was the elevator at the start?

Use with Lesson 9-5. **105**

Name _____

PROBLEM-SOLVING STRATEGY P 9-5

Draw a Picture

Draw a picture to solve the problem. Write the answer in a complete sentence.

1. The sixth graders are constructing a mural. Each student is to draw two triangular segments. The completed segments will be arranged as shown. How many triangles will there be in the mural if 40 students have completed the segments?

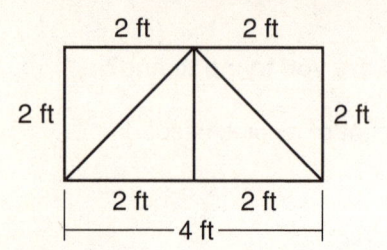

   [Diagram: rectangle 4 ft wide, 2 ft tall, divided into triangles. Labels: 2 ft on top (twice), 2 ft on sides, 2 ft on bottom (twice), 4 ft total width]

   _____
   _____

2. Milo is building bookshelves like those in the diagram. How many inches of shelving material will he need to make a bookshelf with three shelves?

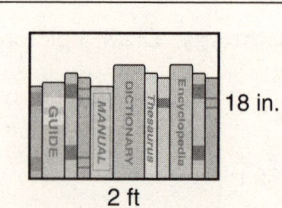

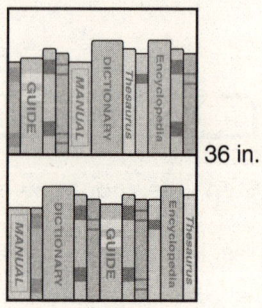

   [Diagram: one-shelf bookshelf, 18 in. tall, 2 ft wide]

   _____
   _____

   [Diagram: two-shelf bookshelf, 36 in. tall, 2 ft wide]

3. Jay is helping his parents tile the floor of their kitchen. The center of the room will have a design like the one in the diagram. If the total design is made up of 15 rows of tiles, how many tiles are in the 1st and 15th rows?

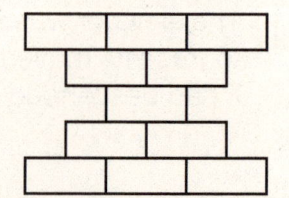

   [Diagram: brick-pattern tile design]

   _____
   _____

Use with Lesson 9-5. **105**

Name _____

Polygons

R 9-6

A **polygon** is a closed figure made up of line segments.

There are special names for some polygons.

A **quadrilateral** has 4 sides.

A **pentagon** has 5 sides.

A **hexagon** has 6 sides.

A **heptagon** has 7 sides.

An **octagon** has 8 sides.

A **nonagon** has 9 sides.

A **decagon** has 10 sides.

A **dodecagon** has 12 sides.

A regular polygon has sides of equal length and angles of equal measure.

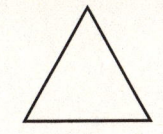

Regular polygon
All sides equal length, all angles equal measure

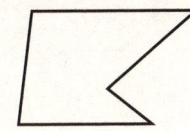

Not regular
Not all sides equal length or angles equal measure

Name each polygon. Then tell if it appears to be a regular polygon.

1.

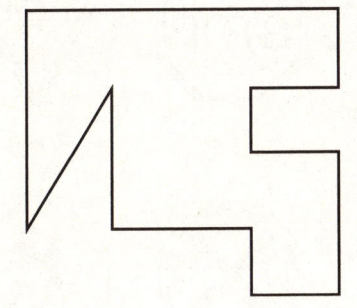

_____
_____

2.

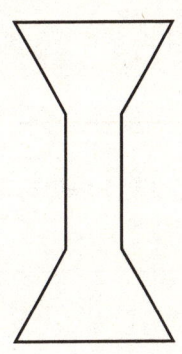

_____
_____

3.

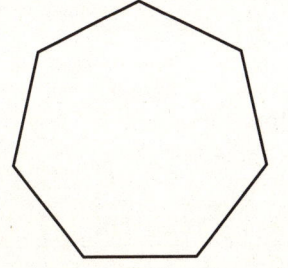

_____
_____

4.

_____
_____

© Pearson Education, Inc. 6

106   Use with Lesson 9-6.

Name _____

Polygons

P 9-6

Name each polygon. Then tell if it appears to be a regular polygon.

1.

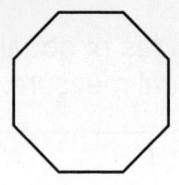

_____

2.

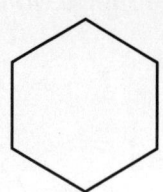

_____

3.

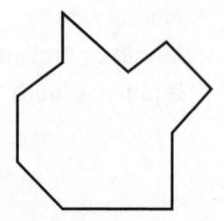

_____

4.

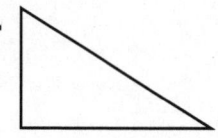

_____

5. Which of the road signs shown are regular polygons?

_____

6. Which of the road signs is not a polygon?

_____

Stop

Yield

Railroad crossing

School zone

Test Prep

7. Which is a characteristic of all regular polygons?

   A. 4 or more sides

   B. 4 or more interior angles

   C. At least one set of parallel sides

   D. All sides of equal length

8. **Writing in Math** Explain how you would construct a regular hexagon using a compass.

_____

_____

_____

Name _____

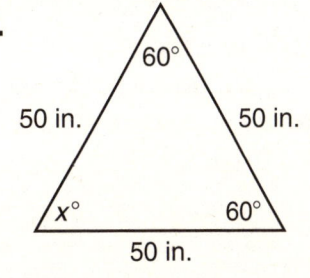

Triangles

R 9-7

Triangles can be classified by their angles or their sides.

Classified by angles

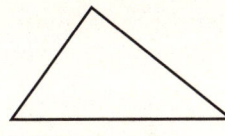

Acute triangle
All three angles are acute angles.

Right triangle
One angle is a right angle.

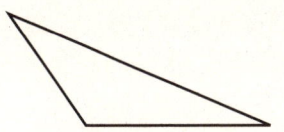

Obtuse triangle
One angle is an obtuse angle.

Classified by sides

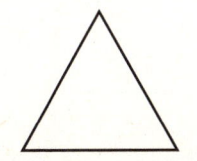

Equilateral triangle
All sides are congruent.

Isosceles triangle
At least two sides are congruent.

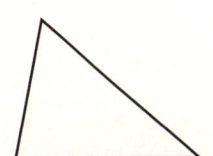

Scalene triangle
No sides are congruent.

How to find angle measures in a triangle:

Find the measure of angle x.

Remember, when you add up all three of the angles, the sum must be 180°.

$x + 110 + 40 = 180$

$x + 150 = 180$

$x = 30$

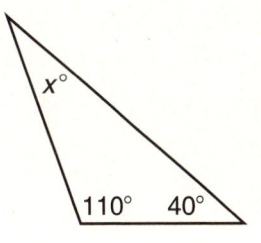

Find the missing angle measure. Then classify the triangle by its angles and by its sides.

1. (triangle with $x°$, 3.4 cm, 7.5 cm, 42°, 5.9 cm, right angle)

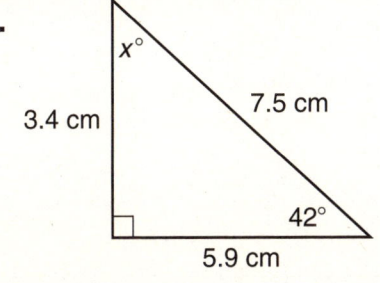

2. (triangle with 60°, 50 in., 50 in., $x°$, 60°, 50 in.)

Use with Lesson 9-7. **107**

Name _____

Triangles

P 9-7

Find the missing angle measure. Then classify the triangle by its angles and by its sides.

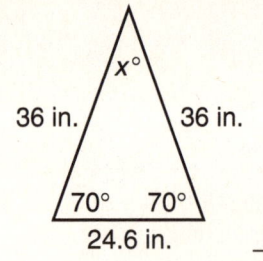

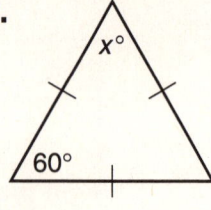

1. (triangle with x°, two sides of 36 in., base 24.6 in., base angles 70° and 70°)

_____

2. (triangle with x°, two tick-marked equal sides, one angle 60°, base with tick mark)

_____

3. **Reasoning** Are all equilateral triangles acute triangles? Why or why not?

_____

4. **Construction** Draw a segment. Label it $\overline{AB}$. Then complete the following construction.

   a. Adjust the compass to a setting equal to $\overline{AB}$. Place the center of the compass at one endpoint of the segment and draw an arc. Repeat from the other endpoint.

   b. Connect the endpoints to the point of intersection of the arcs.

   c. What type of triangle did you construct?

   _____

   _____

Test Prep

5. Which could be the angle measures of a right triangle?

   A. 60°, 60°, 60°   **B.** 90°, 90°, 30°   **C.** 30°, 60°, 90°   **D.** 20°, 80°, 90°

6. **Writing in Math** If you are given the measurement of two angles in a triangle, what steps would you follow to find the measure of the third angle?

   _____

   _____

   _____

Use with Lesson 9-7. **107**

Quadrilaterals

R 9-8

Classifying quadrilaterals

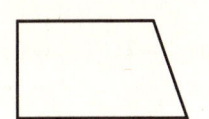

Trapezoid
A quadrilateral with only one pair of parallel sides

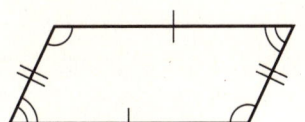

Parallelogram
A quadrilateral with both pairs of opposite sides parallel; Opposite sides and opposite angles are congruent.

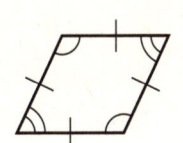

Rhombus
A parallelogram with all sides congruent

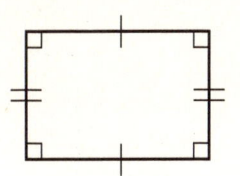

Rectangle
A parallelogram with four right angles

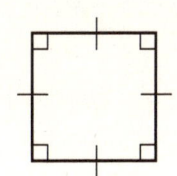

Square
A rectangle with all sides congruent; A square is also a rhombus.

Finding the missing measure of a quadrilateral:

The measures of three angles of a quadrilateral are 115°, 68°, and 45°. Find the measure of the fourth angle.

Remember, the sum of all four angles must be 360°.

$115 + 68 + 45 + x = 360$

$228 + x = 360$

$x = 132$

The measure of the fourth angle is 132°.

Classify each polygon in as many ways as possible.

1.

2.

_____

_____

_____

The measures of three angles of a quadrilateral are given. Find the measure of the fourth angle.

3. 90°, 90°, 90° _____

4. 80°, 60°, 120° _____

5. 70°, 120°, 120° _____

6. 130°, 40°, 50° _____

108 Use with Lesson 9-8.

Name _____

Quadrilaterals

P 9-8

Classify each polygon in as many ways as possible.

1. 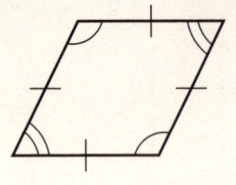 2. 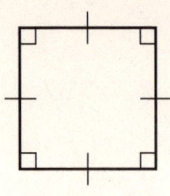 3.

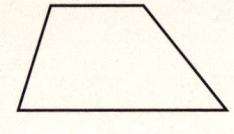

_____   _____   _____
_____   _____   _____
_____   _____   _____

The measures of three angles of a quadrilateral are given. Find the measure of the fourth angle.

4. 90°, 90°, 100° _____

5. 50°, 70°, 100° _____

6. Find the length of JK and the measure of ∠L in the parallelogram.

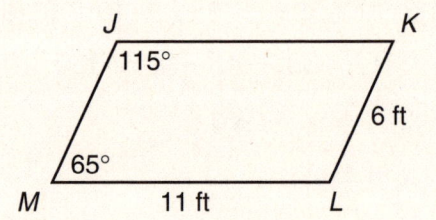

_____

_____

J 115° K
         6 ft
   65°
M   11 ft   L

7. **Construction** Use a ruler and a protractor to draw a square with 3 cm sides.

Test Prep

8. What is true about every quadrilateral?

   A. The angles total 360°.

   B. The angles total 180°.

   C. There are two sets of congruent sides.

   D. There is one set of congruent sides.

9. **Writing in Math** Explain what characteristics would make you classify a quadrilateral as a rhombus and not a square.

_____

_____

108   Use with Lesson 9-8.

Circles

R 9-9

Radius Line segment that connects the center to a point on the circle

Semicircle Arc that connects the endpoints of a diameter

Arc Part of a circle connecting two points of the circle

Diameter Line segment through the center of the circle that connects two points on the circle

Central angle Angle whose vertex is the center; ∠LOM is a central angle.

Sector Region between two radii and an arc

Chord Line segment that connects two points on the circle

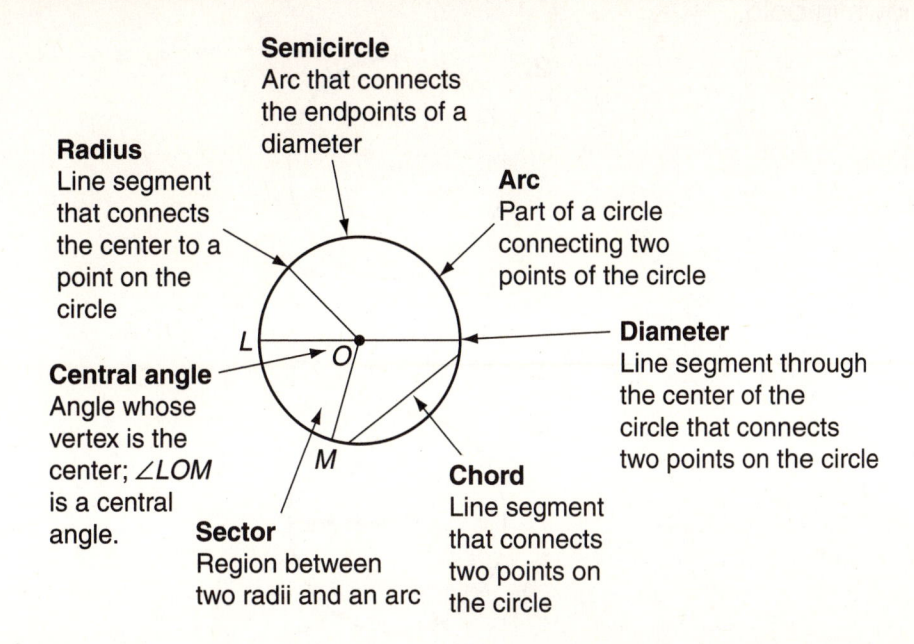

Identify the figure or portion of the figure that is drawn in each circle.

1.

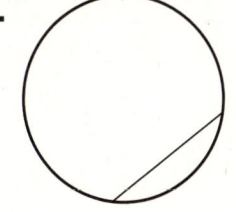

2.

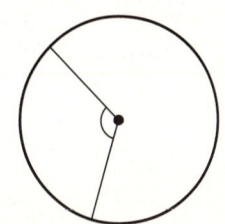

3.

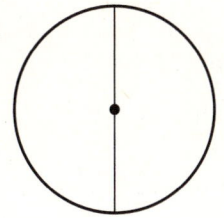

4.

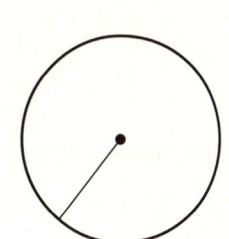

5.

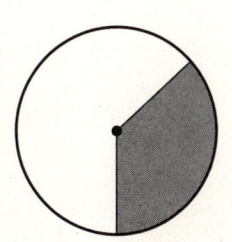

6.

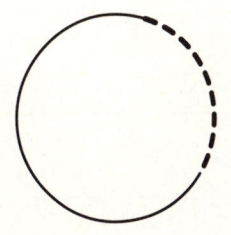

Use with Lesson 9-9. **109**

Name _____

Circles

P 9-9

Identify the figure shown in bold.

1.

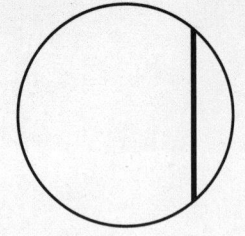

2.

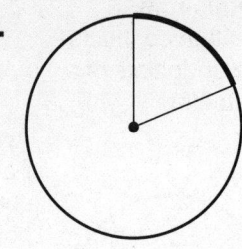

_____

_____

3.

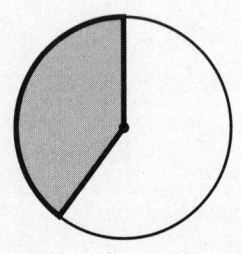

4.

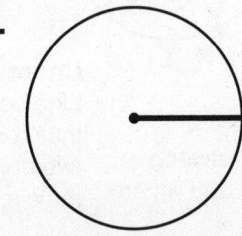

_____

_____

5. **Construction** Construct a circle having a diameter equal to FG.

F•————————•G

6. **Construction** Construct two circles. The arc of one circle should intersect the center of the other.

Test Prep

7. How many degrees are in a circle?

   A. 90°   B. 120°   C. 180°   D. 360°

8. **Writing in Math** Explain how knowing the relationship between the radius and the diameter of a circle helps in construction.

_____

_____

_____

Use with Lesson 9-9.   **109**

Congruent and Similar Figures

R 9-10

Congruent figures have the same size and the same shape. **Similar figures** have the same shape, but may not have the same size. You can use this information to find the measures of different angles and sides.

Congruent Figures

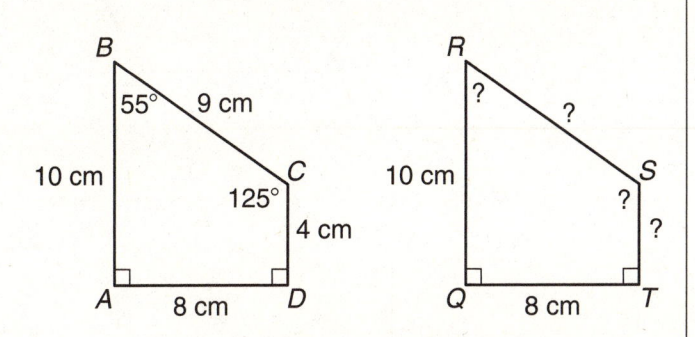

∠ABC ≅ ∠QRS, so ∠QRS = 55°
∠BCD ≅ ∠RST, so ∠RST = 125°
$\overline{BC} ≅ \overline{RS}$, so $\overline{RS}$ = 9 cm
$\overline{CD} ≅ \overline{ST}$, so $\overline{CD}$ = 4 cm

Similar Figures

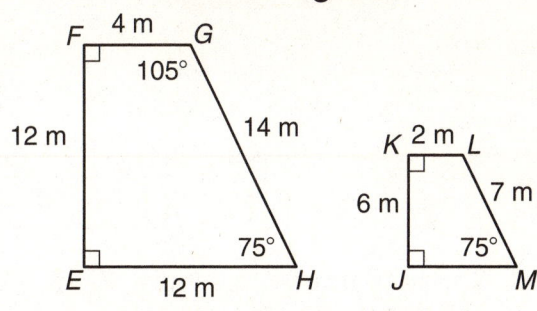

∠FGH ≅ ∠KLM, so ∠KLM = 105°
The corresponding sides are proportional.

$$\frac{\overline{GH}}{\overline{LM}} = \frac{\overline{EH}}{\overline{JM}} \quad \frac{14}{7} = \frac{12}{x}$$

$14x = 84$

$x = 6$

So, $\overline{JM} = 6$.

---

1. These rectangles are congruent. Find $\overline{MP}$ and $\overline{MN}$.

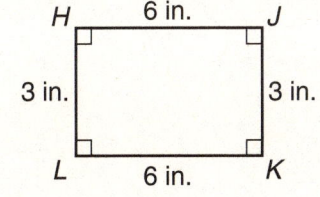

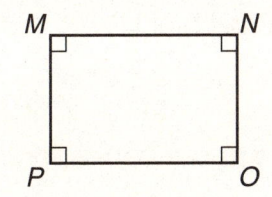

2. These triangles are congruent. Find $\overline{FD}$ and ∠FED.

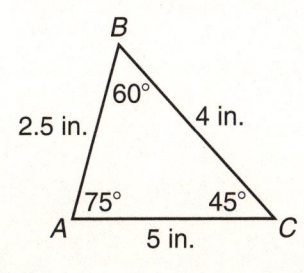

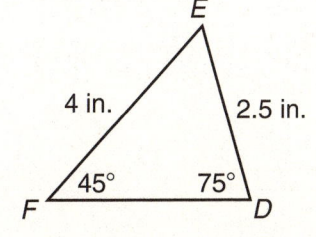

Congruent and Similar Figures

P 9-10

1. These parallelograms are congruent. Find BD, HF, and m∠D.

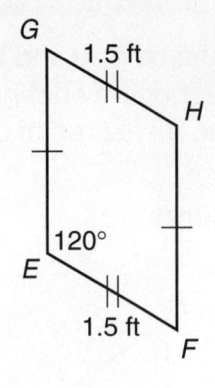

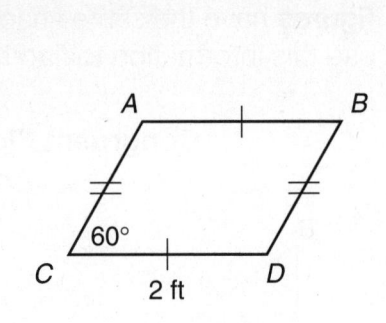

2. These triangles are similar. Find m∠F, DE, and EF.

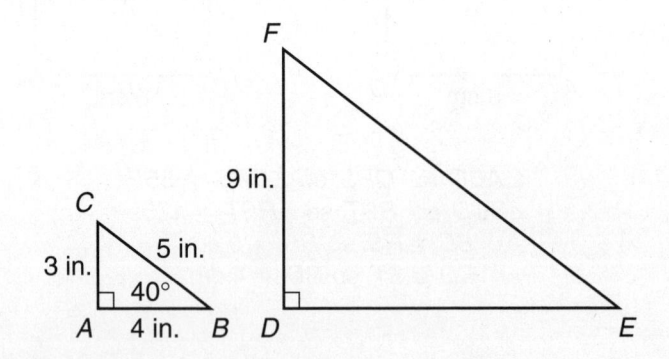

3. Two square building blocks are similar. The large block is 5 in. long. The small block is 3 in. long. How wide is the large block? the small block?

Test Prep

4. In congruent polygons, what is true about corresponding angles?

   A. They are congruent.
   B. They are similar.
   C. They are complementary.
   D. They are supplementary.

5. **Writing in Math** Draw and label two similar triangles. Explain why they are similar.

110 Use with Lesson 9-10.

Name _____

Transformations

R 9-11

Different transformations can be used to move a figure to a new position without changing its size or shape.

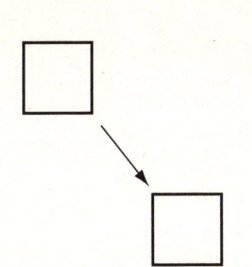

Slide or **translation** moves figure in a straight direction.

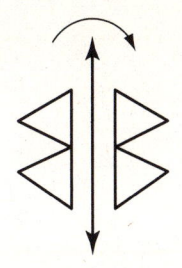

Flip or **reflection** gives a figure its mirror shape.

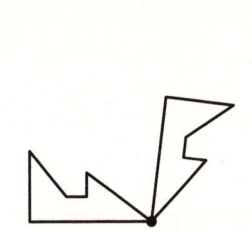

Turn or **rotation** moves a figure about a point.

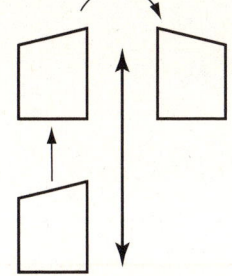

Glide reflection a slide followed by a flip.

Tell whether the figures in each pair are related by a slide, a flip, a glide reflection, or a turn. If it is a turn, describe it.

1.

2.

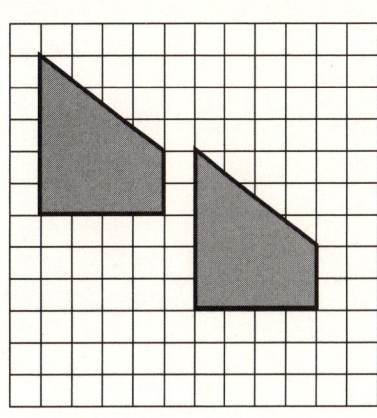

3.

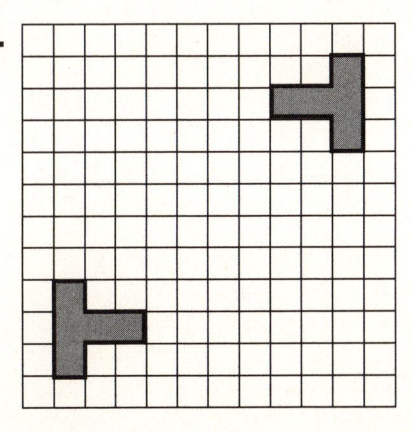

4.

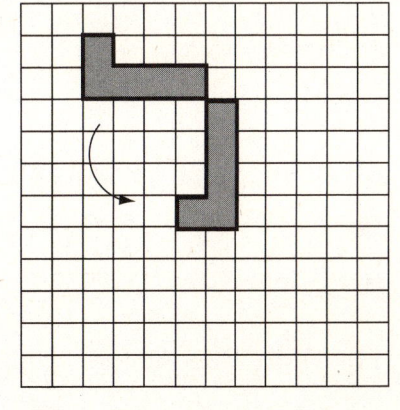

Use with Lesson 9-11. **111**

Name _____

Transformations

P 9-11

Tell whether the figures in each pair are related by a slide, a flip, a glide reflection, or a turn. If a turn, describe it.

1.

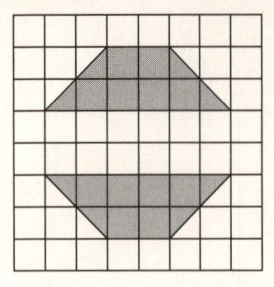

2.

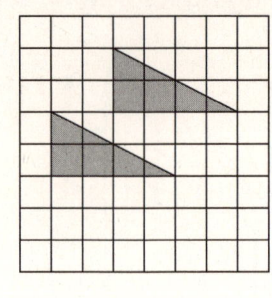

_____

_____

3.

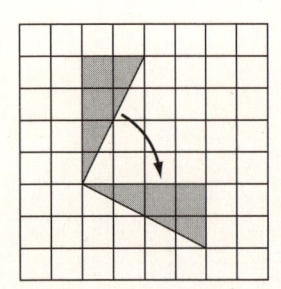

4.

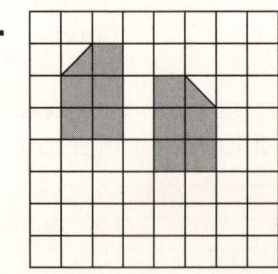

_____

_____

5. Use the grid. Draw a triangle to the left of the y-axis. Then show the triangle flipped over the y-axis.

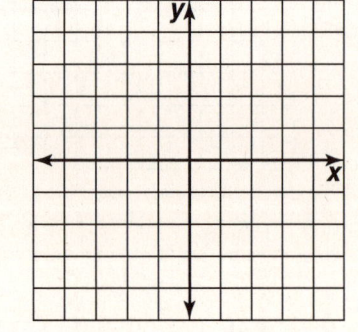

6. **Reasoning** Does a transformation ever change the shape of a figure? Does it ever change the size?

_____

Test Prep

7. Which type of transformation is shown?

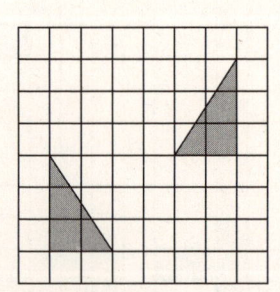

   A. Slide   B. Flip

   C. Glide reflection   D. Turn

8. **Writing in Math** Describe in words a glide reflection.

_____

Use with Lesson 9-11.   **111**

Name _____

PROBLEM-SOLVING SKILL
Writing to Compare

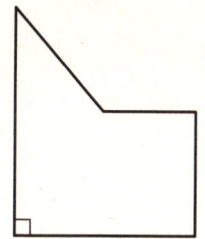

R 9-12

Figure A   Figure B

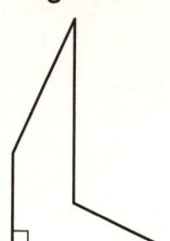

Comparing Write a statement about how the figures above are alike. Then write a statement about how they are different.

Tips for writing geometry comparisons:	**Comparison statements:**
• Compare properties such as length, angle measure, classification, and position. • Use geometry terms to write the statements.	Alike: • Figures A and B each have right angles. • Figures A and B are both pentagons. Different: • Figure A has more right angles than Figure B. • Figure A has a greater area than Figure B.

1. Sangita and Rajit each wrote a number pattern.

   Sangita's pattern is: 43, 53, 63, 73, . . .

   Rajit's pattern is: 30, 40, 50, 60, . . .

a. Write a statement about how the patterns are alike.

_____

_____

b. Write a statement about how the patterns are different.

_____

_____

_____

_____

Use with Lesson 9-12.

Name _____

PROBLEM-SOLVING SKILL   P 9-12
Writing to Compare

1. Compare the two shapes.

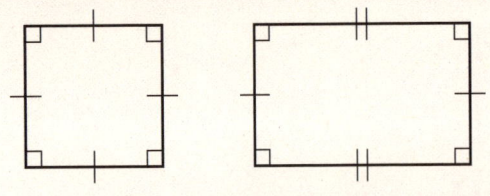

   a. Write two statements about how the shapes are alike.

   _____

   _____

   b. Write two statements about how the shapes are different.

   _____

   _____

2. Compare the two patterns.

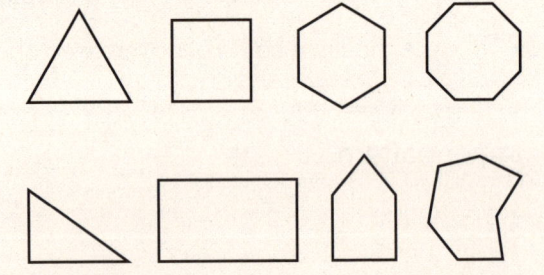

   a. Write a statement about how the patterns are alike.

   _____

   _____

   _____

   b. Write a statement about how the patterns are different.

   _____

   _____

   _____

Use with Lesson 9-12.

Name _____

Symmetry

R 9-13

A figure has **reflection symmetry** if it can be reflected onto itself. The line of reflection is called the **line of symmetry.** Some figures have more than one line of symmetry.

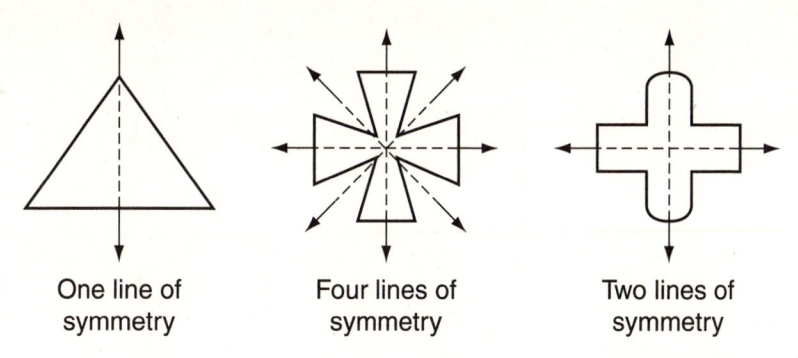

| One line of symmetry | Four lines of symmetry | Two lines of symmetry |

A figure has **rotational symmetry** when it rotates onto itself less than one full turn.

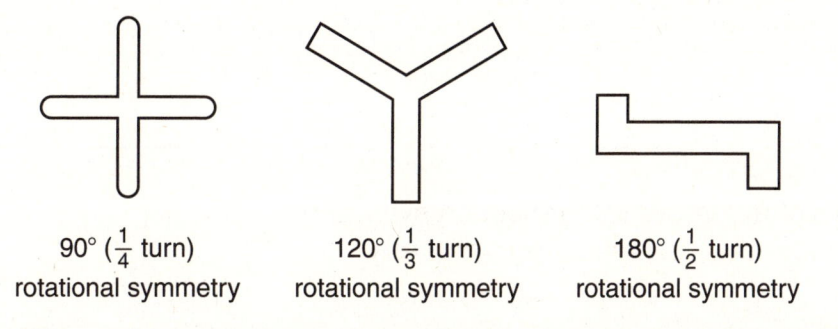

| 90° ($\frac{1}{4}$ turn) rotational symmetry | 120° ($\frac{1}{3}$ turn) rotational symmetry | 180° ($\frac{1}{2}$ turn) rotational symmetry |

Tell if each figure has reflection symmetry, rotational symmetry, or both. If it has reflection symmetry, how many lines of symmetry are there? If it has rotational symmetry, what is the smallest turn that will rotate the figure onto itself?

1. _____
    _____
    _____

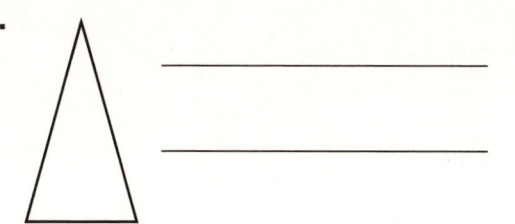

2. _____
    _____
    _____

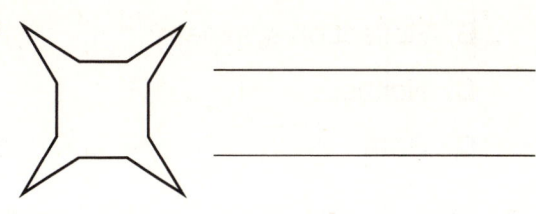

3. _____
    _____
    _____

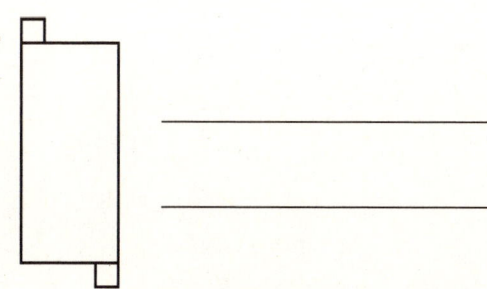

4. _____
    _____
    _____

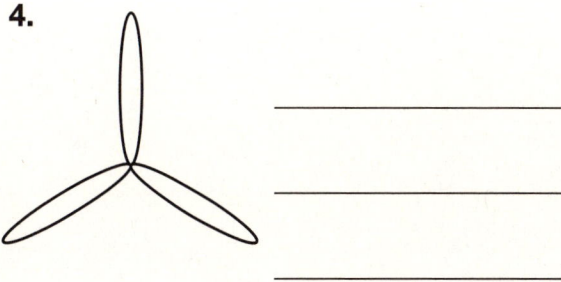

Use with Lesson 9-13. **113**

Name _____

Symmetry

P 9-13

Tell if each figure has reflection symmetry, rotational symmetry, or both. If it has reflection symmetry, how many lines of symmetry are there? If it has rotational symmetry, what is the smallest turn that will rotate the figure onto itself?

1. 
2. 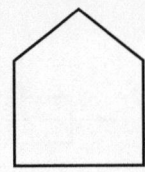
3.

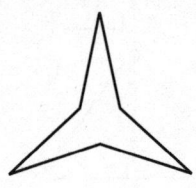

_____   _____   _____

4. **Reasoning** Describe the symmetry of an equilateral triangle.

_____

_____

5. 808 is an example of a number with reflection symmetry. Write another number that has reflection symmetry.

_____

Test Prep

6. Which does the figure have?

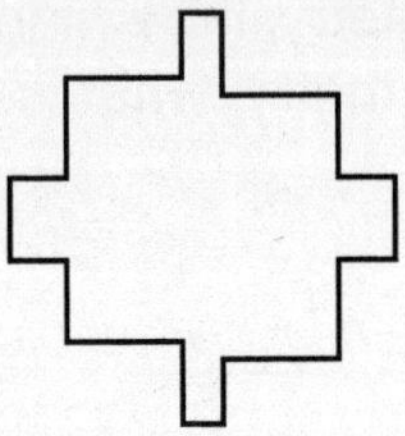

    A. Rotational symmetry
    B. Reflection symmetry
    C. Neither
    D. Both

7. **Writing in Math** Draw a figure with reflection symmetry, and draw the line of symmetry.

Use with Lesson 9-13. **113**

Name _____

Tessellations

R 9-14

A shape **tessellates** if you can place many of them on a plane without any gaps or overlaps.

This shape tessellates:

This shape does not tessellate:

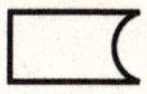

Here is the tessellation:

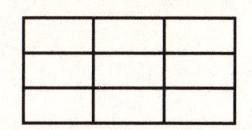

If you try to fill the plane with it, it looks like this:

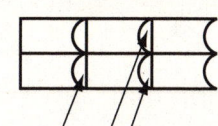

There are no gaps between shapes. None of the shapes overlap.

There are gaps.

How to draw a tessellation using a polygon:

Step 1: Draw the shape.

Step 2: Continue to draw the shape next to the other ones you have drawn. Make sure there are no gaps in between the shapes.

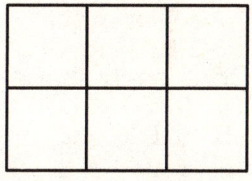

Draw a tessellation made up of the polygon.

1. parallelogram

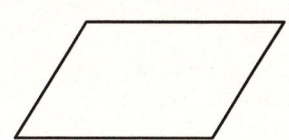

Does each shape tessellate? If so, draw the tessellation.

2. _____

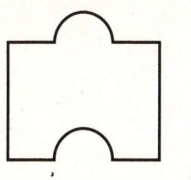

3. _____

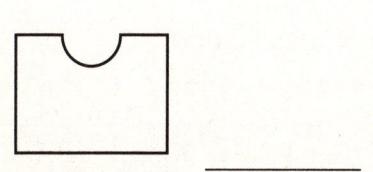

4. **Reasoning** Can an oval tessellate a plane? Explain.

114 Use with Lesson 9-14.

Name _____

Tessellations

P 9-14

Draw a tessellation made up of each polygon.

1. triangle
2. rectangle
3. square

4. **Reasoning** Show a tessellation that involves only slides.

Does each shape tessellate? If so, draw the tessellation.

5.

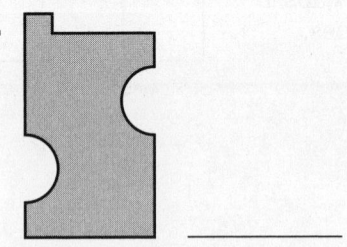

6.

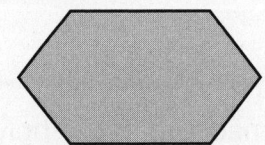

Test Prep

7. Which could NOT be used to tessellate a plane?

   A. Circle

   B. Square

   C. Parallelogram

   D. Right triangle

8. **Writing in Math** In your own words, give a definition of *tessellation*.

_____

_____

_____

114 Use with Lesson 9-14.

Name _____

PROBLEM-SOLVING APPLICATION

New Neighborhood

R 9-15

The city is building a new neighborhood on the outskirts of town. Lisa is helping plan the new neighborhood.

Davis Street intersects Miller Drive, as shown to the right.

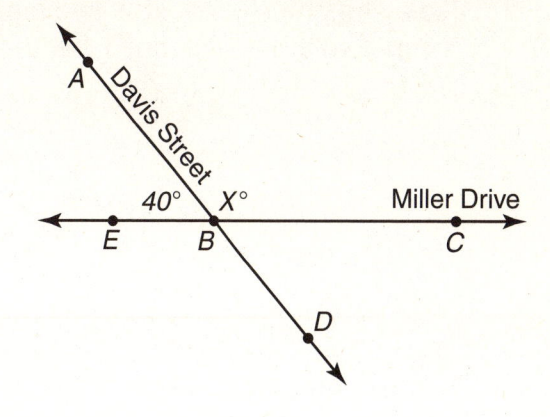

Lisa needs to know the measure of angle x. How can she find the measure?

m∠ABE = 40°, m∠EBC = 180°.
∠ABE and ∠ABC are supplementary.

That is, their measures add up to 180°.

    m∠ABE + m∠ABC = 180°

    40° + x = 180°

    x = 140°

    40° + x = 180°, so m∠ABC = 140°.

1. Lisa thinks a new school should be built on the corner. What is the measure of the angle that forms the corner?

   _____

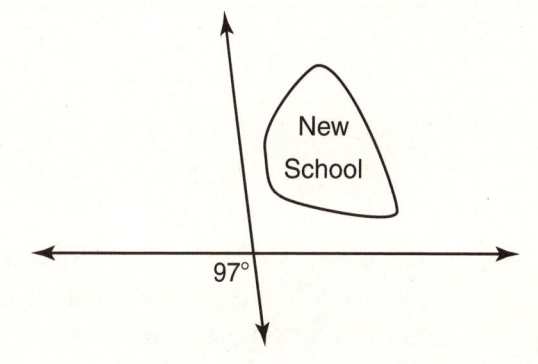

2. Lisa wants the floor of the new library to be a tessellation. Would the shape tessellate? How can you tell?

   _____
   _____
   _____
   _____

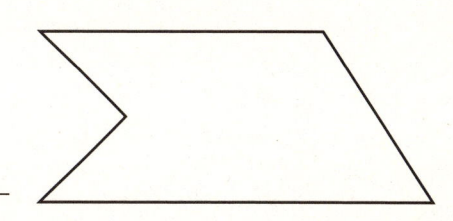

Use with Lesson 9-15. **115**

PROBLEM-SOLVING APPLICATION

P 9-15

Working Construction

1. Use a straightedge to draw two supplementary angles. Use the protractor to measure the angles and label the angles with their measurements.

2. Use a straightedge and a compass to draw two perpendicular lines. Label the lines *AB* and *CD*.

3. Draw a triangle with a 2 in. side between 50° and 40° angles. Label the sides and angles with measurements.

4. Show what your triangle in Exercise 3 would look like after a flip transformation. Label the sides and angles with measurements.

5. Draw a triangle similar, but not congruent, to the triangle in Exercise 3. Label the sides and angles with measurements.

Use with Lesson 9-15.

Name _____

Customary Measurement

R 10-1

Units of Length

foot (ft)	1 ft = 12 in.
yard (yd)	1 yd = 3 ft
	1 yd = 36 in.
mile (mi)	1 mi = 5,280 ft
	1 mi = 1,760 yd

Units of Capacity

cup (c)	1 c = 8 fluid ounces (oz)
pint (pt)	1 pt = 2 c
quart (qt)	1 qt = 2 pt
gallon (gal)	1 gal = 4 qt

How to change from one unit of measurement to another:

To change from larger units to smaller units in the customary system, you have to multiply.

120 yd = _____ ft

1 yd = 3 ft

120 × 3 ft = 360 ft

120 yd = 360 ft

To change from smaller units to larger ones, you have to divide.

256 oz = _____ c

1 c = 8 oz

256 ÷ 8 = 32

256 oz = 32 c

Complete.

1. 36 in. = _____ ft
2. 4 qt = _____ c
3. 5 lb = _____ oz
4. 39 ft = _____ yd
5. 1.5 mi = _____ ft
6. 3.5 gal = _____ qt
7. 2 T = _____ lb
8. 16 pt = _____ qt
9. 64 oz = _____ lb
10. 3 yd = _____ in.
11. 4 gal = _____ pt
12. 55 yd = _____ ft
13. 6.5 lb = _____ oz
14. 20 pt = _____ gal
15. 4.5 qt = _____ c
16. 205 yd = _____ ft

17. **Reasoning** A vendor at a festival sells soup for $1.25 per cup or $3.75 per quart. Which is the better buy?

116 Use with Lesson 10-1.

Customary Measurement

P 10-1

Complete.

1. 3.5 ft = _____ in.
2. 17 yd = _____ ft
3. 1.5 gal = _____ c
4. 4 mi = _____ ft
5. 160 fl oz = _____ qt
6. 72 in. = _____ ft
7. 3 mi = _____ yd
8. 12 pt = _____ qt
9. 180 ft = _____ yd
10. 2 gal = _____ fl oz

11. How many tons are in 35,000 lb? _____

12. **Number Sense** Brian pole vaulted over a bar that was 189 in. high. How many more inches would he need to vault to go over a bar that was 16 ft high?

A paving company was hired to make a 4 mi section of the highway. They need 700 T of concrete to complete the job.

13. How many yards of highway do they need to repave?

14. How many pounds of concrete will they need to repave the highway?

Test Prep

15. Gary's cat weighs 11 lb. How many ounces is that?

    A. 132   B. 144   C. 164   D. 176

16. **Writing in Math** The average car sold in the United States in 2001 could drive 24.5 mi on 1 gal of gas. Explain how to find the number of yards the car can travel on 1 gal of gas.

Name _____

Metric Measurement

R 10-2

Changing from one metric unit to another:

To change from a larger unit to a smaller unit, multiply by a power of ten.

　　3.8 L = _____ mL

A liter is a larger unit than a milliliter. To change from liters to milliliters, multiply.

　　1 L = 1,000 mL

　　3.8 × 1,000 = 3,800

　　3.8 L = 3,800 mL

To change from a smaller unit to a larger unit, divide by a power of ten.

　　100 m = _____ km

The meter is a smaller unit than the kilometer. To change from meters to kilometers, divide.

　　1,000 m = 1 km

　　100 ÷ 1000 = 0.1

　　100 m = 0.1 km

Name the most appropriate metric unit for each measurement.

1. mass of a cow　　　　**2.** length of a carrot　　　　**3.** capacity of a thimble

_____　　　　_____　　　　_____

Complete.

4. 45 g = _____ mg　　　　**5.** 3450 mL = _____ L

6. 4.5 m = _____ mm　　　　**7.** 1.68 L = _____ mL

8. 28 cm = _____ mm　　　　**9.** 7,658 g = _____ kg

10. 600 cm = _____ m　　　　**11.** 5,000 mg = _____ g

12. 5.1 km = _____ m　　　　**13.** 1.780 L = _____ mL

14. 0.780 L = _____ mL　　　　**15.** 4,300 m = _____ km

16. 9,000 cm = _____ m　　　　**17.** 8,000 mg = _____ g

18. Reasoning It is recommended that people have 1 g of calcium each day. How many milligrams of calcium is that?

Use with Lesson 10-2. **117**

Name _____

Metric Measurement

P 10-2

Name the most appropriate metric unit for each measurement.

1. mass of a paperclip _____

2. capacity of a water cooler _____

3. width of a sheet of paper _____

Complete.

4. 2.7 m = _____ cm

5. 1.6 kg = _____ g

6. 9 L = _____ mL

7. 14 m = _____ mm

8. 1.6 cm = _____ mm

9. 5,400 g = _____ kg

10. 1,840 mL = _____ L

11. 32 km = _____ m

12. **Number Sense** The chemist needs 2,220 mL of potassium chloride to complete an experiment. He has 2 L. Does he have enough to complete the experiment? Explain.

_____

13. A computer floppy disk has a mass of 20 g. How many would you need to have a total mass of 1 kg? _____

14. A battery is 5 cm long. How many batteries would you need to line up to get 3 m? _____

Test Prep

15. Which would you do to convert 25 cm to millimeters?

    A. Divide by 10   B. Divide by 100   C. Multiply by 10   D. Multiply by 100

16. **Writing in Math** A banana has a mass of 122 g. Explain how to find the mass of the banana in milligrams.

_____

_____

Use with Lesson 10-2. **117**

Name _____

Units of Measure and Precision

R 10-3

To the nearest inch, the key is 3 in. long.

To the nearest half inch, the key is 3 in. long.

To the nearest quarter inch, the key is $2\frac{3}{4}$ in. long.

To the nearest eighth inch, the key is $2\frac{7}{8}$ in. long.

To the nearest sixteenth inch, the key is $2\frac{14}{16}$ in. long.

To the nearest centimeter, the key is 7 cm long.

To the nearest millimeter, the key is 74 mm long.

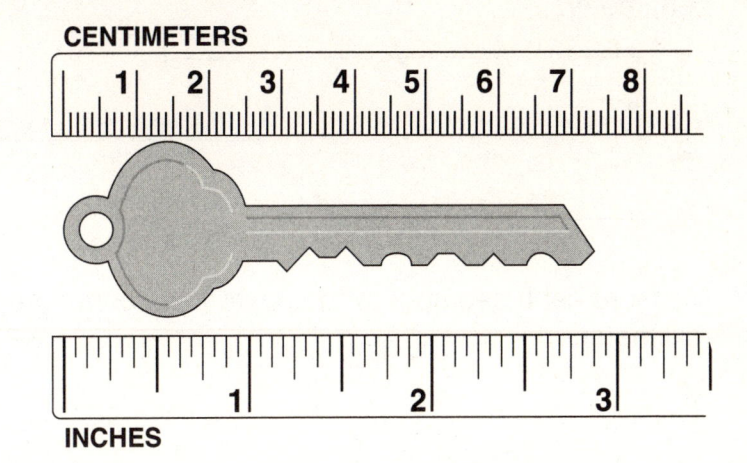

Measure each segment to the nearest eighth inch and nearest centimeter.

1. ⊢—————⊣   _____ , _____

2. ⊢———————⊣   _____ , _____

Measure each segment to the nearest sixteenth inch and nearest millimeter.

3. ⊢——————⊣   _____ , _____

4. ⊢———⊣   _____ , _____

5. **Reasoning** Three different students measured the length of the chalkboard in their classroom. The measurements were 19 ft, 6 yd, and 17 ft 6 in. Which of these measurements is the most precise?   _____

6. Marsha measured a twig. It was $2\frac{5}{8}$ in. long. How long was the twig to the nearest sixteenth inch?   _____

7. A pencil was $7\frac{2}{16}$ in. long. How long was the pencil to the nearest inch?   _____

118 Use with Lesson 10-3.

Name _____

Units of Measure and Precision

P 10-3

Measure each segment to the nearest eighth inch and the nearest centimeter.

1. ⊢──────────────────────⊣   _____

2. ⊢────────────────────────────────⊣   _____

3. ⊢──────────────⊣   _____

Measure each segment to the nearest sixteenth inch and the nearest millimeter.

4. ⊢──⊣   _____

5. ⊢──────────────────────────────────⊣   _____

6. Brian said that milliliters are 100 times more precise than a liter. Is he correct?   _____

7. Julie measured her playground and found that it is 38 m long. Express this length in kilometers and centimeters.

_____

8. A pitcher of fruit punch holds 1,200 mL. Express this capacity in liters.   _____

Test Prep

9. Ben said he was 5 ft 5 in. tall. Jerry said he was 5 ft $6\frac{3}{8}$ in. tall. Robin said he was 5 ft $4\frac{15}{16}$ in. tall. Whose measurement is the most precise?

   A. Ben   **B.** Jerry   **C.** Robin   **D.** Ben and Robin

10. **Writing in Math** The distance from Earth to the Moon is about 385,000 km. Is the kilometer a good unit to use for this measurement? Explain.

_____

_____

_____

Relating Customary and Metric Measurements

R 10-4

You can convert between customary and metric measures using the table below.

Customary and Metric Unit Equivalents

Length	Weight/Mass	Capacity
1 in. = 2.54 cm	1 oz ≈ 28.35 g	1 L = 1.06 qt
1 m ≈ 39.37 in.	1 kg ≈ 2.2 lb	1 gal = 3.79 L
1 mi ≈ 1.61 km	1 metric ton (t) = 1.102 T	

You multiply to convert a larger unit to a smaller unit. For example, multiply when converting from inches to centimeters.

You divide to convert a smaller unit to a larger unit. For example, divide when converting from kilograms to pounds.

4 in. = _____ cm

An inch is larger than a centimeter. To convert from inches to centimeters, multiply.

1 in. = 2.54 cm
4 × 2.54 = 10.16
4 in. = 10.16 cm

171.6 kg = _____ lb

A kilogram is a smaller unit than a pound. To convert from kilograms to pounds, divide.

1 kg ≈ 2.2 lb
171.6 ÷ 2.2 = 78
171.6 kg ≈ 78 lb

Complete. Round to the nearest tenth.

1. 12 gal ≈ _____ L
2. 35 lb ≈ _____ kg
3. 125 in. = _____ m
4. 70 mi ≈ _____ km
5. 34 in. = _____ cm
6. 20 kg ≈ _____ lb
7. 55 oz ≈ _____ g
8. 18 L ≈ _____ qt

9. **Reasoning** Which is a faster speed limit, 65 mi per hour or 100 km per hour?

Use with Lesson 10-4. **119**

Name _____

Relating Customary and Metric Measurements

P 10-4

Complete. Round to the nearest tenth.

1. 100 cm ≈ _____ in.
2. 16.5 gal ≈ _____ L
3. 24.8 kg ≈ _____ lb
4. 375 yd ≈ _____ m
5. 11.5 ft ≈ _____ cm
6. 24 oz ≈ _____ mL

7. **Estimation** Use 1 t ≈ 1.1 T to estimate the number of tons in 10 t. _____

8. **Connections** If a recipe calls for 4 c of milk, and you have 1 L of milk, would it be enough? _____

Convert each. Round to the nearest tenth.

9. The number of feet in the 200 m race _____

10. The number of miles in the 5,000 m race _____

11. The number of miles in the 20 km race _____

12. The phrase *800 lb gorilla* means you are facing a tough task. How might you change this phrase to express it in metric terms?

_____

_____

Test Prep

13. Sarah had 12 oz of milk in her glass. She drank 5 oz. How many mL does she have left?

    A. 2.1   B. 21.1   C. 210   D. 2,100

14. **Writing in Math** Billy wants to ride the roller coaster. A sign says he must be 138 cm tall. Explain how Billy can convert the measurement to feet and inches.

_____

_____

_____

Use with Lesson 10-4.

Elapsed Time

You can use subtraction to find the elapsed time for events, if you know the starting and ending times. You can use addition to find the end time if you know the start time and the elapsed time.

A baseball game started at 7:35 P.M. and lasted 2 hours 48 minutes. When did the baseball game end?

   7 hr 35 min
+ 2 hr 48 min
---
   9 hr 83 min

Rename 83 min as 1 hr 23 min.

So, 9 hr 83 min = 10 hr 23 min.

The game ended at 10:23 P.M.

Mark's class started at 6:30 P.M. and ended at 9:45 P.M. For how long did the class last?

Count the whole hours: 6:30 to 9:30 is 3 hr.

Count the minutes from 9:30 to 9:45.

00:30 to 00:45 is 15 min.

Add the hours and the minutes.

3 hr 15 min

So, the class lasted for 3 hr 15 min.

Find each elapsed time.

1. 6:44 P.M. to 11:07 P.M.

2. 10:28 A.M. to 2:15 P.M.

3. 7:40 P.M. to 1:35 A.M.

4. 5:09 A.M. to 9:05 A.M.

Find each starting time or ending time using the given elapsed time.

5. End Time: 5:22 P.M.
   Elapsed Time: 3 hr 38 min

6. Start Time: 4:45 A.M.
   Elapsed Time: 8 hr 30 min

7. End Time: 1:08 A.M.
   Elapsed Time: 5 hr 10 min

Add or subtract.

8.   2 hr 22 min 50 sec
   + 1 hr 40 min 12 sec

9.   4 hr 32 min 31 sec
   − 2 hr 35 min 40 sec

10.   6 hr 14 min
    − 5 hr 58 min 5 sec

11. **Reasoning** Rename one hour as 59 min _____ sec.

Name _____

Elapsed Time

P 10-5

Find each elapsed time.

1. 8:16 A.M. to 12:35 P.M.   _____

2. 4:22 A.M. to 10:51 A.M.   _____

3. 9:47 P.M. to 2:36 A.M.   _____

Find each starting time or ending time using the given elapsed time.

4. Start time: 11:54 A.M.
   Elapsed time: 6 hr 7 min   _____

5. End time: 5:12 P.M.
   Elapsed time: 3 hr 16 min   _____

6. End time: 4:44 A.M.
   Elapsed time: 1 hr 11 min   _____

Add or subtract.

7.   3 hr 17 min 47 sec
   − 2 hr 18 min 52 sec

8.   4 hr 9 min 31 sec
   + 2 hr 54 min 19 sec

9.   11 hr 22 min 4 sec
   − 5 hr 27 min 11 sec

10. **Number Sense** Nora wants to record a telethon that starts at 6:30 P.M. Her tape has 3 hr 32 min of recording time left. What time will she run out of tape?   _____

Test Prep

11. Bob ran a marathon in 3 hr 52 min. He completed the marathon at 4:42 P.M. At what time did he begin the marathon?

   A. 1:50 P.M.   **B.** 12:50 P.M.   **C.** 12:52 P.M.   **D.** 12:50 A.M.

12. **Writing in Math** Explain how to find the ending time of a movie that begins at 7:05 P.M. and lasts 1 hr and 57 min.

_____
_____
_____
_____

PROBLEM-SOLVING STRATEGY
Use Logical Reasoning

R 10-6

Driving Sherry leaves her home at 10:40 A.M. and drives 50 mi per hour. How far will she have traveled by 3:10 P.M.?

Read and Understand

Step 1: What do you know?

Sherry leaves at 10:40 A.M. and drives until 3:10 P.M. She drives 50 mi per hour.

Step 2: What are you trying to find?

The distance Sherry will have traveled by 3:10 P.M.

Plan and Solve

Step 3: What strategy will you use?

Strategy: Use logical reasoning

First find the elapsed time for Sherry's drive. The elapsed time from 10:40 A.M. until 3:10 P.M. is 4 hr 30 min, or 4.5 hr.

For each hour that Sherry drives, she travels 50 mi.

Multiply Sherry's time and speed to find the distance she travels.

$4.5 \times 50 = 225$

Sherry could drive 225 mi in the given time.

Look Back and Check

Step 4: Is your answer reasonable?

Yes. 11:00 A.M. to 3:00 P.M. = about 4 hr. 50 + 50 + 50 + 50 = 200 mi. The answer of 225 mi is reasonable.

---

1. Amanda leaves her home at 10:00 A.M. and needs to get to a meeting 90 mi away by 11:30 A.M. How fast must Amanda travel?

Use with Lesson 10-6. **121**

Name _____

PROBLEM-SOLVING STRATEGY   P 10-6
Use Logical Reasoning

A method of keeping time around the world is called Universal Time, Coordinated, or UTC. The table below shows how UTC relates to the U.S. time zones. The time 8:00 A.M. is written as 0800 hours in UTC. To convert 3:00 P.M. to UTC, add 3 to 12 to get 15. Write 1500 hours.

1. Seattle, Washington, is in the Pacific time zone. What is the UTC time when it is midnight in Seattle?

   _____

Time Zone (standard)	Hours Behind UTC
Hawaii	10
Alaska	9
Pacific	8
Mountain	7
Central	6
Eastern	5

2. Every day, Steve gets on the subway at 5:12 P.M. to go home. Steve lives in New York City, which is in the Eastern time zone. What is the UTC time when Steve gets on the subway?

   _____

3. Harriet lives in Chicago, Illinois, in the Central time zone. She takes a plane from Chicago at 11:21 A.M. and lands in Denver, which is in the Mountain time zone, at 12:55 P.M. What is the UTC time when Harriet lands? _____

4. The chess club is holding 3 tournaments. The finalists in Tournament 1 are Kyle and Gina. The finalists for Tournament 2 are Beth and David. The finalists for Tournament 3 are Joel and Nancy. List all the possible combinations of players that could win the tournaments.

   _____

   _____

5. Simion, Yvonne, Peter, and Gail each have a different pet. The pets are a fish, a parrot, a cat, and a lizard. Simion is allergic to fur. Gail's pet has feathers. Peter's pet lives in an aquarium. List each person with his or her pet.

   _____

   _____

Use with Lesson 10-6.

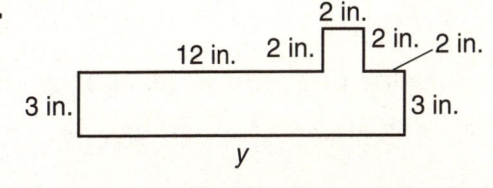

Perimeter

R 10-7

Find the perimeter of the figure below.

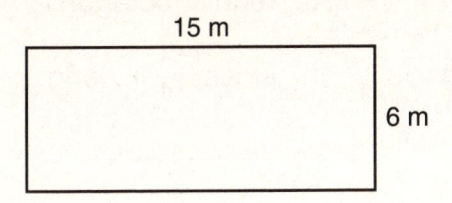

[Rectangle: 15 m by 6 m]

By using a formula:

There are two equal lengths and equal widths, so you can use the formula

$P = 2l + 2w.$

$P = 2(6) + 2(15)$

$= 12 + 30$

$= 42$

The perimeter is 42 m.

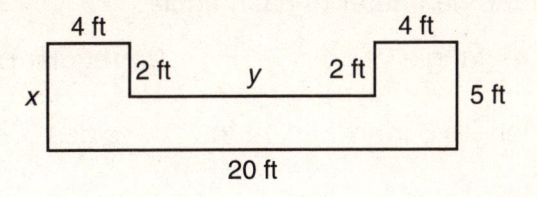

[Figure with sides: 4 ft, 2 ft, y, 2 ft, 4 ft on top; x on left; 5 ft on right; 20 ft on bottom]

Sometimes you are not given the lengths of all the sides of a polygon.

Side x is the same size as the side parallel to it. So, side x = 5 ft.

You can figure out the length of side y by looking at the side parallel to it. That side is 20 ft.

$4 \text{ ft} + 4 \text{ ft} + y \text{ ft} = 20 \text{ ft}$

$8 \text{ ft} + y \text{ ft} = 20 \text{ ft}$

$8 \text{ ft} + 12 \text{ ft} = 20 \text{ ft}$

So, y = 12 ft.

Now you can add up all the sides to find the perimeter.

$4 + 2 + 12 + 2 + 4 + 5 + 20 + 5 = 54$

$P = 54 \text{ ft}$

Find the perimeter of each figure.

1. rectangle, length 5.1 ft, width 7.4 ft

2. regular octagon, sides 4.6 cm long

Find the length of each unknown side. Then find the perimeter.

3. [L-shaped figure with sides: 5 m (top), x, 10 m, 4 m (right), 15 m (bottom), 7 m (left)]

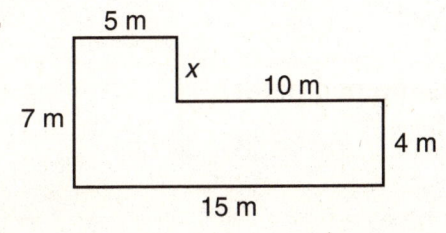

4. [Figure with sides: 12 in., 2 in., 2 in., 2 in., 2 in., 3 in. (right), y (bottom), 3 in. (left)]

122 Use with Lesson 10-7.

Perimeter

P 10-7

Find the perimeter of each figure.

1. rectangle

   length 6 in., width 14 in.

2. regular pentagon

   sides 3.3 cm long

3. regular octagon

   sides $8\frac{3}{4}$ in. long

Estimate the perimeter of each figure. Then find the perimeter.

4. 11.97 m, 8.21 m

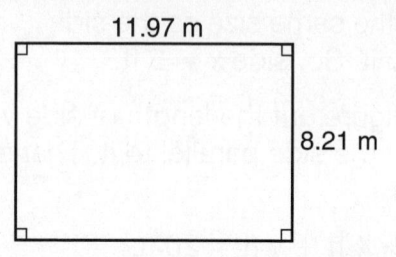

5. 21.46 cm, 16.03 cm, 15.41 cm, 18.9 cm

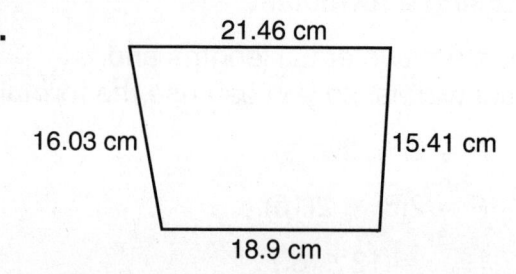

Find the length of each unknown side. Then find the perimeter.

6. y, 18 mm, 15 mm, 4 mm, z, 39 mm

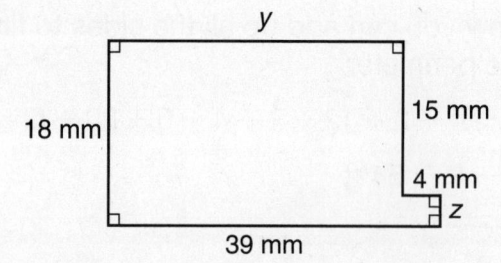

7. 12 ft, j, 14 ft, 9 ft, 6 ft, k

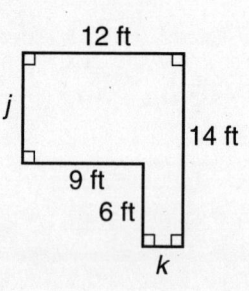

Test Prep

8. One side of a regular hexagon is 18 cm. Which is the perimeter?

   A. 108 cm   **B.** 96 cm   **C.** 72 cm   **D.** 36 cm

9. **Writing in Math** A square and a rectangle each have a perimeter of 100 ft. Explain how this is possible.

Use with Lesson 10-7.

Name _____

Area of Squares and Rectangles

R 10-8

You can use formulas to find the area of a square or rectangle.

Find the area of a square that is 7.2 m on each side.

Use the formula $A = s^2$.

$A = (7.2)^2$

$A = 51.84$

The area is 51.84 m².

Find the area of a rectangle with a length (*l*) of 4 cm and a width (*w*) of 12 cm.

Use the formula $A = l \times w$.

$A = 4 \times 12$

$A = 48$

The area is 48 cm².

Find the area of each figure.

1. 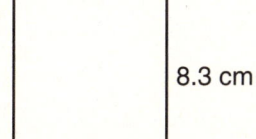 8.3 cm

2. 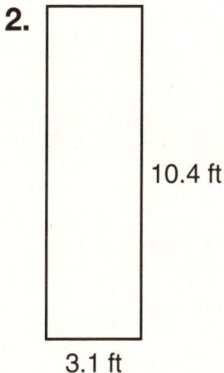 10.4 ft, 3.1 ft

3. 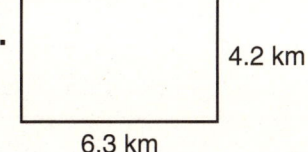 4.2 km, 6.3 km

4. 8.8 ft

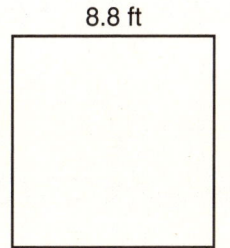

5. **Reasoning** What is the length of a rectangle that has an area of 120 ft² and a width of 8 ft? _____

6. **Number Sense** What is the area of a square that is 12.4 cm on each side? _____

Use with Lesson 10-8.

Name _____

Area of Squares and Rectangles

P 10-8

Find the area of each figure.

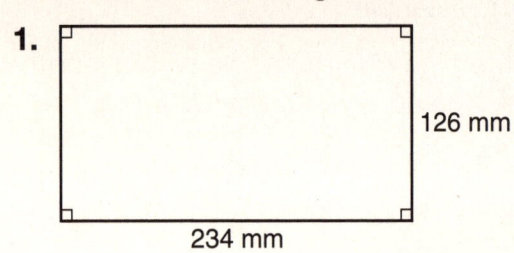

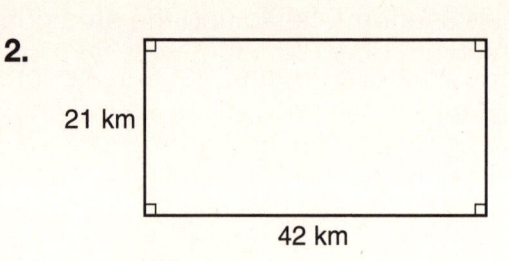

1.
126 mm
234 mm

_____

2.
21 km
42 km

_____

The rules state that the length of a soccer field must be no greater than 130 yd and no less than 100 yd. The width cannot be greater than 100 yd nor less than 50 yd.

3. According to the rules, what is the maximum area of a soccer field? _____

4. According to the rules, what is the minimum area of a soccer field? _____

A professional football field is shown.

5. What is the area of the whole field?

_____

6. What is the area of each end zone?

_____

Diagram: End zones 10 yd each, field width $53\frac{1}{3}$ yd, total length 120 yd.

7. What is the area of the field, not including the end zones? _____

Test Prep

8. Which is the area of a square with sides of 11.1 km?

   A. 124 km^2 **B.** 123.7 km^2 **C.** 123.21 km^2 **D.** 122.52 km^2

9. **Writing in Math** If you know the perimeter of a rectangle but not the length of its sides, can you calculate its area? Explain.

_____

Use with Lesson 10-8.

Relating Area and Perimeter

R 10-9

A rectangle's perimeter is 16 cm. Find the dimensions of the rectangle with the greatest area.

Strategy: Draw different rectangles that have a perimeter of 16 cm. Find the one that has the greatest area.

6 cm / 2 cm
A = 12 cm²

7 cm / 1 cm
A = 7 cm²

4 cm / 4 cm
A = 16 cm²

l = 4, w = 4

A rectangle's area is 24 cm². Find the dimensions of the rectangle with the shortest perimeter.

Strategy: Draw different rectangles that have an area of 24 cm². Find the one that has the shortest perimeter.

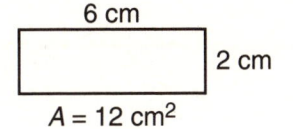

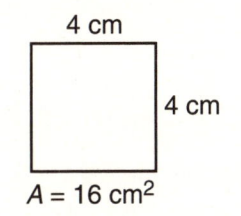

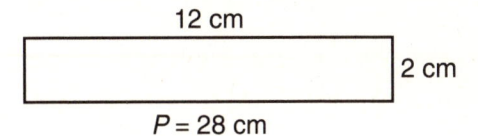

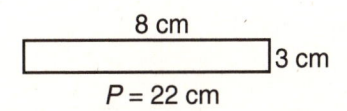

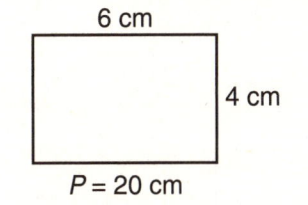

12 cm / 2 cm
P = 28 cm

8 cm / 3 cm
P = 22 cm

6 cm / 4 cm
P = 20 cm

l = 6, w = 4

Using whole units and the perimeter given, find the dimensions of the rectangle with the greatest area.

1. P = 30 _____ ; _____
2. P = 60 _____ ; _____
3. P = 20 _____ ; _____
4. P = 150 _____ ; _____

Using whole units and the area given, find the dimensions of the rectangle with the shortest perimeter.

5. A = 36 _____ ; _____
6. A = 45 _____ ; _____
7. A = 60 _____ ; _____
8. A = 160 _____ ; _____

9. **Number Sense** The side of a square measures 12 in. What is the area in square inches? _____

Use with Lesson 10-9.

Name _____

Relating Area and Perimeter

P 10-9

Using whole units and the perimeter given, find the dimensions of the rectangle with the greatest area.

1. P = 24 _____
2. P = 28 _____
3. P = 26 _____
4. P = 42 _____

Using whole units and the area given, find the dimensions of the rectangle with the shortest perimeter.

5. A = 75 _____
6. A = 56 _____
7. A = 81 _____
8. A = 132 _____

The illustration shows 4 rugs. Rug A costs $513. Rug B costs $360. Rug C costs $72. Rug D costs $51.

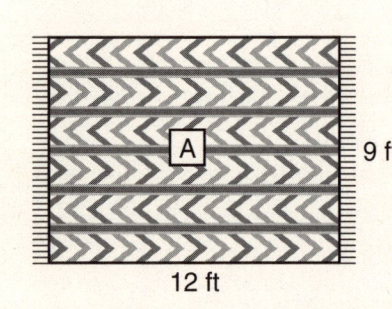

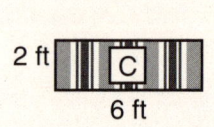

Rug A: 12 ft × 9 ft
Rug B: 8 ft × 10 ft
Rug C: 6 ft × 2 ft
Rug D: 3 ft × 5 ft

9. What is the cost per square foot of Rug A? _____

10. What is the cost per square foot of Rug B? _____

11. How much more expensive per square foot is Rug C than Rug D? _____

Test Prep

12. Which is the greatest possible area of a rectangle with a perimeter of 38 ft?

    A. 90 ft^2
    B. 81 ft^2
    C. 72 ft^2
    D. 66 ft^2

13. **Writing in Math** The blocks in a neighborhood are the same rectangular size. Explain how to find the greatest area of blocks if you rode your bike around a perimeter of 44 blocks.

_____

_____

_____

124 Use with Lesson 10-9.

Area of Parallelograms and Triangles

R 10-10

Finding the area of a parallelogram:

Find the area of the parallelogram below.

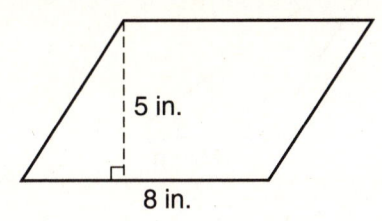

5 in.
8 in.

Use the formula $A = bh$.

$A = 8 \times 5$

$A = 40$ in^2

The area of the parallelogram is 40 in^2.

Finding the area of a triangle:

Find the area of the triangle below.

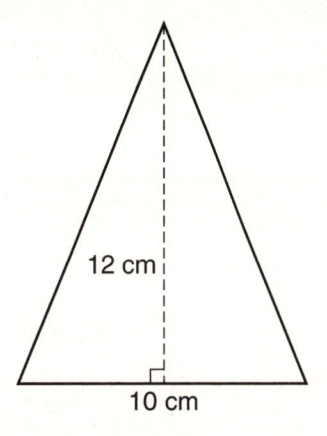

12 cm
10 cm

Use the formula $A = \frac{1}{2}bh$.

$A = \frac{1}{2} \times 10 \times 12$

$A = 5 \times 12$

$A = 60$

The area of the triangle = 60 cm^2.

Find the area of each parallelogram or triangle.

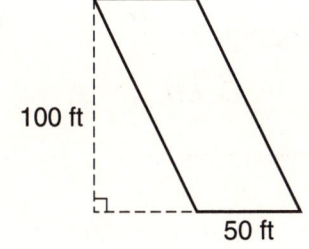

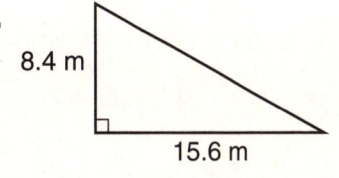

1. 100 ft
    50 ft

2. 8.4 m
    15.6 m

3. triangle: $b = 3$ ft, $h = 9$ ft

4. parallelogram: $b = 18$ m, $h = 13$ m

5. triangle: $b = 7$ ft, $h = 7$ ft

6. **Number Sense** A parallelogram has a base of 9 in. and a height 14 in. What is its area?

Use with Lesson 10-10.

Name _____

Area of Parallelograms and Triangles

P 10-10

Find the area of each parallelogram or triangle.

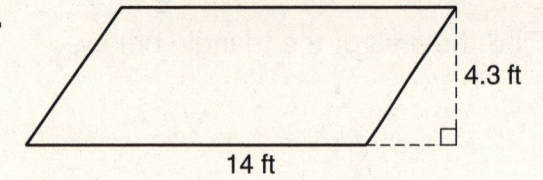

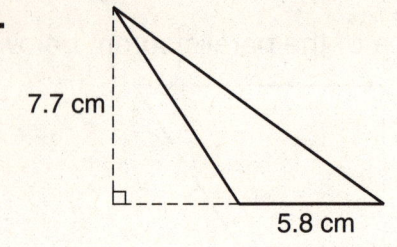

1. [parallelogram: base 14 ft, height 4.3 ft]

2. [triangle: height 7.7 cm, base 5.8 cm]

_____   _____

3. triangle

   b: 18 in.

   h: $2\frac{1}{4}$ in.

4. triangle

   b: 11.2 yd

   h: 4 yd

5. parallelogram

   b: $7\frac{1}{4}$ ft

   h: $5\frac{1}{2}$ ft

_____   _____   _____

6. **Number Sense** A parallelogram has a base of 4 m and a height of 3 m. Find the area of the parallelogram in square centimeters.

_____

Test Prep

7. Which shows the correct formula for finding the area of a triangle?

   A. $bh = (\frac{1}{2})A$ **B.** $(\frac{1}{2})h = A$ **C.** $2bh = A$ **D.** $bh(\frac{1}{2}) = A$

8. **Writing in Math** Tony says that he does not have enough information to find the area of the parallelogram to the right. Is he correct? Explain.

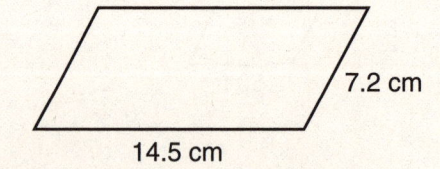

   [parallelogram: side 14.5 cm, side 7.2 cm]

_____
_____
_____

Use with Lesson 10-10.   **125**

Circumference

R 10-11

Finding the circumference of a circle:

Find the circumference.

Diameter = 8 m

Since you know the diameter, use the formula $C = \pi d$.

$C = \pi d$
$C = 3.14 \times 8$
$ = 25.12$ m

So, the circumference is 25.12 m.

Find the circumference.

Radius = 12 m

Since you know the radius, use the formula $C = 2\pi r$.

$C = 2\pi r$
$C = 2 \times \pi \times 12$
$ = 2 \times 3.14 \times 12$
$ = 6.28 \times 12$
$ = 75.36$

So, the circumference is 75.36 m.

Finding the diameter or radius of a circle:

Find the diameter.

Circumference = 65.94 m

Use the formula $C = \pi d$.

$65.94 = \pi d$
$65.94 = 3.14 d$
$\frac{65.94}{3.14} = \frac{3.14}{3.14} d$
$21 = d$

So, the diameter is 21 m.

Find the radius.

Circumference = 40.82 ft

Use the formula $C = 2\pi r$.

$40.82 = 2 \times \pi \times r$
$40.82 = 2 \times 3.14 \times r$
$40.82 = 6.28\, r$
$\frac{40.82}{6.28} = \frac{6.28}{6.28} r$
$6.5 = r$

So, the radius is 6.5 ft.

Find each circumference. Use $\frac{22}{7}$ or 3.14 for π.

1. 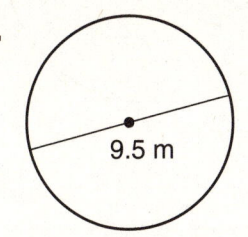 9.5 m

2. 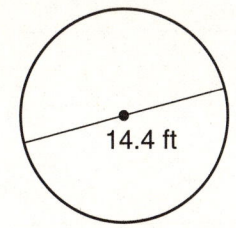 14.4 ft

3. 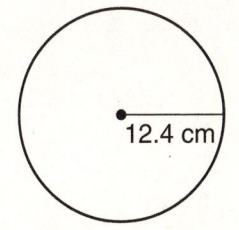 12.4 cm

_____   _____   _____

Find the missing measurements for each circle. Round to the nearest hundredth.

4. $C = 39.25$ ft,

    $d =$ _____

5. $C = 63.3024$ m,

    $r =$ _____

6. $r = 5.95$ yd,

    $C =$ _____

126 Use with Lesson 10-11.

Name _____

Circumference

P 10-11

Find each circumference. Use 3.14 or $\frac{22}{7}$ for π.

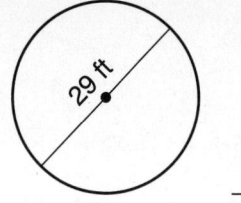

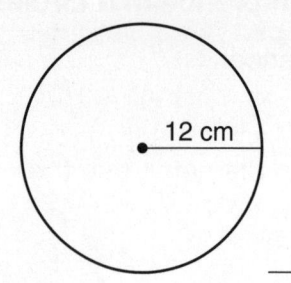

1. (circle with 29 ft diameter)   _____

2. (circle with 12 cm radius)   _____

Find the missing measurement for each circle. Round to the nearest hundredth.

3. C = 60.288 cm, d = _____

4. C = 11.304 m, r = _____

5. **Estimation** CDs have a diameter of about 5 in. Estimate the circumference of a CD.

_____

Test Prep

6. Angela baked an apple pie that had a radius of 6 in. She wants to cut the pie into eight equal slices. How wide at the outer end will each piece of pie be?

   A. 5.2 in.   **B.** 4.7 in.   **C.** 4.4 in.   **D.** 4.2 in.

7. **Writing in Math** Based on the diagram, is it correct to say that the smaller circle has one half the circumference of the larger? Why?

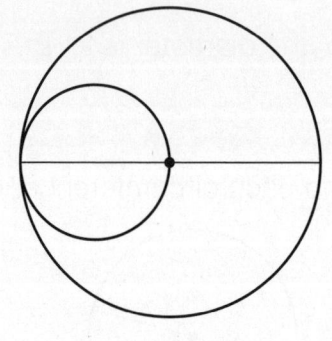

126 Use with Lesson 10-11.

Name _____

Area of a Circle

R 10-12

A circular bucket has a radius of 6 in. Find the area of the bottom of the bucket. The formula for finding the area of a circle is $A = \pi r^2$.

One Way

Use 3.14 for π.

$A = \pi r^2$

$\approx 3.14 \times 6^2$

$\approx 3.14 \times 36$

≈ 113.04 in^2

Another Way

Use $\frac{22}{7}$ for π.

$A = \pi r^2$

$\approx \frac{22}{7} \times 6^2$

$\approx \frac{22}{7} \times 36$

$\approx \frac{22}{7} \times \frac{36}{1}$

$\approx \frac{792}{7}$

≈ 113.14 in^2

With a Calculator

Press: [π] [×] [6] [x²] [=]

Display: 113.09734

The bucket's area is about 113 in^2.

Find the area of each circle to the nearest whole number. Use 3.14 or $\frac{22}{7}$.

1. 16 cm _____

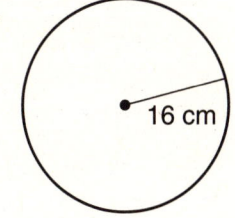

2. 18.4 m _____

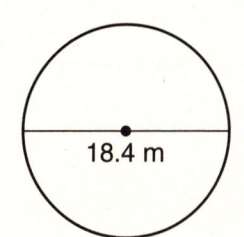

3. $5\frac{1}{4}$ in. _____

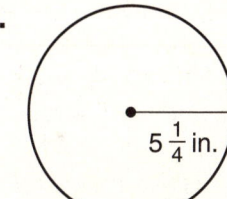

4. $r = 9$ yd _____

5. $d = 20$ m _____

6. $r = 14$ cm _____

7. $d = 2.4$ ft _____

8. $r = 22$ cm _____

9. $d = 8.8$ m _____

10. $d = 32$ cm _____

11. $r = 5.3$ m _____

12. **Reasoning** If the circumference of a circle is 18π, what is the area of the circle? _____

Use with Lesson 10-12.   **127**

Name _____

Area of a Circle

P 10-12

Find the area of each circle to the nearest whole number.
Use 3.14 or $\frac{22}{7}$.

1. $18\frac{1}{2}$ in. (radius)

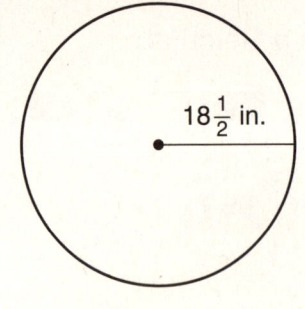

2. 2.4 km (diameter)

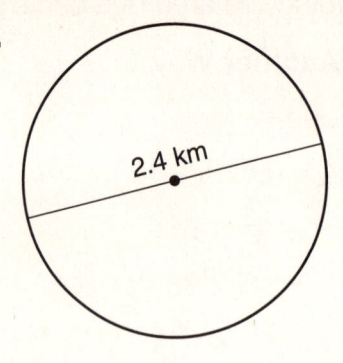

3. 23.7 cm (radius)

_____   _____   _____

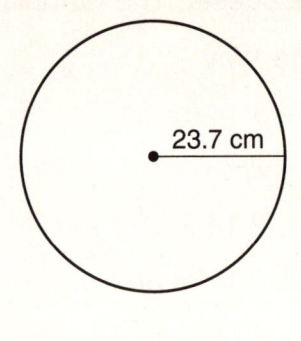

4. $d = 14$ in.   5. $r = 11.25$ cm   6. $d = 2$ mi

_____   _____   _____

Brian's dad wants to put a circular pool in their backyard. He can choose between pools with diameters of 15 ft, 17 ft, or 22 ft. Round to the nearest square foot.

7. How many more square feet would the 17 ft pool use than the 15 ft pool? _____

8. How many more square feet would the 22 ft pool use than the 17 ft pool? _____

Test Prep

9. On a water ride at the amusement park, a rotating valve sprays water for 15 ft in all directions. What is the area of the circular wet patch it creates?

   A. 30 ft²   **B.** 31.4 ft²   **C.** 94.2 ft²   **D.** 706.5 ft²

10. **Writing in Math** Explain how to find the radius of a circle with an area of 50.24 mi.

_____

_____

_____

Use with Lesson 10-12.   **127**

Name _____

PROBLEM-SOLVING SKILL
Extra or Missing Information

R 10-13

Tiles Marlena is going to tile her kitchen floor with square tiles that are 1 ft on each side. Marlena's kitchen is 13 ft long, 10 ft wide, and 8 ft tall. How many tiles will Marlena need to cover her floor?

Read and Understand

Step 1: What do you know?

The tiles are 1 ft by 1 ft. The kitchen is 13 ft by 10 ft by 8 ft.

Step 2: What are you trying to find?

The number of tiles needed to cover the kitchen floor

Plan and Solve

Step 3: Is there enough information?

There is enough information to solve the problem.

The kitchen floor is 13 ft by 10 ft, so the area is 130 ft^2.

Since each tile is 1 ft by 1 ft, each tile will cover an area of 1 ft^2. Marlena will need 130 tiles to cover the kitchen floor.

Look Back and Check

Step 4: Is the answer reasonable?

Yes. The tiles each cover 1 ft^2, so 130 tiles are needed to cover the 130 ft^2 area of the kitchen floor.

Decide if the problem has extra or missing information. Solve if you have enough information.

1. One rectangle has a perimeter of 24 cm. A second rectangle has a perimeter of 26. Which rectangle has the larger area?

   _____

2. One square has an area of 36 m^2. Another square has an area of 25 m^2. Which square has the larger perimeter?

   _____

   _____

128 Use with Lesson 10-13.

Name _____

PROBLEM-SOLVING SKILL P 10-13

Extra or Missing Information

Decide if each problem has extra or missing information. Solve if you have enough information.

The table shows an estimate of the world's population in various years.

World Population	Year
600,000,000	1700
900,000,000	1800
1,500,000,000	1900
6,000,000,000	2000

1. As a percentage, about how many more people were there in the year 2000 than in the year 1600?

_____

_____

2. The world's population will increase in the future. During which 100-year period did the world's population increase the most?

_____

3. Wendi is making a wooden box to store her trading cards. She has about 1,000 trading cards. The box will have 4 compartments. The base will be 10 in. wide. What is the area of the base?

_____

_____

4. The circumference of the front wheel on Mike's bike is 50.24 in. Mike's bike is red and has a new seat. What is the area of the front wheel of the bike?

_____

5. Kylie works in a bakery. There are rectangular and circular baking pans. Of the circular baking pans, there are three sizes: large, medium, and small. The diameter of the small baking pan is 8 in. and the diameter of the medium baking pan is 10 in. What is the circumference of the large baking pan?

_____

Use with Lesson 10-13.

Name _____

Solid Figures

R 10-14

There are a variety of different solid figures.

Triangular prism 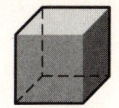 Cube 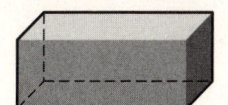 Rectangular prism

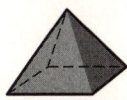

Rectangular pyramid  Triangular pyramid  Hexagonal pyramid

Cylinder  Cone  Sphere

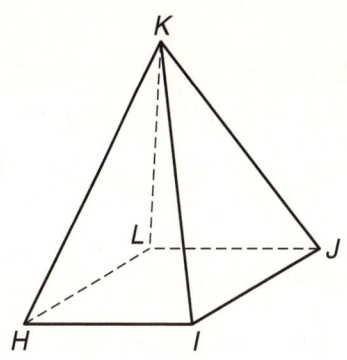

The polyhedron above is a square pyramid. The vertices are H, I, J, K, and L. The edges are HI, IJ, JL, LH, HK, IK, JK, and LK. The faces are HIJL, HIK, IJK, JLK, and HLK.

Classify the polyhedron. Name all vertices, edges, and faces.

1.

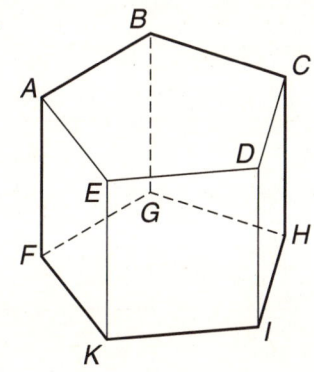

_____

_____

_____

_____

_____

Use with Lesson 10-14. **129**

Name _____

Solid Figures

P 10-14

Classify the polyhedron. Name all vertices, edges, and faces.

1. _____
_____
_____
_____

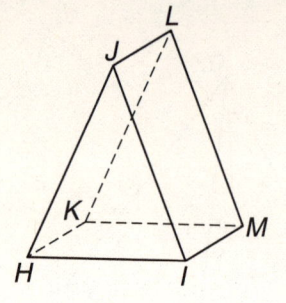

Identify the solid represented by each net.

2. _____

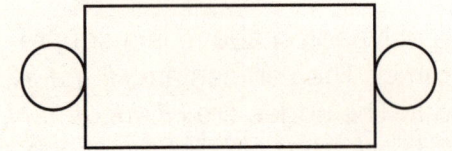

3. _____

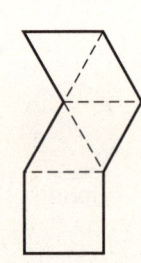

4. Which solid figure is a round cake? _____

5. How many total faces are on 6 number cubes? _____

6. Factories often buy the boxes they need in the form of flat nets. Can you think of what advantage this might have?

_____
_____

Test Prep

7. Which is the name of this polyhedron?

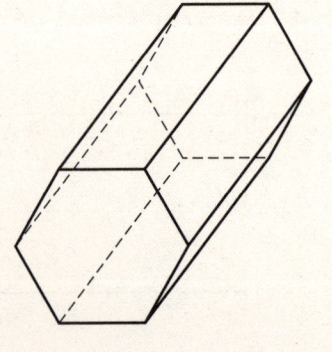

   A. Rectangular prism
   B. Hexagonal prism
   C. Pentagonal pyramid
   D. Octagonal pyramid

8. **Writing in Math** Describe the similarities of a pentagonal pyramid and a pentagonal prism.

_____
_____

Use with Lesson 10-14. 129

Name _____

Surface Area

R 10-15

You can use formulas to find the surface area of different solid figures.

Rectangular prism

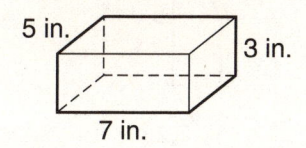

5 in., 3 in., 7 in.

$SA = 2lw + 2lh + 2wh$
$= 2(5 \times 7) + 2(5 \times 3) + 2(7 \times 3)$
$= 70 + 30 + 42$
$= 142$

The surface area is 142 in².

Triangular prism

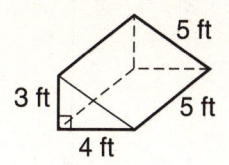

5 ft, 3 ft, 5 ft, 4 ft

$SA = 2(\frac{1}{2} \times 4 \times 3) + (3 \times 5) + (4 \times 5) + (5 \times 5)$
$= 12 + 15 + 20 + 25$
$= 72$

The surface area is 72 ft².

Find the surface area of each solid.

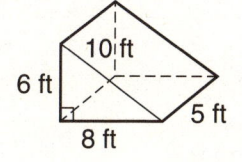

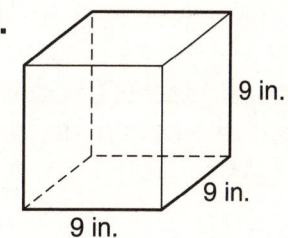

1. (triangular prism: 10 ft, 6 ft, 8 ft, 5 ft)

2. (cube: 9 in., 9 in., 9 in.)

_____   _____

Find the surface area of each rectangular prism.

3. $l = 5.5$ cm, $w = 4.5$ cm, $h = 3.5$ cm   _____

4. $l = 15$ in., $w = 9$ in., $h = 3.8$ in.   _____

5. $l = 2$ yd, $w = 6$ yd, $h = 1.7$ yd   _____

6. **Reasoning** Write the dimensions of two different rectangular prisms that have the same surface area.

_____

_____

_____

130 Use with Lesson 10-15.

Name _____

Surface Area

P 10-15

Find the surface area of each solid.

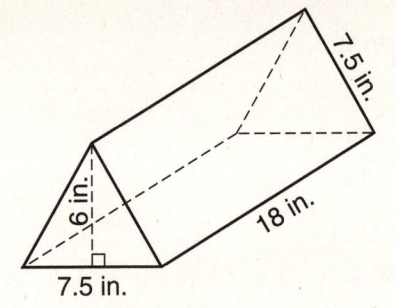

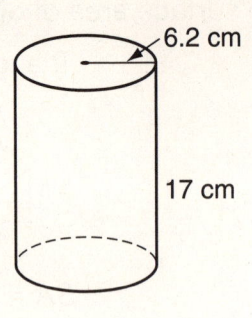

1. [triangular prism: 7.5 in., 6 in., 7.5 in. base; 18 in. length]

2. [cylinder: radius 6.2 cm, height 17 cm]

3. [rectangular prism: 5.8 m, 3.7 m, 2.2 m]

_____   _____   _____

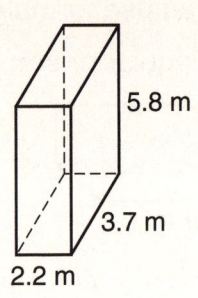

Find the surface area of each rectangular prism.

4. l = 6.9 mm, w = 8.2 mm, h = 14 mm   _____

5. l = 3.4 cm, w = 12.7 cm, h = 16.5 cm   _____

6. l = 5.7 yd, w = 9 yd, h = 12.9 yd   _____

7. **Reasoning** Margaret wants to cover a footrest in the shape of a rectangular prism with cotton fabric. The footrest is 18 in. × 12 in. × 10 in. She has 1 yd² of fabric. Can she completely cover the footrest?

_____

_____

_____

Test Prep

8. Which is the surface area of a rectangular prism with a length of 2.3 in., a width of 1.1 in., and a height of 3 in.?

   A. 26.48 in²   **B.** 25.46 in²   **C.** 24.58 in²   **D.** 21.5 in²

9. **Writing in Math** A square pyramid has 2 m sides on the base. Each face is a triangle with a base of 2 m and a height of 1.5 m. Explain how to find the surface area.

_____

_____

_____

130 Use with Lesson 10-15.

Name _____

Volume

R 10-16

Cylinder

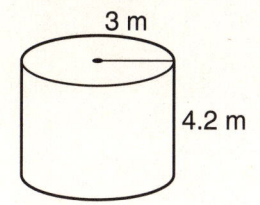

3 m
4.2 m

Step 1: Find the area of the base.

$B = \pi r^2$

$B \approx 3.14 \times 3^2$

$B \approx 28.26$

Step 2: Use the volume formula.

$V = B \times h$

$\approx 28.26 \times 4.2$

≈ 118.7

The volume is about 118.7 m³.

Triangular prism

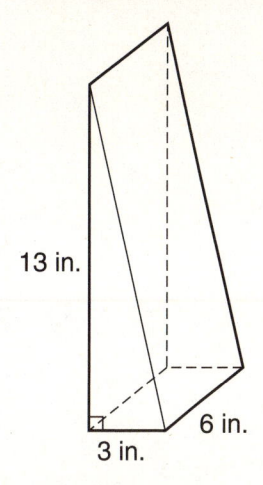

13 in.
6 in.
3 in.

$V = B \times h$

$= (\frac{1}{2} \times 3 \times 13) \times 6$

$= 19.5 \times 6$

$= 117$

The volume is 117 in³.

Find the volume of each solid.

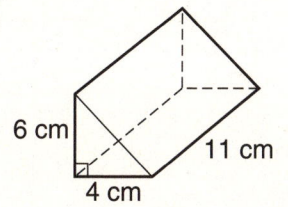

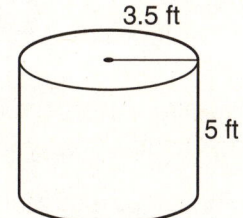

1. 6 cm, 11 cm, 4 cm

2. 3.5 ft, 5 ft

3. hexagonal prism, $B = 16.3$ m², $h = 3$ m _____

4. cube, $s = 4$ ft _____

5. **Reasoning** If a cube with $s = 5$ in. is placed inside a rectangular box with $l = 8$ in., $w = 6$ in., and $h = 9$ in., how much space is left over inside the box? _____

Use with Lesson 10-16.   **131**

Name _____

Volume

P 10-16

Find each volume. Round to the nearest tenth.

1. [cylinder: 15 cm height, 6 cm radius]

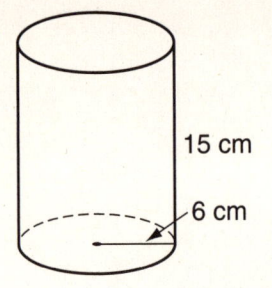

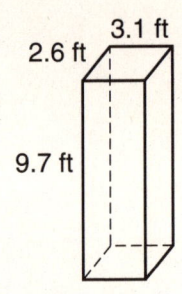

2. [rectangular prism: 3.1 ft, 2.6 ft, 9.7 ft]

_____   _____

3. [triangular prism: 22.5 mm, 44.4 mm, 38.8 mm]

_____

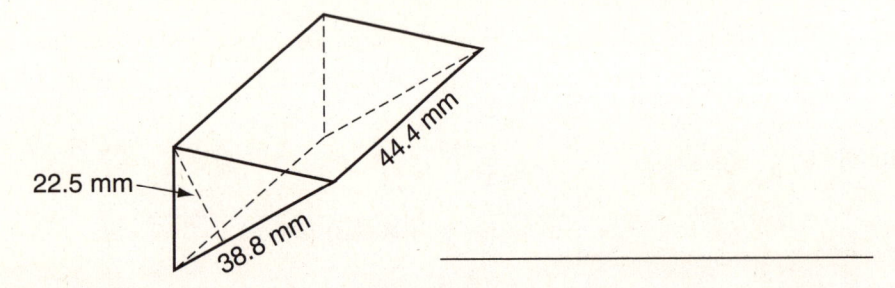

4. octagonal prism: $B = 77.9$ cm^2, $h = 127$ cm   _____

5. triangular prism: $B = 2.4$ mm^2, $h = 11.1$ mm   _____

6. cylinder: $B = 17.2$ yd^2, $h = 44$ yd   _____

7. **Number Sense** Suppose a box has a volume of 1 yd^3. What is its volume in cubic feet?   _____

A Frenchman named Nicolas Appert is credited with inventing a way to store food in cans to prevent spoiling. Today, many kinds of food are stored in cans.

8. What is the capacity in cubic centimeters of a can with a base with a radius of 2.8 cm and a height of 12 cm?   _____

Test Prep

9. A cylinder has a volume of 200.96 cm^3. Which are the cylinder's dimensions?

   A. $r = 4$ cm, $h = 2$ cm   **B.** $r = 2$ cm, $h = 4$ cm

   C. $r = 4$ cm, $h = 4$ cm   **D.** $r = 2$ cm, $h = 2$ cm

10. **Writing in Math** Two measurements are required to determine the volume of a cylinder or prism. Name them and provide the equation for determining volume.

_____

Use with Lesson 10-16. **131**

Name _____

PROBLEM-SOLVING APPLICATION   R 10-17
The Candle Company

The Martin Candle Company makes different-shaped candles. What is the volume of their special Sports Candle?

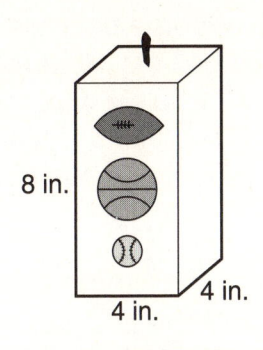

$V = Bh$

$ = (4 \times 4) \times 8$

$ = 16 \times 8$

$ = 128$

So, the volume of the Sports Candle is 128 in³.

---

1. Meghan bought a rectangular-prism-shaped candle for her dining room table. What is the volume of the candle?

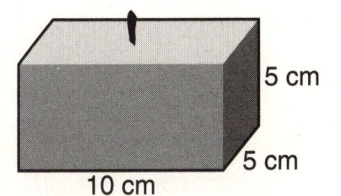

   _____

2. The candle company buys string to use as wicks. What is the length of the wick to the nearest centimeter? To the nearest millimeter?

   _____

3. Ramon runs one of the machines that makes candles. It takes 6 hr 13 min to make a batch of Tea Light Candles. If Ramon starts making the candles at 8:25 A.M., at what time will the batch of candles be finished?

   _____

4. As the company grew, it moved into a larger factory. What is the perimeter of the new factory?

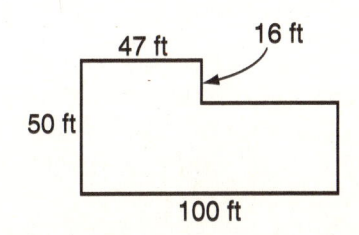

   _____

© Pearson Education, Inc. 6

132 Use with Lesson 10-17.

Name _____

PROBLEM-SOLVING APPLICATION P 10-17

Bus Route

Solve each problem. Write the answer in a complete sentence.

1. George boarded a bus in Milwaukee, Wisconsin, on Monday at 3:47 P.M. He arrived in Nashville, Tennessee, Monday night at 11:52 P.M. George got on a bus in Nashville and arrived in New Orleans, Louisiana, on Tuesday at 11:11 A.M. How long did George's bus trip from Milwaukee to New Orleans take?

_____

2. At the bus depot in New Orleans, the crew works to maintain the buses. Necia, Carl, Lois, and Jay are assigned to Bus No. 156. Four jobs need to be completed: inspect the engine, wash the bus, vacuum the interior, and change a tire. Follow the clues to find which job each crew member did.

   • Necia did not work inside the bus.
   • Carl took the old tire to the recycling center when he finished.
   • Jay used a water hose to finish his job.

_____

_____

_____

3. A parking lot where passengers board the buses is shown. Find the perimeter and the area of the parking lot.

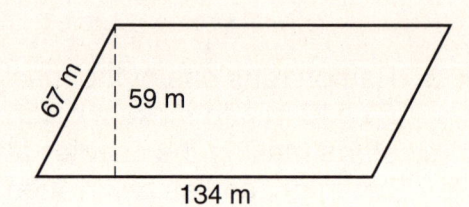

   (parallelogram: 67 m side, 59 m height, 134 m base)

_____

_____

4. The dimensions of the luggage compartment on a bus are shown. What is the volume of the luggage compartment?

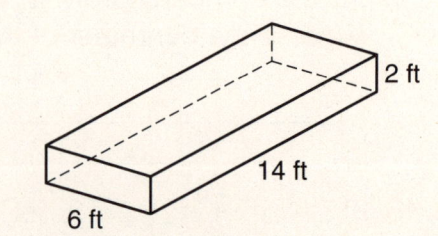

   (rectangular prism: 6 ft × 14 ft × 2 ft)

_____

_____

132 Use with Lesson 10-17.

Name _____

Samples and Surveys

R 11-1

Data about an **entire population** is often collected and analyzed. For example, all of the students in a school may be asked to answer questions about their favorite subjects. It would be possible to ask every student a question.

Sometimes only a part of the population is studied. This is called a **sample**. When it would be too difficult to study every member of the population, a sample is used. For example: Studying whether every single box of cereal in a state has raisins.

In Exercises 1–3, identify the population studied. Then tell whether you think the statistics are drawn from a sample or from the entire population. Explain your thinking.

1. Steve figured out that 34% of the loaves of bread sold in the United States are wheat bread.

   _____
   _____
   _____

2. Ms. Davis calculated that the average age of the students in her class was 8 years, 3 months.

   _____
   _____
   _____

3. The Rocking Horse Company stated that 65% of its employees arrive at work before 8:00 A.M. each morning.

   _____
   _____
   _____

4. Zachary poured 4 oz of cereal mix out of the box. He found that 1 oz was bran cereal. About what percent of the cereal mix in the box is bran cereal?

   _____

Use with Lesson 11-1.

Name _____

Samples and Surveys

P 11-1

In Exercises 1 and 2, identify the population studied. Then tell whether you think the statistics are drawn from a sample or from the entire population. Explain your thinking.

1. In a large city in Sweden, 77% of adults had fair hair.

   _____

   _____

   _____

2. Out of all the members of a string quartet, 50% had day jobs.

   _____

   _____

   _____

3. Buster has a collection of 1,400 marbles. Out of 100, 17 of the marbles are clear. About what percent of the 1,400 marbles are clear? _____

4. A juice maker reports that 0.23% of the cartons produced have part of the package torn. How many cartons can the juice maker sell if 240,000 cartons are produced?

   _____

Test Prep

5. A survey of 700 retired individuals in a city revealed that 342 had grandchildren. Out of 34,000 retired citizens in the city, how many probably had grandchildren?

   A. 12,452   B. 14,843   C. 16,612   D. 17,212

6. **Writing in Math** Explain how a person taking a survey to find the percent of sports fans who chose baseball as their favorite sport might get a biased sample.

   _____

   _____

Use with Lesson 11-1.   **133**

Name _____

Mean, Median, Mode, and Range

R 11-2

The chart below shows Yuri's scores on his first 8 math tests.

Test	1	2	3	4	5	6	7	8
Points	85	72	94	85	95	94	85	76

Find the range, mean, median, and mode of Yuri's scores.

How to find the range:

Subtract the minimum number in the set from the maximum number in the set.

95 − 72 = 23

The range is 23.

How to find the mean:

Add up all of the numbers. Then divide the sum by the number of values.

85 + 72 + 94 + 85 + 95 + 94 + 85 + 76 = 686

686 ÷ 8 = 85.75
The mean is 85.75.

How to find the median:

Arrange the numbers in order. Find the number exactly in the middle. If there are two numbers in the middle, find the mean of those middle numbers.

72 76 85 **85 85** 94 94 95

There are two middle numbers, 85 and 85.

85 + 85 = 170. 170 ÷ 2 = 85

The median is 85.

How to find the mode:

Choose the number that occurs most often. Sometimes there is no mode, and sometimes there is more than one mode.

72 76 **85 85 85** 94 94 95

85 is the number that occurs most often, so the mode is 85.

Find the mean, median, mode, and range of each data set. Round decimal answers to the nearest hundredth.

1. 8, 4, 3, 9, 7, 4, 3, 3, 7 _____

2. 25, 26, 24, 21, 25, 21, 23, 21, 26, 21, 20 _____

3. $2, $4, $5, $10, $1, $3, $4, $10, $10 _____

4. 0.2, 0.3, 0.9, 0.8, 0.9, 0.8, 0.4, 0.9 _____

5. The two middle numbers in a set are 56 and 78. What is the median? _____

Name _____

Mean, Median, Mode, and Range   P 11-2

Find the mean, median, mode, and range of each data set. Round the decimal answers to the nearest hundredth.

1. 4, 6, 4, 5, 2, 3, 6, 7, 4 _____

2. 0.6, 0.9, 0.5, 0.3, 0.6, 0.4 _____

3. 32 mL, 42 mL, 88 mL, 35 mL, 40 mL, 73 mL, 88 mL, 17 mL

   _____

4. If you told someone that the greatest depth in Lake Superior was 1,333 ft, would you be expressing a number similar to mode, median, mean, or range?

The chart shows the number of keys on several different kinds of musical instruments with keyboards.

5. To the nearest whole number, find the mean in the number of keys listed for each instrument.

Instrument	Keys
Average spinet piano	88
Hammond organ	122
Clavichord	60
Harpsichord	48
Average grand piano	88

6. For this data set, which is greater, the median or the mode?

Test Prep

7. The mean of a batting average of a baseball player for 5 years was 0.281. Four of his batting averages were 0.301, 0.299, 0.287, and 0.243. What was the fifth average?

   A. 0.303   B. 0.286   C. 0.277   D. 0.275

8. **Writing in Math** Sheila said that in any data set, the median and the mean are usually very similar in value. Is she correct? Explain.

Name _____

Frequency Tables and Line Plots

R 11-3

Officer Harris recorded the speeds of drivers on Elk Road. Here are the speeds he recorded:

55 mph, 32 mph, 46 mph, 61 mph, 57 mph, 43 mph, 41 mph, 38 mph, 52 mph, 59 mph, 34 mph, and 47 mph.

He represented this data in a frequency table.

Speed	Tally	Frequency
30–39 mph	III	3
40–49 mph	IIII	4
50–59 mph	IIII	4
60–69 mph	I	1

Note that Officer Harris first made groups, or intervals. Then he made a tally mark for each data value and wrote how many tally marks there were for each group.

He then represented this data in a line plot.

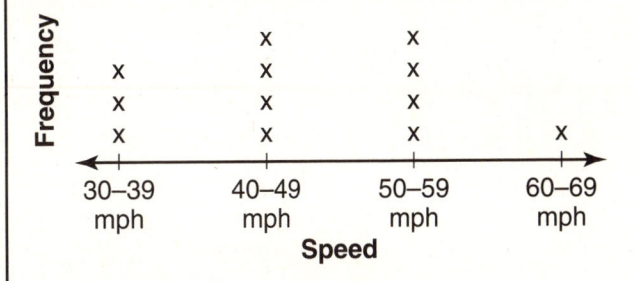

```
Frequency
              x         x
    x         x         x
    x         x         x
    x         x         x         x
  30–39     40–49     50–59     60–69
   mph       mph       mph       mph
              Speed
```

Most scores cluster in the 40s and 50s. There are no gaps in the data. The speed of 61 is different from the rest of the data, so it is an outlier.

Here are the lowest temperatures recorded in Mel's town, in °F:
18, 43, 36, 39, 47, 35, 33, 32, 34, 37.

1. Complete the frequency table and line plot in order to represent this data.

Temperature (in °F)	Tally	Frequency
10–19		
30–39		
40–49 mph		3

Frequency

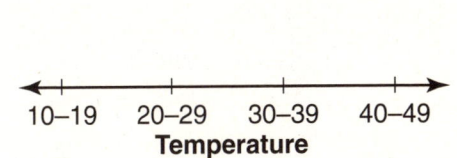

10–19   20–29   30–39   40–49
          Temperature

2. Identify any clusters, gaps, and outliers.

_____

3. Number Sense What is the mean of the data above? _____

Use with Lesson 11-3. **135**

Frequency Tables and Line Plots

P 11-3

1. Use the data set to complete the line plot.

Weights in Pounds of Boxes

168	174	198	202	188
214	201	207	212	222
194	171	218	205	224

Weights of Boxes

Frequency

160–169, 170–179, 180–189, 190–199, 200–209, 210–219, 220–229

Pounds

The chart to the right shows the heights of U.S. mountains.

U.S. Mountain Heights in Meters

6,194	4,418	1,605	2,665	3,979	4,350
5,037	4,351	1,917	3,812	4,350	3,602

2. Use the data set to complete the frequency table.

U.S. Mountains

Height	Frequency

Test Prep

3. Which of the following statements relating to line plots and frequency tables is not correct?

   A. The tallest column of Xs in a line plot indicates the mean of the data set.

   B. An outlier in a data set is usually preceded, or followed, by a gap.

   C. A line plot can be used to determine the mean, median, mode, and range of a data set.

   D. An interval is a variable data range used to differentiate data sets.

4. **Writing in Math** Explain the relationship between gaps and outliers.

Use with Lesson 11-3. **135**

Name _____

Stem-and-Leaf Plots

R 11-4

The data file shows how many minutes the students in Mr. Anchor's class have read so far this week.

Data File

Minutes Read by Students in Mr. Anchor's Class:

35, 23, 27, 31, 26, 24, 19, 41

Here is how to represent the data in a stem-and-leaf plot:

Step 1 Write a title.

Step 2 Draw two columns and label them *Stem* and *Leaf*.

Step 3 Write the tens digit from the data in order from least to greatest in the *Stem* column.

Step 4 Next to each tens digit, in the *Leaf* column, write the ones digit for each data value from least to greatest.

Minutes

Stem	Leaf
1	9
2	3 4 6 7
3	1 5
4	1

1. Complete the stem-and-leaf plot to represent the data below.

Green Family Height (in inches)		
49	48	54
57	53	72
68	62	64

Green Family Heights

Stem	Leaf

2. Find the median, mode, and range of the data.

_____

3. **Reasoning** If you remove the greatest height, will the range increase or decrease? Explain.

_____

_____

_____

136 Use with Lesson 11-4.

Stem-and-Leaf Plots

P 11-4

The chart at the right shows how far the girls in Shelly's Girl Scout troop could throw a softball.

Softball Throw Distance (Ft)

44	40	48	35	38	51
55	36	32	47	29	28
54	33	42	36	50	41

1. Represent the data as a stem-and-leaf plot.

2. Find the median, mode, and range of the data.

The prices of items in dollars in two stores are displayed in the stem-and-leaf plots.

Store 1

Stem	Leaf
1	0 1 2 4
2	1 3 6 7 8
3	0 1 2 2 2 4 8
4	0 1 2 5

Store 2

Stem	Leaf
2	0 1 8 9 9
3	1 3 7 8
4	0 1 2 3 4 6 7 9
5	5 7 8

3. What is the range of prices for each store?

4. Which store has the greater mean?

Test Prep

5. Use the stem-and-leaf plots above. Which is the mode for Store 2?

   A. 29   B. 21   C. 20   D. 9

6. **Writing In Math** Explain what a store owner might learn by doing a stem-and-leaf plot of the prices of items in her store.

Name _____

Bar Graphs

R 11-5

The double bar graph to the right shows the number of hours Frida and Tayib spent doing homework over a two-week period.

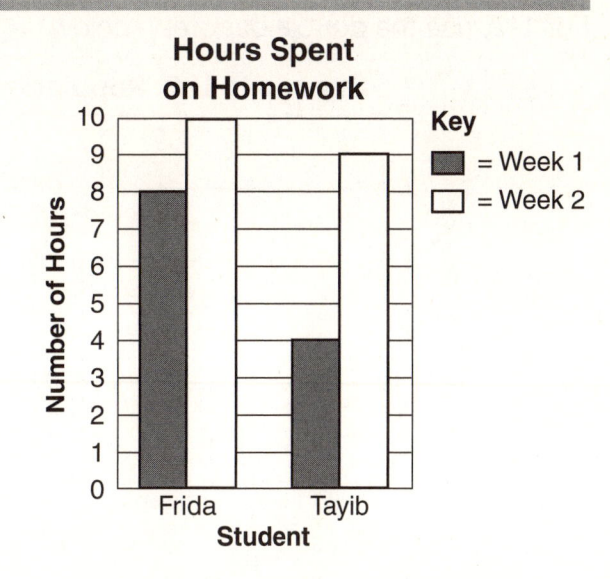

Hours Spent on Homework

Key
■ = Week 1
□ = Week 2

Which student spent more time on homework during Week 1? <u>Frida</u>

Which student spent less time on homework during Week 2? <u>Tayib</u>

How many total hours did Frida spend on her homework? <u>18 hr</u>

The double bar graph shows the number of shoes sold last month at three shoe shops.

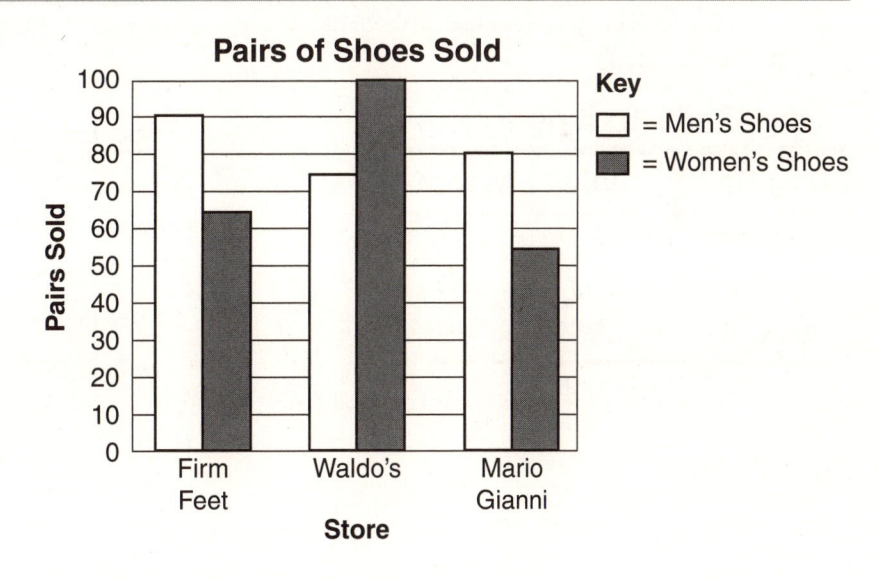

Pairs of Shoes Sold

Key
□ = Men's Shoes
■ = Women's Shoes

1. Which shoe store sold the greatest number of men's shoes? _____

2. Which shoe store sold the fewest number of women's shoes? _____

3. **Number Sense** How many more pairs of men's shoes did Firm Feet sell than Mario Gianni? _____

Use with Lesson 11-5. **137**

Name _____

Bar Graphs

P 11-5

For 1–2, use the double bar graph below.

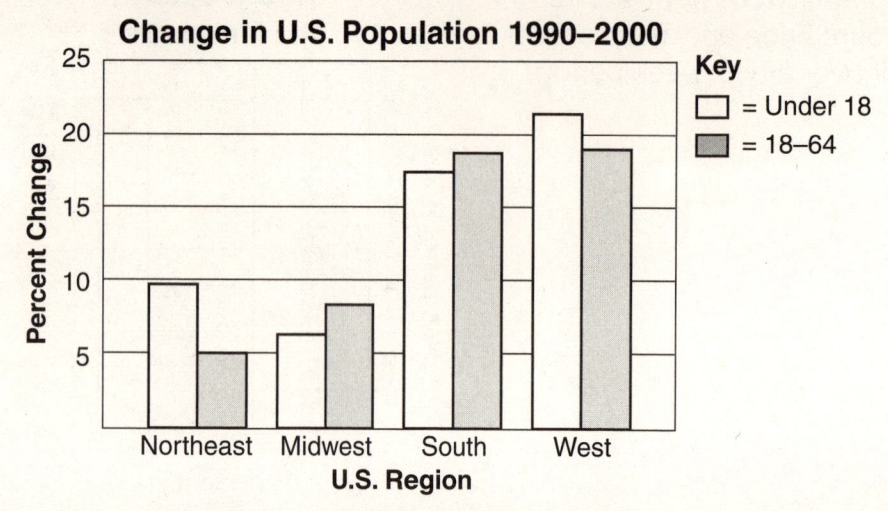

Change in U.S. Population 1990–2000

Key:
☐ = Under 18
▨ = 18–64

(Bar graph showing Percent Change by U.S. Region: Northeast, Midwest, South, West)

1. Which region showed the greatest growth in the age group under 18? _____

2. Which region showed the least growth in the age group from 18 to 64? _____

3. Complete the graph. Use the data below for 3–4.

Dog Visits to Dog Parks

Dog Park	July	March
Bow Wow	320	165
Hey Rover	260	230
Fetch It	395	285

Key:
☐ = July
▨ = March

Dog Visits to Dog Parks

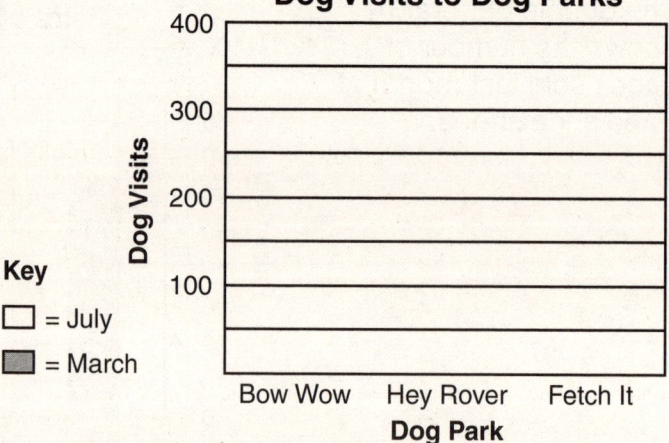

(Blank bar graph with Dog Visits axis 0–400, Dog Parks: Bow Wow, Hey Rover, Fetch It)

Test Prep

4. Which dog park had the greatest number of dog visits?

   A. Bow Wow   **B.** Hey Rover   **C.** Fetch It   **D.** Drop by Park

5. **Writing in Math** Explain why a key is so important to a bar graph.

_____

_____

Use with Lesson 11-5.   **137**

Name _____

Line Graphs

R 11-6

The chart shows the car dealer's sales of cars in the two most popular colors. Show the data on a double line graph.

Car Sales

Year	Red	Blue
1999	100	25
2000	125	50
2001	75	175
2002	25	225

Step 1: Write a title.

Step 2: Label the horizontal and vertical axis.

Step 3: On the horizontal axis, mark equal time intervals.

Step 4: On the vertical axis, mark equal intervals beginning with 0.

Step 5: Draw grid lines.

Step 6: Choose your colors and make a key to show what each color represents.

Step 7: Plot a point for each value of data. Join the points with line segments.

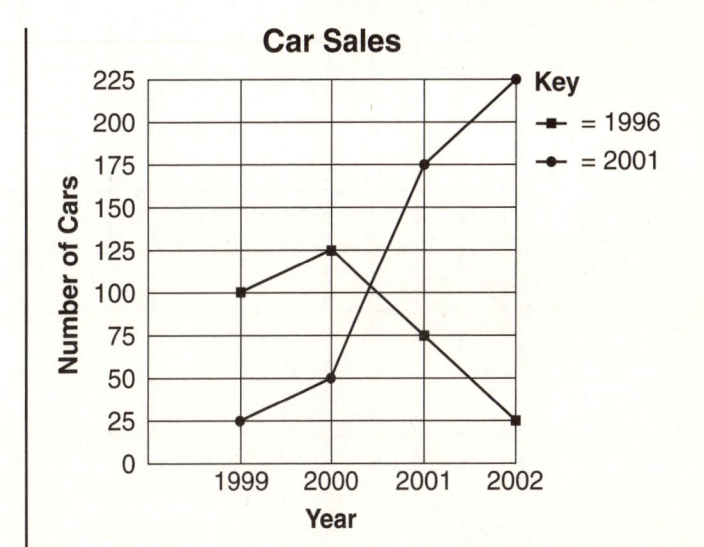

Car Sales graph with Key: ■ = 1996, ● = 2001

1. Use the snowfall data to complete the double line graph.

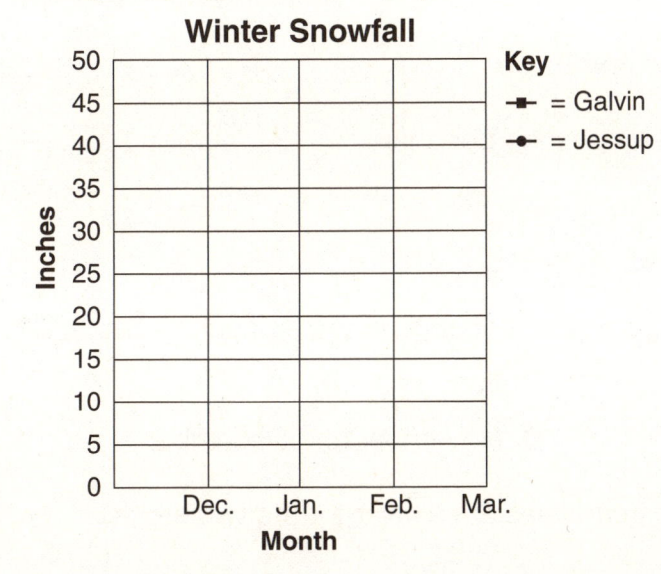

   Winter Snowfall graph (empty), Key: ■ = Galvin, ● = Jessup

Winter Snowfall

Month	Galvin	Jessup
Dec.	20	5
Jan.	30	3
Feb.	45	15
Mar.	35	5

2. **Reasoning** During which month did both towns have the greatest amount of snow?

_____

138 Use with Lesson 11-6.

Name _____

Line Graphs

P 11-6

The table below shows the price of two stocks on the last day of each month.

	Jan	Feb	Mar	Apr	May	Jun	Jul	Aug	Sep	Oct	Nov	Dec
Stock A	$17	$10	$10	$16	$17	$14	$12	$8	$6	$7	$11	$11
Stock B	$33	$27	$24	$28	$31	$29	$28	$20	$12	$13	$13	$14

1. Complete the double line graph of the data.

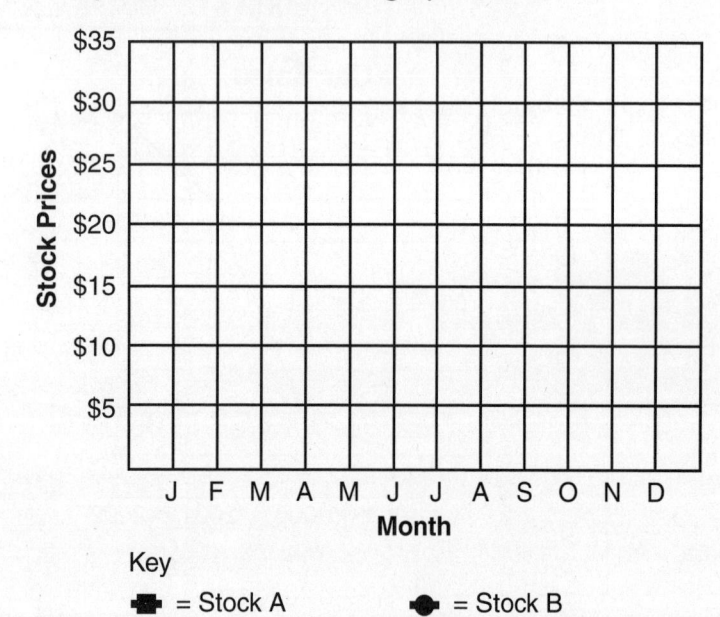

   Key
   ■— = Stock A   ●— = Stock B

2. During which month did both companies have the highest price per share? _____

3. Describe the overall trend for both companies. _____

4. Which company showed the greater change per share? _____

Test Prep

Use the double line graph above for Exercises 5 and 6.

5. Between which two months did the greatest change in price occur for Stock B?

   A. May and June
   B. June and July
   C. August and September
   D. November and December

6. **Writing in Math** Explain how the trend lines are similar for the two stocks.

_____

_____

138 Use with Lesson 11-6.

Name _____

Circle Graphs

R 11-7

There are 50 students in the school choir. The circle graph shows the makeup of the choir.

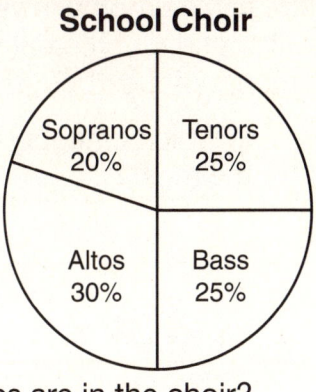

School Choir

- Sopranos 20%
- Tenors 25%
- Altos 30%
- Bass 25%

How many altos are in the choir?

30% of the choir is made up of altos.

Estimate: 30% of 50 is about $\frac{1}{3}$ of 50, or 16.

You know there are 50 choir members.

Multiply: $0.3 \times 50 = 15$

So, there are 15 altos in the choir.

How many sopranos are in the choir?

20% of the choir is made up of sopranos.

Estimate: 20% of 50 is about $\frac{1}{4}$ of 50, or 12.5.

You know there are 50 choir members.

Multiply: $0.2 \times 50 = 10$

So, there are 10 sopranos in the choir.

The circle graph to the right shows how water is used each day at the Clarkson Ranch. The ranch uses about 200 gal every day.

Clarkson Ranch Water Usage

- Horses' Drinking Water 35%
- Human Drinking 21%
- Cooking 5%
- Human Washing 23%
- Washing Stables 16%

1. What is most of the water used for?

   _____

2. About how much water is used for cooking?

   _____

3. About how much water do the humans drink each day?

   _____

4. **Estimation** About how much water is used for washing?

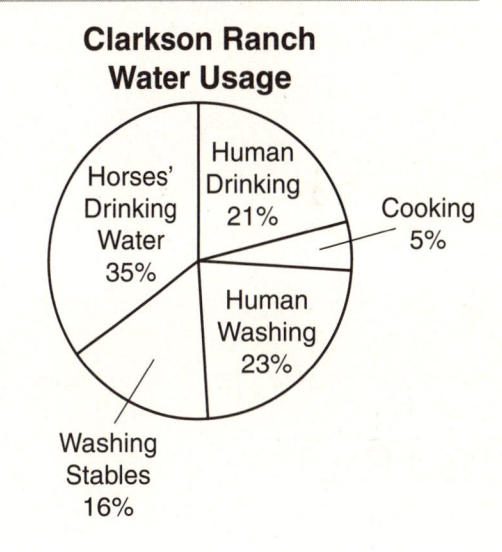

   _____

Use with Lesson 11-7. **139**

Name _____

Circle Graphs

P 11-7

The circle graph shows the amount the Johnson family will spend on different categories this year. The total amount of their budget is $10,000.

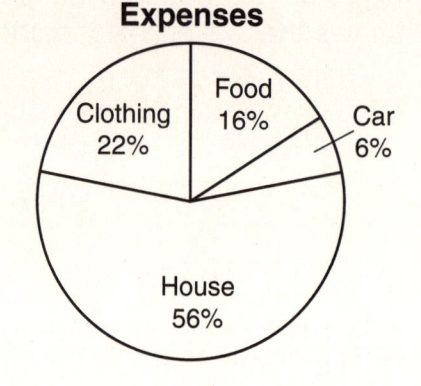

Expenses

Clothing 22% | Food 16% | Car 6% | House 56%

1. In which category will the Johnson family spend the most?

   _____

2. How much will be spent on clothing?

   _____

3. How much will be spent on food?

   _____

4. **Estimation** Estimate the amount of money that will be spent on the house.

   _____

5. Make a circle graph of the data given in the table.

Books Sold

Mystery	2,035
Western	407
Science Fiction	2,442
Adventure	3,256
TOTAL	8,140

Test Prep

6. Jane spent 62% of her school budget on books. In degrees, what measurement would that section be on a circle graph?

   A. 62°   **B.** 162°   **C.** 177°   **D.** 223°

7. **Writing in Math** Jane has a budget of $290. Explain how you would find the amount Jane spent on books.

   _____

   _____

Use with Lesson 11-7. **139**

PROBLEM-SOLVING STRATEGY

Make a Graph

R 11-8

Here is how students at Sinclair Elementary get to school each day: 15% ride bikes, 45% ride in cars, 10% go by foot, and 30% take the bus. Make the most appropriate graph to show the data.

Read and Understand

Step 1: What do you know?

15% bike; 45% ride in a car; 10% walk; 30% ride the bus

Step 2: What are you trying to do?

Make the best display of the data

Plan and Solve

Step 3: What strategy will you use?

Strategy Make a graph

Since the data is in the form of percentages, make a circle graph.

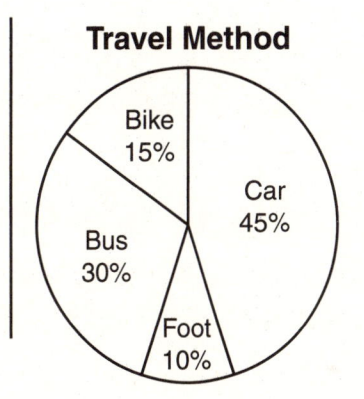

Travel Method

Bike 15%, Car 45%, Foot 10%, Bus 30%

Look Back and Check

Step 4: Is your answer reasonable?

Yes, a circle graph is the best choice to show percentages.

---

1. Make the most appropriate graph to show the data below.

Miles Jogged

Week	Ramón	Glenda
1	10	5
2	20	10

PROBLEM-SOLVING STRATEGY

Make a Graph

P 11-8

Solve each problem.

1. The table shows the average test scores for two classes in a middle school. Make the most appropriate graph to show the data.

Middle School Test Scores

Subject	Class A	Class B
Math	88	82
Science	86	81
English	80	90
Social Studies	82	89

2. Which class tested better in math and science?

3. Which class tested better in English and social studies?

4. Determine the overall test average for both classes. Which class tested better overall?

140   Use with Lesson 11-8.

Name _____

Misleading Graphs

R 11-9

Biking Flora claimed that she biked twice as many miles as Quentin. Is her claim correct?

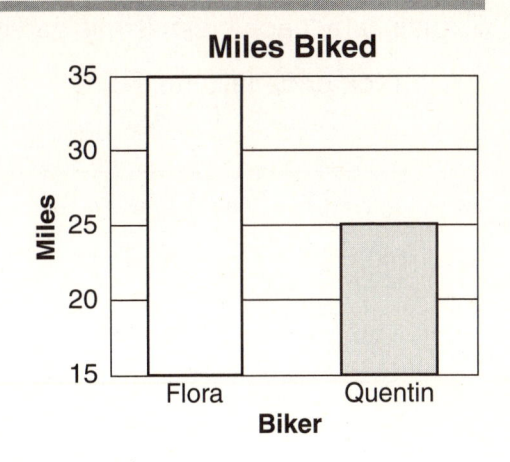

Miles Biked

(Bar graph showing Flora at 35 miles and Quentin at 25 miles, with vertical scale from 15 to 35)

The bar for Flora is about twice as tall as for Quentin, but Flora only biked 10 mi more than Quentin. The claim is incorrect.

The graph is misleading because the vertical scale does not begin at zero.

Explain why the claim is misleading.

1. The population declined sharply.

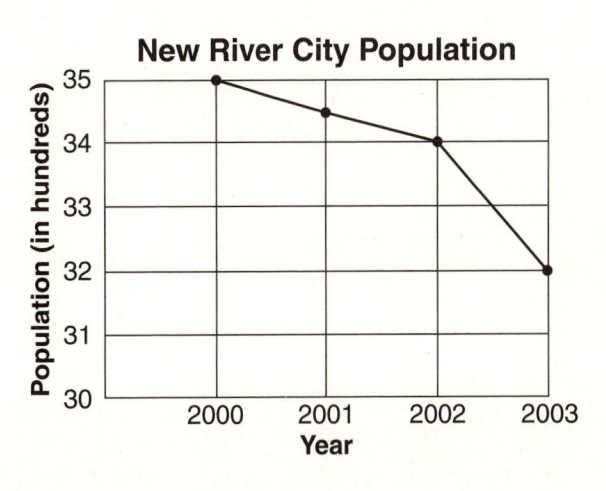

New River City Population

(Line graph showing population in hundreds from 2000-2003: 35, 34.5, 34, 32, with vertical scale from 30 to 35)

_____
_____
_____

2. **Reasoning** Write a claim that is more accurate for the population graph.

_____
_____

Use with Lesson 11-9. **141**

Misleading Graphs

P 11-9

Explain why each claim is misleading.

1. Stock price falls fast!

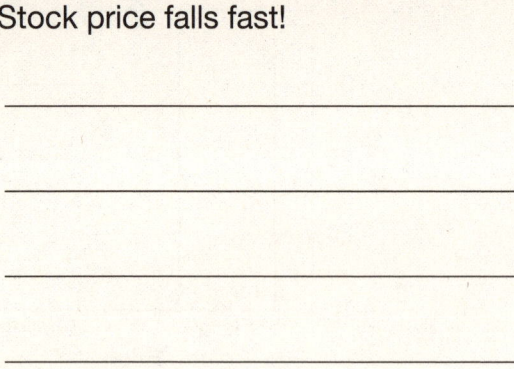

   _____
   _____
   _____
   _____

2. Arthur spends more of his free time playing.

   _____
   _____
   _____
   _____

Test Prep

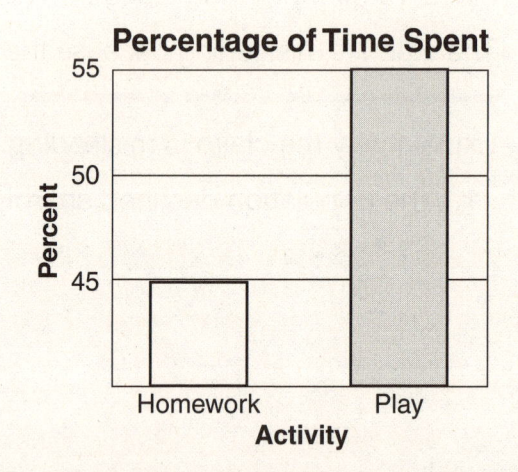

3. Which statement about misleading graphs is true?

   A. Circle graphs can be misleading by having a larger circle.

   B. Double bar graphs cannot be misleading.

   C. Line graphs and bar graphs can be misleading by having scales that are too great or too small.

   D. Line graphs cannot be misleading.

4. **Writing in Math** Explain why someone selling CDs might want to create a misleading graph.

   _____
   _____

Use with Lesson 11-9. **141**

Counting Methods

R 11-10

How many possible outcomes are there if you spin both spinners? You can count the different possibilities by making an organized list or using multiplication.

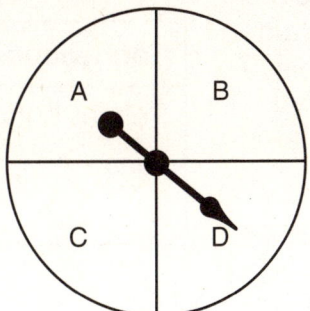

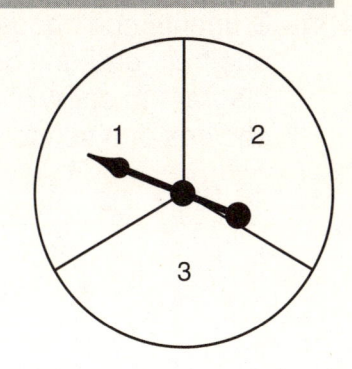

Make an organized list:

A1, A2, A3,

B1, B2, B3,

C1, C2, C3,

D1, D2, D3

Use multiplication:

Choices for 1st spinner	Choices for 2nd spinner	Total Number of Possible Outcomes
4 ×	3 =	12

There are 12 possible outcomes.

1. Pablo is filling fruit baskets. Each basket must have a small, medium, and large fruit. Use multiplication to find out how many possible combinations he could make. Show your work.

Small	Medium	Large
Strawberry	Plum	Orange
Cherry	Apricot	Banana
Blueberry	Kiwi	Pear

_____

_____

_____

2. **Number Sense** Each member of the club will receive a "member code" made of one letter and one number. The numbers are 2, 4, 6, and 8; the letters are W and Z. Make a list to find the total number of possible codes if the numbers and letters may repeat.

_____

_____

_____

142 Use with Lesson 11-10.

Counting Methods

P 11-10

1. Students can choose one sandwich, one fruit, and one drink. Make a tree diagram to show all the possible choices of a school lunch.

School Lunches

Sandwiches	Fruits	Drinks
Peanut butter	Apple	Milk
Tuna	Orange	Juice
	Banana	Water

_____

2. Show how you could use multiplication to find the outcome.

_____

Use any counting method you like.

3. How many possible outcomes are there if you spin each spinner once?

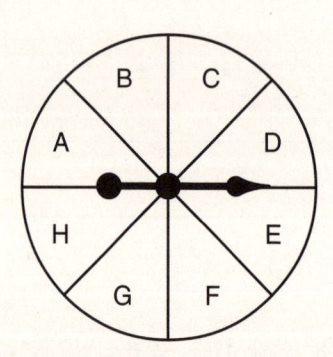

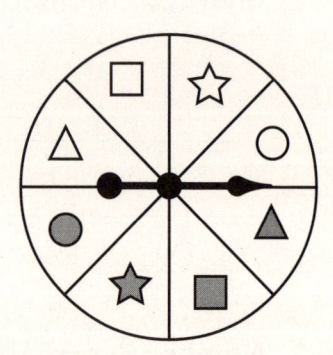

_____

Test Prep

4. Sandra has four color cards: one blue, one red, one green, and one yellow. If she puts them in a box, in how many different orders could she draw them out?

   A. 16   **B.** 24   **C.** 32   **D.** 64

5. **Writing in Math** A basketball team needs 5 players. The team can choose from a group of 7 players. Explain how to find the number of combinations of players that can be on the team.

_____

142 Use with Lesson 11-10.

Permutations and Combinations

R 11-11

Guido the chef can prepare three different dishes: soup, beef, and olives. He must decide which two to serve at the meal. In how many different ways can he choose?

One dish will be served first, and the other second, so the order is important.

Use the counting principle.

Choices for first dish	Choices for second dish	Number of ways to choose
3	× 2	= 6

Make a list.

SB, SO, BO, BS, OB, OS

There are 6 ways to choose.

In how many ways can Guido choose two of the three dishes to serve? The order does not matter.

Make a list.

SB, SO, BO

There are 3 different ways.

Find the number of ways to choose the objects in each situation. Remember to consider whether order matters.

1. Oliver is choosing 3 of his 4 hats to take on vacation. _____

2. Ivy is choosing 2 of 5 pictures to hang on 2 different walls. _____

Find the number of possible arrangements for each situation.

3. Four people are sitting on a bench. _____

4. Six students are standing in line. _____

5. Five different colored markers are in a box. _____

6. Eight different plants are in a row. _____

Use with Lesson 11-11.

Permutations and Combinations

P 11-11

Find the number of ways to choose the objects or events in each situation. Remember to consider whether order matters.

1. Salvatore is choosing which 2 games to watch out of a group of 8 games at a basketball tournament. _____

2. Carla is choosing 2 of her 12 bracelets to wear to dinner. _____

Find the number of possible arrangements for each situation.

3. The farmer has 6 horses in 6 stalls. _____

4. William has 8 model cars on his shelf. _____

Most radio and television stations in the United States that are east of the Mississippi River have a set of 4 call letters, such as WWOR or WKZO.

5. How many possible arrangements of the call letters WKZO could there be? _____

6. Suppose a station wanted to have vowels as the second and third letters and W and V as the other letters. The vowels can be used twice. Do not count "Y" as a vowel. How many possible permutations are there? _____

Test Prep

7. A car company offers 4 different car models, 4 different inside colors, and 6 different outside colors. How many variations could a buyer choose from?

   A. 96 **B.** 48 **C.** 36 **D.** 24

8. **Writing in Math** Carlos has a CD player that can hold 8 CDs. He has 8 CDs he wants to put in the player. Is the order he puts them in the player an example of a combination or a permutation? Explain.

_____

_____

_____

Name _____

Probability

R 11-12

The probability of an event is the number that describes the likelihood that an event will occur.

An impossible event = 0.

A certain event = 1.

P(event) = number of favorable outcomes/number of possible outcomes

Finding probability:

There are 10 marbles in a bag. 7 are red and 3 are green. If Jamie selects one marble from the bag without looking, what is the probability she will select a red marble?

$P(red) = \frac{7}{10}$ ← There are 7 marbles.
← There are 10 marbles total.

The probability of getting a red marble is $\frac{7}{10}$.

This can also be expressed as a decimal, 0.7, or a percent, 70%.

Hannah gets one spin on the spinner. Find each probability as a fraction, decimal, and a percent rounded to the nearest whole percent.

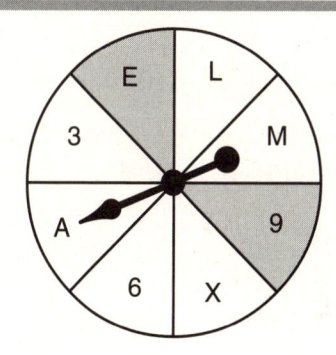

1. P(number) _____

2. P(prime number) _____

3. P(vowel) _____

4. P(letter not shaded) _____

5. **Reasoning** Name an event that is impossible to spin on the spinner.

_____

_____

144 Use with Lesson 11-12.

Name _____

Probability

P 11-12

Find each probability as a fraction, decimal, and percent rounded to the nearest whole percent.

1. P(star) _____ ; _____ ; _____

2. P(shaded shape) _____ ; _____ ; _____

3. P(number) _____ ; _____ ; _____

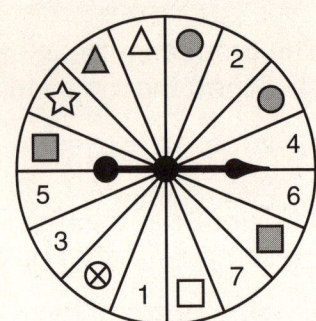

In Exercises 4 and 5, draw a set of 10 number cards that could yield each probability.

4. $P(4) = \frac{3}{10}$

5. P(odd number) = 70%

Test Prep

6. A box holds 2 green cards, 3 blue cards, 7 orange cards, 1 red card, and 5 yellow cards. Which is NOT the probability that you will draw a blue card?

   A. $\frac{1}{6}$ B. 17%   C. 0.167   D. $\frac{3}{20}$

7. **Writing in Math** Corina said that she had a greater chance of getting heads on the second flip of a penny if the first flip was tails. Is she correct? Explain.

_____

_____

Use with Lesson 11-12.

Name _____

Predictions and Probability

R 11-13

Using probability to make predictions:

Near the end of the school year, each of the 120 sixth graders spins the spinner once to determine what special privilege he or she will get. How many rulers might the principal, Mr. Wiggins, expect to give away?

School Privileges

Multiply the probability by the number of spins.

$\frac{1}{6} \times 120 = \frac{1}{\cancel{6}_1} \times \frac{\cancel{120}^{20}}{1} = \frac{20}{1} = 20$

So, Mr. Wiggins might expect to give away about 20 rulers.

---

1. If you flip a coin 1,000 times, about how many times might you expect to get tails? Do you think it will happen exactly that many times?

   _____

2. About how many times might you expect to get a number greater than 4 when you toss a number cube 400 times?

   _____

3. About how many times can you expect to spin B in 250 spins?

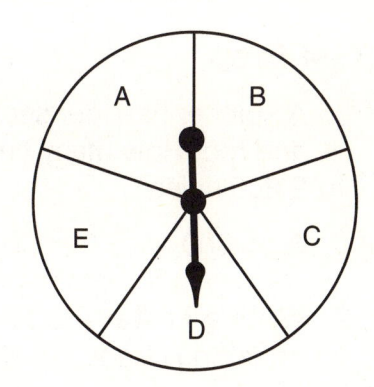

   _____

4. **Number Sense** About how many times can you expect to spin a vowel in 500 spins?

   _____

Use with Lesson 11-13. **145**

Name _____

Predictions and Probability

P 11-13

1. You have 26 number cards, numbered from 1 to 26. How many times might you expect to draw the 24 card in 1,300 tries? _____

2. If you had a jar with 166 white marbles and 2 red marbles, and you reached in without looking, how many times might you select a red marble after 1,000 tries? _____

3. **Reasoning** Gene said that if you toss a number cube 420 times, you will get a 1 about 70 times. Is he correct? Explain.

_____

_____

_____

In baseball, a player's batting average is found by dividing the number of hits by the number of times he or she has been at bat. The batting average is therefore an expression of experimental probability.

4. Casey had 637 at bats last season, and he got hits on 213 of those at bats. What is the experimental probability that he will get a hit the next time he has an at bat? _____

5. Sam has a batting average of .346. How many base hits can he expect to get in 544 at bats? _____

Test Prep

6. A spinner has four sections of equal size: blue, green, yellow, and red. How many times might you expect to spin green out of 2,200 spins?

   A. 1,000   **B.** 700   **C.** 550   **D.** 500

7. **Writing in Math** Explain how to find the experimental probability of getting heads in 100 coin flips.

_____

_____

_____

Use with Lesson 11-13. **145**

Adding Probabilities

R 11-14

If two events cannot happen at the same time, they are called **mutually exclusive.** You can add to find the probability.

The 8 marbles are placed in a bag and 1 is drawn at random. Decide if the event is mutually exclusive. Then find the probability expressed as a fraction.

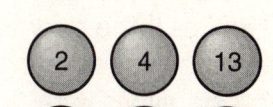

Find P(multiple of 2 or number greater than 20)

The only number greater than 20 is 25, which is not a multiple of 2, so the event is mutually exclusive. There are 4 multiples of 2: 2, 4, 16, 20.

P(multiple of 2) = $\frac{4}{6}$; P(number greater than 20) = $\frac{1}{6}$; $\frac{4}{6} + \frac{1}{6} = \frac{5}{6}$

The probability of getting a multiple of 2 or a number greater than 20 is $\frac{5}{6}$.

If two events can happen at the same time, they are *not* mutually exclusive. For example:

Find P(multiple of 2 *or* multiple of 5).

P(multiple of 2) = $\frac{4}{6}$; P(multiple of 5) = $\frac{2}{6}$

Add the probabilities and subtract the probability of the outcome they share in common. The number 20 is a multiple of 2 and 5.

$\frac{4}{6} + \frac{2}{6} - \frac{1}{6} = \frac{5}{6}$

The probability of getting a mulltiple of 2 or 5 is $\frac{5}{6}$.

The 10 marbles are placed in a bag and 1 is drawn at random. Decide if the event is mutually exclusive. Then find the probability expressed as a fraction.

1. P(multiple of 6 or shaded)

   _____

2. P(multiple of 2 or multiple of 9)

   _____

146 Use with Lesson 11-14.

Name _____

Adding Probabilities

P 11-14

Fifteen slips of paper showing boys' and girls' names are placed into a box and drawn at random. Decide if the events are mutually exclusive. Then find each probability expressed as a fraction.

Bob	Sue	Carol	Ed	Tom
Bill	Laura	Pam	Jennifer	Juan
Cathy	Mike	Sarah	Kyle	Eric

1. P(boys' name or name of 4 letters)

   _____

2. P(name of 3 letters or name that starts with J)

   _____

3. **Reasoning** What is the probability that you would select either a 2-letter name, an 8-letter name, or a 4-letter name? Express your answer as a percentage. _____

A bag holds 25 marbles: 3 blue, 4 red, 6 green, 8 orange, and 4 yellow.

4. What is the probability that you will draw either a blue marble or a red marble? _____

5. What is the probability that you will draw a marble that is not yellow? _____

Test Prep

6. Which are NOT mutually exclusive events?

   A. The weather today will be rainy or sunny.

   B. The president is a man or the president is a woman.

   C. You won the spelling bee or you did not win the spelling bee.

   D. A square pyramid is a polyhedron or a polyhedron has five faces.

7. **Writing in Math** If you tossed two number cubes, what sum has the greatest probability of occurring? Explain.

   _____

   _____

146 Use with Lesson 11-14.

Name _____

Multiplying Probabilities

R 11-15

Independent events:

Joe draws one marble from the bag without looking. He then replaces the marble and draws another one.

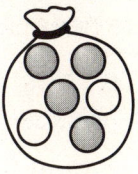

What is the probability of his drawing two shaded marbles in a row?

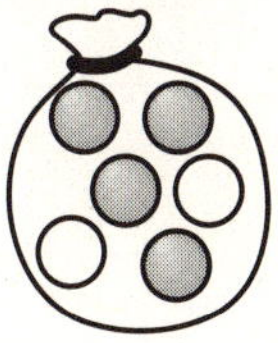

P(shaded, shaded)

= P(shaded on 1st draw) × P(shaded on 2nd draw)

= $\frac{4}{6} \times \frac{4}{6} = \frac{16}{36}$

= 44%

1st draw

2nd draw

Dependent events:

Joe draws one marble from the bag without looking. He does not replace the marble, then draws another one.

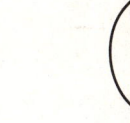

What is the probability of his drawing two shaded marbles in a row?

P(shaded, shaded)

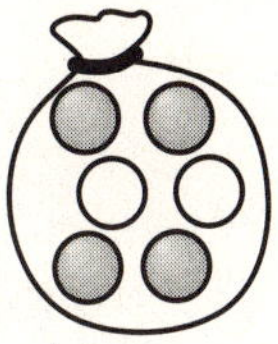

= P(shaded on 1st draw) × P(shaded on 2nd draw)

= $\frac{4}{6} \times \frac{3}{5} = \frac{12}{30}$

= 40%.

1st draw

2nd draw

In Exercises 1–4, give each probability as a fraction and a percent. Round to the nearest tenth of a percent as needed.

W	X	E	E	Z
O	A	B	M	G

You select one letter without looking, replace it, and then select another.

1. Find P(E, Z). _____

2. Find P(vowel, W). _____

You select one letter without looking, do not replace it, and then select another.

3. Find P(M, consonant). _____

4. Find P(B, vowel). _____

Use with Lesson 11-15. **147**

Name _____

Multiplying Probabilities
P 11-15

In Exercises 1–4, give each probability as a fraction and as a percent rounded to the nearest tenth of a percent.

Counters:
- Row 1: Blue, Red, Green, Green
- Row 2: Red, Green, Blue, Red
- Row 3: Green, Yellow, Red, Green

You select a counter without looking at it, replace it, then select another.

1. Find P(green, red). _____

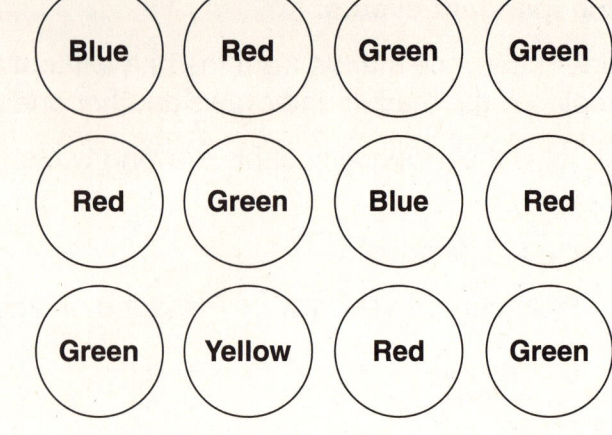

2. Find P(blue, yellow). _____

You select a counter without looking at it, do not replace it, then select another.

3. Find P(green, yellow). _____

4. Find P(blue, green). _____

5. On a TV game show there are three doors. The grand prize for the day is behind one of them. Use a fraction and a percent to express the probability that contestants will guess the correct door on the next two shows. _____

Test Prep

6. When two events are dependent, what changes?

   A. The probability of one of the events
   B. The number of possible outcomes
   C. The sample space
   D. The number of events

7. **Writing in Math** Of a group of 20 color cards, 5 each are red, blue, green, and yellow. If each of the 3 cards Jake has turned over are blue, is the probability of him turning over another blue card an independent or dependent event? Explain.

_____

Use with Lesson 11-15. **147**

PROBLEM-SOLVING SKILL

Writing to Describe

R 11-16

The table shows the results of a survey about favorite colors. Ken made the bar graph below to show the number of students who prefer each color. Nigel made the circle graph to show the percent of students who prefer each color.

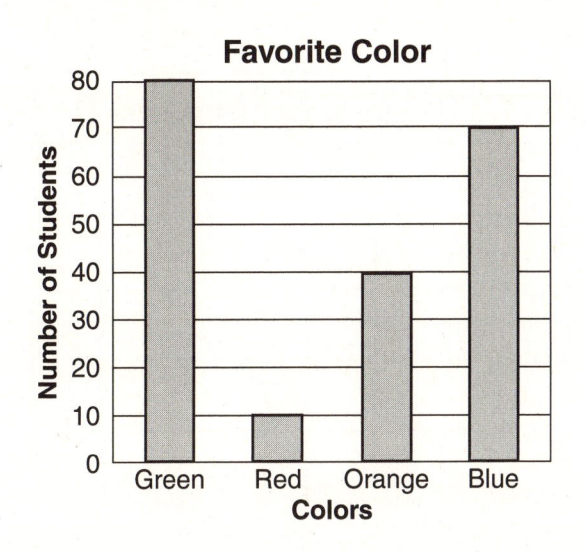

Favorite Color

Color	Number of Students
Green	80
Red	10
Orange	40
Blue	70

Favorite Color (bar graph)

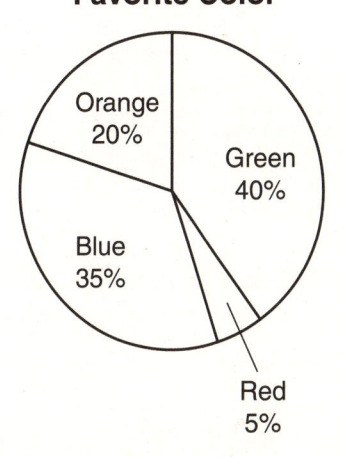

Favorite Color (circle graph)
- Green 40%
- Blue 35%
- Orange 20%
- Red 5%

The circle graph more clearly shows that almost half the students prefer green. In a circle graph, you can see how these numbers compare to the whole. You can see that the green section is almost half.

Stem	Leaf
1	8 8 8 8 8
2	0 1

Number of Sit-Ups in 1 Minute

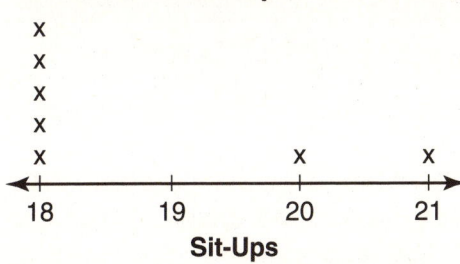

```
x
x
x
x
x           x       x
←——+———+———+———+→
   18  19  20  21
         Sit-Ups
```

1. Which graph more clearly shows that most of the students in the group did 18 sit-ups in 1 min? Describe the characteristics of the graph to justify your decision.

148 Use with Lesson 11-16.

Name _____

PROBLEM-SOLVING SKILL   P 11-16

Writing to Describe

The chart shows the number of wins for a basketball team for the past 6 years.

Year	Wins
1998	11
1999	14
2000	16
2001	18
2002	20
2003	22

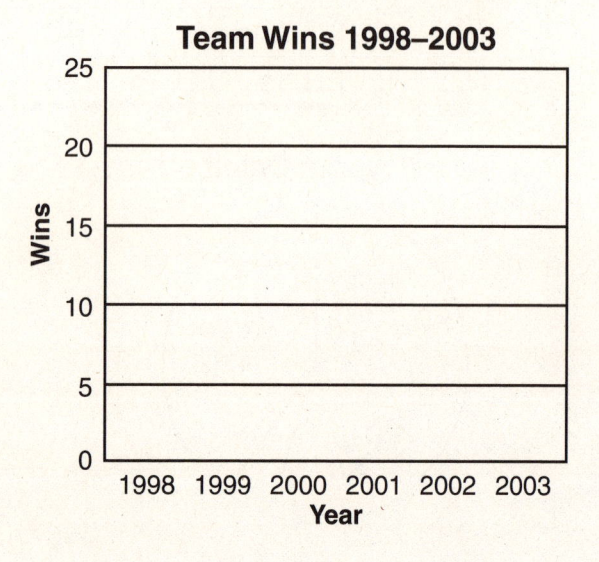

1. Using the data in the chart, complete the bar graph and the line graph.

Team Wins 1998–2003

Team Wins 1998–2003

2. Describe which graph more clearly shows how the number of wins has changed over the past 6 years. Describe the characteristics of the graph that justify your decision.

_____

_____

_____

3. Katie is a sportswriter for a local newspaper. Describe how she can use the two graphs to predict the number of games the team will win next year.

_____

_____

_____

148 Use with Lesson 11-16.

Name _____

PROBLEM-SOLVING APPLICATION   R 11-17
Melba Gets Healthy

Melba jogs twice each day: once in the morning before work, and once in the late afternoon before dinner. The graphs show how many miles she jogged on each run.

Miles Jogged Per Day

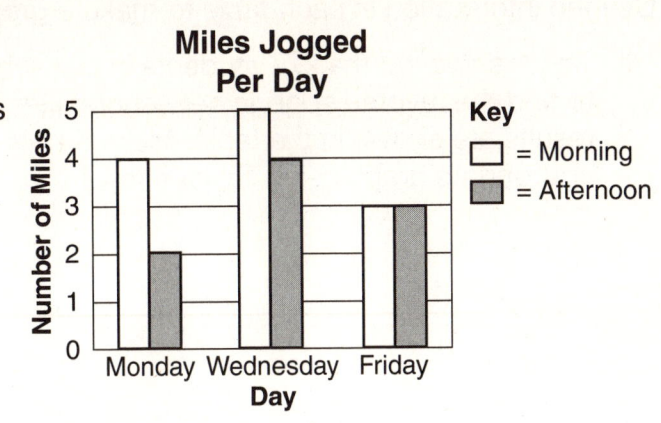

Key:
- ☐ = Morning
- ▨ = Afternoon

On which day did Melba jog a total of 9 mi? <u>Wednesday</u>

On which day did Melba jog the same number of miles in the morning and afternoon? <u>Friday</u>

---

1. Each morning Melba does push-ups to increase her strength. The number she did is recorded in the stem-and-leaf plot to the right. What was the greatest number of push-ups she did? What was the fewest number she did?

   _____

   Push-Ups

Stem	Leaf
1	6 7
2	4 5
3	2

2. What is the median of the push-up data? _____

3. What is the range of the push-up data? _____

4. Melba kept track of what she ate during each week. If she ate 38 lb of food in one week, how many pounds were fruits and vegetables?

   _____

   Food Eaten in One Week 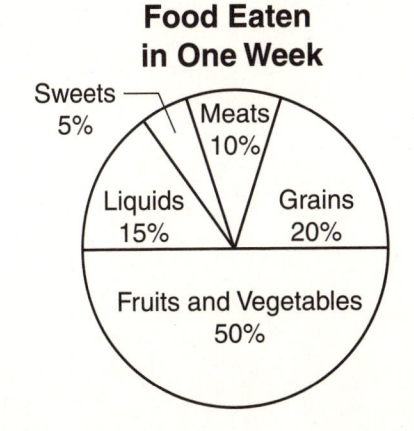
   - Sweets 5%
   - Meats 10%
   - Liquids 15%
   - Grains 20%
   - Fruits and Vegetables 50%

5. About how many pounds were meats?

   _____

Use with Lesson 11-17. **149**

PROBLEM-SOLVING APPLICATION
Graph Construction

P 11-17

Use the information in each table to make a graph.

1. Taylor surveyed the 277 students in her school to find the favorite sport in her school. Her results are shown in the table. Make an appropriate graph using Taylor's results.

Favorite Sport

Sport	Votes
Basketball	119
Baseball/Softball	55
Football	47
Soccer	38
Volleyball	18

2. Ned is a delivery driver. The table shows the number of packages he delivers each day of the week. Make an appropriate graph using Ned's delivery information.

Deliveries

Day	Packages
Monday	47
Tuesday	38
Wednesday	29
Thursday	45
Friday	49
Saturday	12

Use with Lesson 11-17.

Name _____

Graphing Inequalities

R 12-1

Naming solutions to an inequality:

Any number that makes an inequality true is a solution to the inequality.

Here is an inequality: $y \leq 13$. This is read "y is less than or equal to 13."

To come up with some solutions, think: What numbers are less than or equal to 13?

Some solutions to $y \leq 13$ are 13, 12, 10, 9, and 7. Any number equal to or less than 13 is a solution.

Graphing an inequality on a number line:

Graph $y \leq 13$.

- Draw a closed circle at 13 on the number line. This shows that 13 is a solution.
- Find several solutions and graph those on the number line. Start at the closed circle and draw a thick line over the solutions.
- Draw an arrow to show that the solutions go on forever.

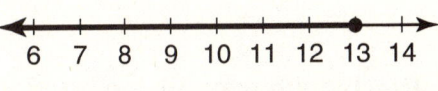

Here is how to graph $v > 5$:

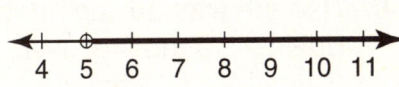

There is an open circle at 5. This shows that 5 is not a solution, but numbers close to 5 are.

Name three solutions to each inequality and graph the inequality on a number line.

1. $b > 9$ _____

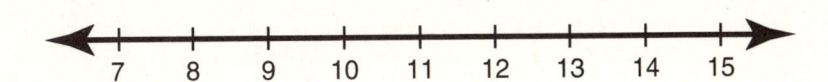

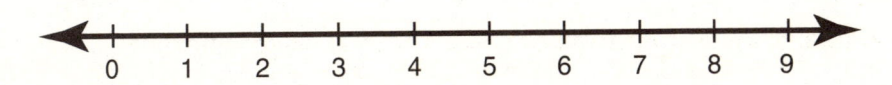

2. $t \leq 8$ _____

3. **Number Sense** Is 3.96 a solution to the inequality $x < 4$? Explain how you know.

_____

_____

Name _____

Graphing Inequalities

P 12-1

Name 3 solutions of each inequality. Then graph the inequality on a number line.

1. $c < 5$ _____ 2. $s \leq 9$ _____

3. $a > 14$ _____ 4. $m \geq 21$ _____

5. **Number Sense** Is 2.25 a solution to the inequality $x > 2$? Explain how you can tell.

_____

6. Hannah was driving her car at 55 mi per hour, then she slowed down. Use the inequality $s < 55$ to find three possible speeds of Hannah's car after she slowed down.

_____

7. All of the shoes in Abbot's Shoe Store cost $15.00 or more. Use the inequality $p \geq 15$ to find three possible prices of shoes.

_____

Test Prep

8. Which are three possible solutions for the inequality $y > 12$?

   A. 5, 7, 9   **B.** 10, 12, 14   **C.** 13, 17, 22   **D.** 12, 22, 32

9. **Writing in Math** Explain how the graphs of $g \leq 4$ and $g < 4$ are different.

_____
_____
_____
_____

Solving Inequalities

R 12-2

Solve $x + 4 \leq 12$. Then graph the solution.

$x + 4 \leq 12$

$x + 4 - 4 \leq 12 - 4$ Undo addition by subtracting 4 from both sides.

$x \leq 8$

The solution is $x \leq 8$.

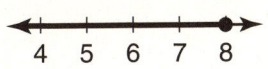

<-----|----|----|----|----•----->
      4   5   6   7   8

Check: Test a point on the graph, like 6.

$x + 4 \leq 12$

$6 + 4 \leq 12$

$10 \leq 12$

The inequality is true, so $x \leq 8$.

Solve $5n \leq 30$. Then graph the solution.

$5n \leq 30$

$\frac{5n}{5} \leq \frac{30}{5}$ Undo multiplication by dividing both sides by 5.

$x \leq 6$

The solution is $x \leq 6$.

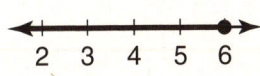

<-----|----|----|----|----•----->
      2   3   4   5   6

Check: Test a point on the graph, like 2.

$5n \leq 30$

$5(2) \leq 30$

$10 \leq 30$

The inequality is true, so $x \leq 6$.

Solve each inequality. Graph and check the solution.

1. $k + 1 < 9$

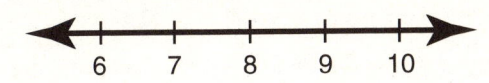

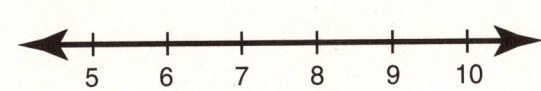

<-----|----|----|----|----|----->
      6   7   8   9   10

2. $3r \geq 21$

<-----|----|----|----|----|----->
      5   6   7   8   9   10

3. Number Sense Would the solutions for $x - 3 < 9$ be to the left or to the right of 12 on a number line? Explain.

_____

_____

_____

_____

Name _____

Solving Inequalities

P 12-2

Solve each inequality. Graph and check the solution.

1. $z + 2 < 12$ _____

2. $p - 4 > 5$ _____

3. $6x \geq 18$ _____

4. $\frac{r}{4} \geq 10$ _____

5. **Number Sense** How can you tell that $x = 18.5$ is NOT a solution of $x - 13.5 > 18.5$ without adding?

_____
_____
_____

The quiz show awards prizes based on the number of questions a contestant answers correctly.

Quiz Show Prizes	
Correct answers ≥ 30	Car
Correct answers ≥ 25	Stereo
Correct answers ≥ 20	Movie tickets

6. What prize will Whitney get if she answers 27 questions correctly?

_____

7. What prize will Abraham get if he answers 24 questions correctly?

_____

Test Prep

8. Which is a value of f if $f + 8 > 35$?

   A. 23   B. 25   C. 27   D. 31

9. **Writing in Math** Explain how you would solve the inequality $3x \geq 27$.

_____
_____

Use with Lesson 12-2.

PROBLEM-SOLVING STRATEGY
Try, Check, and Revise

R 12-3

Brothers Gary is twice as old as his brother Leroy. The sum of their ages is 27. How old is each person?

Read and Understand

Step 1: What do you know?

Gary is twice as old as his brother Leroy. The sum of their ages is 27.

Step 2: What are you trying to find?

The age of each person

Plan and Solve

Step 3: What strategy will you use?

Strategy: Try, check, and revise

Try: 20 and 7. 20 is more than twice as much as 7, so 20 and 7 does not work.

Try: 19 and 8. 19 is more than twice as much as 8, so 19 and 8 does not work.

Try: 18 and 9. 18 is twice as much as 9, so 18 and 9 works.

Answer: Gary is 18 and Leroy is 9.

Look Back and Check

Step 4: Is your work correct?

Yes. 18 is twice as much as 9, and 18 + 9 = 27.

Solve. Write your answers in a complete sentence.

1. Find three consecutive odd integers whose sum is between 95 and 105.

2. There are 21 fish in the aquarium. Out of every 3 fish, 1 is a goldfish. The rest are black mollies. How many goldfish are there?

Name _____

PROBLEM-SOLVING STRATEGY   P 12-3

Try, Check, and Revise

Solve. Write your answer in a complete sentence.

1. Zora has 128 books to put in 8 boxes. Write and solve an equation to find how many books go in each box.

   _____
   _____

2. There are 32 crayons in the art supply box. Three out of every four are green crayons. The rest are orange crayons. How many green crayons are there?

   _____
   _____

3. Find three consecutive integers whose sum is between 35 and 45.

   _____
   _____

4. A van traveled for 3 days. It traveled 320 mi the first day and 280 mi the second day. It traveled a total of 760 mi. How far did it travel the third day?

   _____
   _____

5. **Writing in Math** The length of the long side of a rectangle is 3 times the length of the short side. If the long side is 36 ft, explain how you would write an equation to find the length of the short side.

   _____
   _____
   _____
   _____

152 Use with Lesson 12-3.

PROBLEM-SOLVING SKILL
Translating Words to Expressions

R 12-4

Write as an algebraic expression.

17 less than 6 times a number

Step 1

Start with "6 times a number."

6n is the algebraic expression for "6 times a number."

Step 2

"17 less" means you need to subtract 17.

6n − 17

Write as an algebraic expression.

one third the sum of a number and 37

Step 1

Start with "the sum of a number and 37."

n + 37 is the algebraic expression for "the sum of a number and 37."

Step 2

"$\frac{1}{3}$ the sum" means to multiply the sum by $\frac{1}{3}$. $\frac{1}{3}(n + 37)$

Write an algebraic expression for each.

1. 35 more than 10 times a number

2. 4 times a number minus 25

3. 12 less than the quotient of a number and 3

4. the quotient of 5 times a number and 9

5. 8 less than the sum of a number and 55

6. One chair costs $25.50 more than twice as much as another one.

7. One bed costs $100 less than three times as much as another bed.

8. The product of 9 and n

9. 87 more than 15 times a number

10. the quotient of 8 times a number and 3

Use with Lesson 12-4. **153**

Name _____

PROBLEM-SOLVING SKILL   P 12-4
Translating Words to Expressions

Write an algebraic expression for each.

1. 50 more than 8 times a number _____

2. 5 times a number minus 7 _____

3. 4 less than the quotient of a number and 2 _____

4. the quotient of 9 times a number and 6 _____

5. the sum of a number and 15 divided by 4 _____

6. 12 less than the sum of a number and 20 _____

7. one book costs $1.25 more than four times as much as another one _____

8. one clock costs $3.00 less than twice as much as another clock _____

9. 40 more than 6 times a number _____

10. 7 less than 4 times a number _____

11. a dog weighs 3 lb more than twice a cat's weight _____

12. 5 more than the quotient of a number and 7 _____

13. **Writing in Math** Write a word phrase for the expression $5n - 13$.

_____

_____

_____

Use with Lesson 12-4.   **153**

Solving Two-Step Equations

R 12-5

Some equations have more than one operation. When you solve a two-step equation, you should undo operations in the following order:

- First, undo addition or subtraction.
- Then, undo multiplication or division.

Solve $5x - 10 = 95$.

Step 1: Undo subtraction by adding 10 to both sides.

$5x - 10 = 95$
$5x - 10 + 10 = 95 + 10$
$5x = 105$

Step 2: Undo multiplication by dividing both sides by 5.

$5x = 105$
$\frac{5x}{5} = \frac{105}{5}$
$x = 21$

Step 3: Check.

$5x - 10 = 95$
$5(21) - 10 = 95$
$105 - 10 = 95$
$95 = 95$

It checks.

Solve $10 = \frac{n}{5} + 6$.

Step 1: Undo addition by subtracting 6 from both sides.

$10 = \frac{n}{5} + 6$
$10 - 6 = \frac{n}{5} + 6 - 6$
$4 = \frac{n}{5}$

Step 2: Undo division by multiplying both sides by 5.

$4 = \frac{n}{5}$
$4 \times 5 = \frac{n}{5} \times 5$
$20 = n$

Step 3: Check.

$10 = \frac{n}{5} + 6$
$10 = \frac{20}{5} + 6$
$10 = 4 + 6$
$10 = 10$

It checks.

Solve each equation and check your solution.

1. $8b + 16 = 64$ _____

2. $2y - 4 = 24$ _____

3. $\frac{q}{10} + 5 = 10$ _____

4. $\frac{m}{3} + 2 = 17$ _____

5. **Number Sense** Is the solution to $4x + 12 = 36$ greater than or less than 36? Explain.

_____

_____

Use with Lesson 12-5.

Name _____

Solving Two-Step Equations

P 12-5

Solve each equation and check your solution.

1. $12a + 24 = 48$ _____

2. $4z - 8 = 32$ _____

3. $\frac{x}{5} - 10 = 2$ _____

4. $\frac{p}{3} + 6 = 42$ _____

5. $5b + 15 = 30$ _____

6. $7n + 14 = 21$ _____

7. $\frac{c}{4} + 3 = 5$ _____

8. $\frac{g}{2} - 4 = 18$ _____

For 9 and 10, write an equation to solve.

9. Yoshi's age is twice Bart's age plus 3. Yoshi is 13 years old. How old is Bart?

_____

10. Caleb and Winona both traveled by car to their friend's wedding. The distance Winona traveled was 124 mi less than twice the distance Caleb traveled. If Winona traveled 628 mi, how far did Caleb travel?

_____

Test Prep

11. Which is the value of n when $4n + 16 = 64$?

    A. $n = 4$ **B.** $n = 8$ **C.** $n = 12$ **D.** $n = 16$

12. **Writing in Math** Explain, in complete sentences, how you solve the equation $6x - 3 = 39$.

_____

_____

_____

Patterns and Equations

R 12-6

You can use an equation to complete a table. The equation shows the pattern in the table, or how the x- and y-values are related. For example:

The equation is $y = 3x + 7$.

x	2	4	10	20
y				

As the table shows, the x-value is already given. What is y when x = 2? Plug the x-value into the equation to find out.

$y = 3x + 7$

$y = 3(2) + 7$

$y = 6 + 7$

$y = 13$

Use the same process to complete the rest of the table.

x	2	4	10	20
y	13	19	37	67

Complete each table.

1. $y = 4x + 6$

x	3	8	10	50
y				

2. $y = 8x - 9$

x	2	4	6	8
y				

3. $y = \frac{1}{4}x + 5$

x	16	20	36	48
y				

4. **Number Sense** If the equation is $y = 1x - 25$, will the value of y increase or decrease as x increases? _____

Use with Lesson 12-6. **155**

Name _____

Patterns and Equations

P 12-6

Complete each table.

1. $y = 2x + 4$

x	1	2	3	4
y				

2. $y = 4x - 3$

x	1	4	6	7
y				

3. $y = 10x - 5$

x	2	4	5	10
y				

4. $y = 9x + 1$

x	2	3	4	5
y				

5. **Number Sense** Is 5 a reasonable solution for y when x = 1 in the equation $y = 2x + 6$? Why or why not?

_____

_____

6. Whitney is making a quilt. She is using blue and red squares of fabric. The equation $r = 2b - 1$ represents the number of red squares she uses for each blue square. If Whitney uses 15 blue squares, how many red squares will she use?

_____

Test Prep

7. Which number completes the table for $y = 5x - 10$?

   A. 80   B. 85
   C. 90   D. 95

x	5	10	15	20
y	15	40	65	

8. **Writing in Math** Explain how finding patterns can help you solve equations.

_____

_____

_____

Use with Lesson 12-6. **155**

Equations and Graphs

R 12-7

To graph a two-step equation, first make a T-table and fill in the values. Then use the coordinate pairs to graph the equation.

$y = 2x - 4$

x	y
1	−2
2	0
3	2

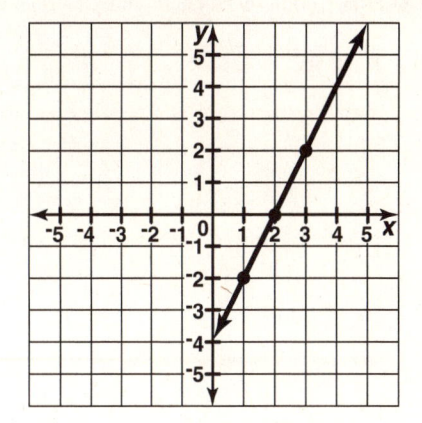

Solve the equation $-1 = 3 - x$.

The value of y is −1, so first go to −1 on the y-axis. Then move across to the right. When you reach the graph line, move up to the x-axis. The x value is 4. So, when $y = -1$, $x = 4$.

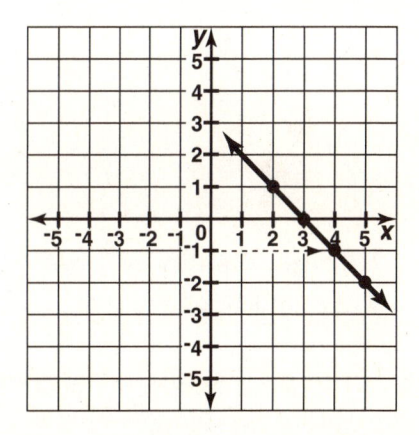

---

1. Complete the T-table, then graph the equation.

$y = 4x - 7$

x	y
1	
2	
3	

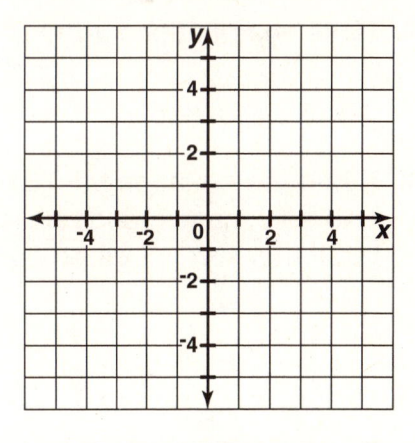

Use the graph of $y = 5 - 2x$ at the right to solve each equation.

2. $-5 = 5 - 2x$ _____

3. $-1 = 5 - 2x$ _____

4. $-3 = 5 - 2x$ _____

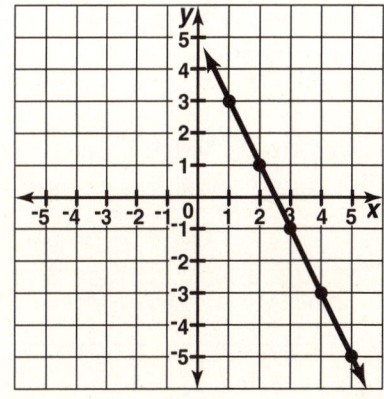

156 Use with Lesson 12-7.

Equations and Graphs

P 12-7

Make a T-table. Then graph the equation.

1. $y = 3x - 5$

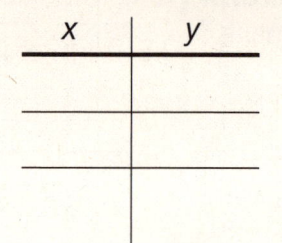

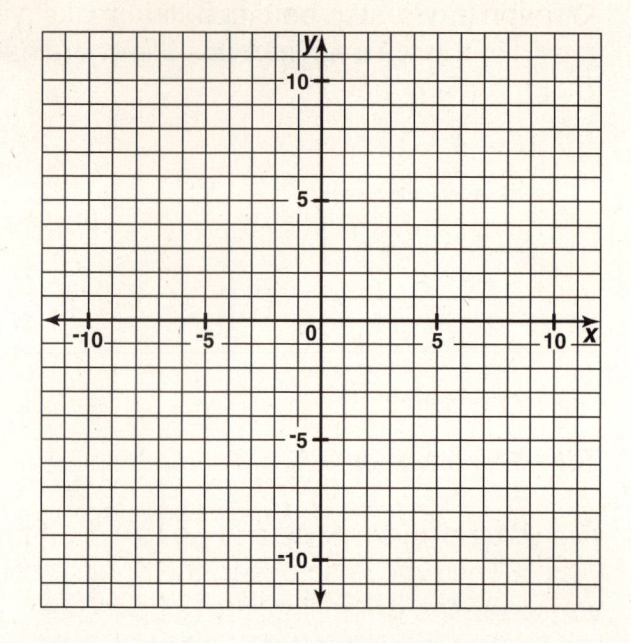

x	y

2. **Number Sense** Without graphing, tell whether the solution to $-4 = 3x + 2$ is positive or negative. _____

The toy store has a bin of green and orange balls. The graph shows the relationship of green balls to orange balls.

3. Write an equation for the line.

   _____

4. Using the equation from Exercise 3, find how many orange balls are in the bin if there are 12 green balls.

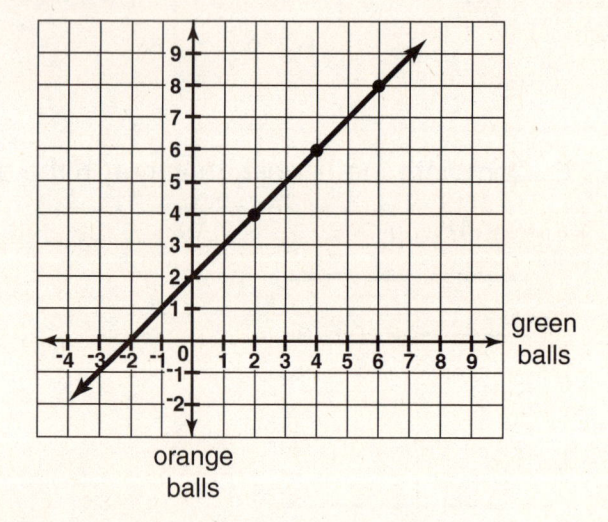

   _____

Test Prep

5. Which is a solution for the equation $y = 3x + 7$?

   A. (3, 17)   B. (4, 19)   C. (3, 19)   D. (4, 17)

6. **Writing in Math** For the equation $y = x - 4$, as the x value increases, will the y value increase or decrease? Explain.

   _____

156 Use with Lesson 12-7.

Temperature

R 12-8

Converting Fahrenheit to Celsius

What is 65°F in Celsius?

Use $C = \frac{5}{9}(F - 32)$.

$C = \frac{5}{9}(65 - 32)$

$C = \frac{5}{9}(33)$

$C = \frac{165}{9}$

$C = 18\frac{1}{3}$

$C = 18$

So, 65°F is about 18°C.

Converting Celsius to Fahrenheit

What is 15°C in Fahrenheit?

Use $F = \frac{9}{5}C + 32$.

$F = \frac{9}{5}(15) + 32$

$F = 27 + 32$

$F = 59$

So, 15°C is about 59°F.

Find each temperature in degrees Fahrenheit.

1. 35°C _____

2. 20°C _____

3. 14°C _____

4. 25°C _____

5. 45°C _____

Find each temperature in degrees Celsius, to the nearest whole degree.

6. 76°F _____

7. 28°F _____

8. 62°F _____

9. 44°F _____

10. 86°F _____

11. **Number Sense** Is 13°C warmer or colder than 50°F? _____

Temperature

P 12-8

Find each temperature in degrees Fahrenheit, to the nearest whole degree.

1. 25°C _____
2. 40°C _____
3. 18°C _____
4. −9°C _____

Find each temperature in degrees Celsius, to the nearest whole degree.

5. 84°F _____
6. 92°F _____
7. 5°F _____
8. −12°F _____

9. **Number Sense** Damon's new coat keeps him warm in temperatures down to −15°F. Will he be warm if the temperature is −30°C? Explain.

_____

_____

The table shows the high and low temperatures for two months in Fargo, North Dakota.

Find the following in degrees Celsius, to the nearest whole degree.

Month	Average High	Average Low
January	15°F	−3°F
July	83°F	58°F

10. the average low temperature in January _____

11. the average high temperature in July _____

Test Prep

12. Which is equal to −15°C?

    A. −5°F   B. 0°F   C. 5°F   D. 10°F

13. **Writing in Math** If the temperature is 3°C, is 10°F or 40°F a better estimate for the temperature? Explain.

_____

_____

Use with Lesson 12-8.

Name _____

PROBLEM-SOLVING APPLICATION   R 12-9
Kelly's Orchard

Kelly is planting an orchard. He has 192 trees to plant in 12 rows. Write an equation to find how many trees he should plant in each row.

Let x = the number of trees in each row.

$12x = 192$

$\dfrac{12x}{12} = \dfrac{192}{12}$

$x = 16$

So, Kelly should plant 16 trees in each row.

Solve. Write your answer in a complete sentence.

1. Kelly can sell 1 basket of apples for $2. Write an equation to find out how many baskets he will have to sell to earn $300.

   _____

   _____

2. Kelly is planting peach, pecan, and apple trees in his orchard. He will plant a total of 192 trees. One out of every 6 trees is an apple tree. How many apple trees is he planting?

   _____

3. Find three consecutive even integers whose sum is between 70 and 80.

   _____

   _____

Solve each equation.

4. $5x + 8 = 68$ _____   5. $\dfrac{x}{4} + 3 = 13$ _____

6. In 1 month, Kelly picked a total of 360 pieces of fruit from 2 of his trees. He picked twice as many apples as he did pears. How many of each fruit did he pick?

   _____

Use with Lesson 12-9.

PROBLEM-SOLVING APPLICATION P 12-9

Expressions

Solve. Write your answer in a complete sentence.

1. Venus has 216 pieces of fruit to put in 18 baskets. Write and solve an equation to find how many pieces of fruit she should put in each basket.

2. Find three consecutive integers whose sum is between 70 and 80.

3. Robert is half as old as Yvonne minus 2. How old is Yvonne if Robert is 11?

4. For every 6 frames Ethan sells, he gets $20 minus the $5 he spent making the frames. If Ethan made $75, how many frames did he sell?

Write an algebraic expression for each.

5. 40 more than 6 times a number _____

6. 8 times a number minus 12 _____

7. one car costs $500 less than twice as much as another one _____

8. one orchard has 40 more than 3 times the number of trees another orchard has _____

9. 12 more than 3 times a number _____

10. 21 less than the quotient of 400 and a number _____